Tell Me Something,
Tell Me Anything,
Even If It's a Lie

Tell Me Something, Tell Me Anything, Even If It's a Lie

A Memoir in Essays

STEVE WASSERMAN

HEYDAY
50

BERKELEY, CALIFORNIA

Portions of this work originally appeared, sometimes in slightly
different form, in the following publications:

*The American Conservative, California Monthly, The Center Magazine,
Columbia Journalism Review, Critical Quarterly, The Economist,
Los Angeles Review of Books, Los Angeles Times Book Review, Los Angeles Times,
The Nation, The New Republic, Opera News, The Progressive,
The Threepenny Review, The* (London) *Times Literary Supplement,
Truthdig,* and *The Village Voice.*

Several essays were first delivered as talks sponsored by the Berlin Institute for
Cultural Inquiry, College of the Redwoods, Guadalajara International Book Fair,
Los Angeles Central Library, Los Angeles Institute for the Humanities,
New York Institute for the Humanities, and the Niebyl-Proctor Marxist Library;
others as posts on Facebook.

Library of Congress Cataloging-in-Publication Data
Names: Wasserman, Steve, 1952- author.
Title: Tell me something, tell me anything, even if it's a lie :
a memoir in essays / Steve Wasserman.
Description: Berkeley : Heyday, 2024. | Includes index.
Identifiers: LCCN 2024005623 (print) | LCCN 2024005624 (ebook) |
ISBN 9781597146470 (hardcover) | ISBN 9781597146487 (epub)
Subjects: LCSH: Wasserman, Steve, 1952— | Wasserman, Steve, 1952—Books
and reading. | Book editors—United States—Biography. | Editors—United
States—Biography. | LCGFT: Autobiographies. | Essays.
Classification: LCC PN149.9.W36 A3 2024 (print) | LCC PN149.9.W36 (ebook)
| DDC 070.5092 [B]—dc23/eng/20230313
LC record available at https://lccn.loc.gov/2024005623
LC ebook record available at https://lccn.loc.gov/2024005624

Cover Art: Salamander Hill Design Studio
Cover Design: Salamander Hill Design Studio
Interior Design/Typesetting: Archie Ferguson
Endpapers: *Still-life* by Whitney Green, Santa Monica, California

Published by Heyday
P.O. Box 9145, Berkeley, California 94709
(510) 549-3564
heydaybooks.com

Printed in East Peoria, Illinois, by Versa Press, Inc.

10 9 8 7 6 5 4 3 2 1

For Robert Scheer,
Susan Sontag, and
Christopher Hitchens

Hallelujah. Yodellayheehoo.
Everyman for himself.
Golden cities. Golden towns.
Thanks for the ride.
—LAURIE ANDERSON

John and I wasted fifteen years eating macrobiotic
and drinking soy milk,
when all I wanted was a little half-and-half.
—YOKO ONO

Live all you can: It's a mistake not to.
—HENRY JAMES

Contents

Introduction

GEOGRAPHY IS FATE. In the fall of 1964, a year after my parents left a hamlet of two thousand souls in central Oregon for the cosmopolitan seductions of Berkeley, the Free Speech Movement burst forth. A kid on the cusp of adolescence, I learned to run a Gestetner printing machine from David Lance Goines, the printer for the Free Speech Movement, a former student of classical antiquity who'd been kicked out for his activism. (Goines would go on to design the original poster for Alice Waters's restaurant, Chez Panisse. And in that trajectory, perhaps, the odyssey of an entire political and cultural movement is inscribed, from militants who used to debate with alarming intensity how many Trotskyites might dance on the head of a Stalinist pin to very often the same folks who decades later argued with similar passion which street-corner bakery had the best croissants.)

Although the media largely chose to report Berkeley's irruptions of dissent as singular, the truth was that Berkeley had a long history of protest. Even Robert S. McNamara, who graduated Cal in 1937, a principal architect of the Vietnam War, later would recall with considerable affection the heated political ferment of the university he knew as an undergraduate. But Berkeley, the city, was more conservative. Many of its residents regarded the political passions of students in their midst as dangerously provocative.

Not so my parents. They sought out the friendship—dare I say comradeship—of malcontents and bohemians who had made their way over the years to the town, whose early boosters had dubbed it the "Athens of the West." Jessica Mitford, the quixotic muckraker with the aristocratic English pedigree, regularly punctured the pompous and the duplicitous with her instinct for the jugular and her unerring wit and withering irony. Fred Cody was another. A stand-up guy with an unabashed and unapologetic love for the unfiltered cigarettes that one day would kill him, he had made his way west from the impoverished hill country of West Virginia by way of Columbia University on the GI Bill. He and his wife, Pat, started a bookstore, which he named after himself. He banished the distinction between paperbacks and hardcovers and, like Ferlinghetti's City Lights in San Francisco, championed the independent press, the neglected, the offbeat, and the marginal writers, poets, and other misfits who gathered in the Bay Area. Cody's radical patriotism and socially conscious literary aesthetics had much in common with the ethos that informed James Agee and Walker Evans's *Let Us Now Praise Famous Men.* His best friend, John Dunbar, who'd been at Columbia with him and found a job teaching English at the California College of Arts and Crafts, had survived being shot down by the Germans over Nazi-occupied France, and had published a memorable account of his harrowing trek alone over the Pyrenees. His son, Robbie, a precocious guitarist with a high school band called the Purple Earthquake, inspired by the English rock 'n' roll of the Yardbirds and the Rolling Stones, became my best friend.

Czeslaw Milosz, the great Polish poet who dissected the fate of intellectuals under Stalinism in *The Captive Mind,* was another Berkeley iconoclast, albeit of a different sort. Although Milosz was troubled by what he regarded as the hopeless naiveté of student militants, something in his melancholy Central European temperament found common ground with activists hammered by the tragic collision of history with hope. I knew him through his sons, especially Peter, whom I had met in acting class while we were at Berkeley High School. I was dimly aware that their father had written a famous book about the Orwellian world that had so deformed the Communist dream. For me, at that time, he was the father we had to beware didn't catch us smoking pot in the garage of their Grizzly Peak home. I regret that I didn't enroll in his class on Dostoyevsky at Cal.

I spent my afternoons delivering the *Berkeley Daily Gazette*, a right-wing rag, to subscribers living in what is now Berkeley's Gourmet Ghetto, an appellation that has recently been consigned to history's linguistic dustbin by the woke police. On weekends, I hawked Max Scherr's underground *Berkeley Barb* along Telegraph Avenue, using my meager profits to buy the books I lusted for at Moe's, Shakespeare's, and a hole-in-the-wall shambles of a secondhand shop called Creed's. (I was also a teenage thief, having successfully and brazenly stolen from Moe's an oversized art book whose contents I found irresistible: Dugald Stermer's *The Art of Revolution*, a compendium of dazzling political and film posters by Cuban artists, which was introduced by Susan Sontag in an essay that she was too embarrassed to reprint in any subsequent collection of her writings.) Whenever I tried to sell books to cigar-chomping Moe, I could count on his unsentimental eye to separate wheat from chaff. If he accepted more books than he rejected, you felt you'd passed your oral exams. He was my strictest teacher and the one to whom I owe the most.

It was impossible to grow up in Berkeley and not be drawn to the archipelago of bookstores that shaped the era. Despite California's fetish for the new and its widespread disdain for history, the reverence for old books among some was palpable. Used bookstores were as ubiquitous as they are now few and far between, many owned by ersatz bohemians who'd migrated to the Bay Area, feeling at home in the region's cosmopolitan maritime mash-up. They often resembled hoarders reluctant to part with the treasures they needed to sell to stay in business. You'd enter their shops, often musty, woody places with dim lighting, chockablock with mysterious tomes in leather bindings, some behind locked bookcases, others displayed in glass vitrines. You felt you had to pass some secret and invisible test to pass muster as a potential buyer.

This breed of bookseller was not only to be found in Berkeley. Years later, in my midtwenties, Susan Sontag told me of a renowned secondhand and antiquarian bookstore on Amsterdam Avenue across from Columbia University. Called the Ideal Bookstore, it was run by an erudite Romanian Jew, a Holocaust survivor. Specializing in literature, philosophy, antiquity, and the Middle Ages, with a fine selection of poetry, the shop attracted scholars and writers and collectors from around the world. Susan told me that, upon entering the store, I should be sure that the proprietor saw me as he was deaf in one ear, and God forbid he wouldn't know you were there and then, startled by your presence, have a stroke. The guilt for killing off the last living remnant of Romanian Jewry would be unbearable.

I wandered among the shelves and after an hour or so made my selection. I came to the cash register and placed my small pile of books on the counter. The owner examined each of the books and then looked me full in the face and said he couldn't sell them to me. I said I had enough cash to make the purchase if he didn't want to take my credit card. No, he said, it's not your money. What was it then?

"You're not ready."

It was a familiar feeling. All my life I had wanted to be a grown-up. I remember as a young boy of eleven stealing out of my bed to huddle, shivering, in the hallway of our Berkeley apartment, trying to make sense of the murmured conversation at the dinner parties my parents would occasionally host. In Berkeley, I was soon surrounded by people, not much older than myself but who seemed impossibly sophisticated, who had decided to tilt at the status quo, to live the future they tried mightily to create. I was swept into the vortex of heated debate and perfervid efforts to make history. The French student slogan of May 1968—Be realistic, demand the impossible—was especially compelling.

In my senior year at Cal, I began seeing a woman who lived in a house with others of radical bent and provenance, including Robert Scheer, the former editor of *Ramparts* in whose 1966 campaign for Congress I had worked as a foot soldier. (It was then that I met Alice Waters, a newly minted graduate of the Free Speech Movement, who also was bending her every effort to elect Scheer.) One evening we all went to see Chris Evert battle Billie Jean King at the Virginia Slims tournament in San Francisco, stopping first to have a Chinese meal at the Yenching, then buying a bottle of cheap rum at a nearby bodega, passing it back and forth during the tennis match. Afterward, we went back to Berkeley. Scheer and I spent half the night playing chess and smoking cigars. Early next morning, he asked me to become his researcher on a book he was writing for McGraw-Hill. His editor was Joyce Johnson. I knew she'd been Jack Kerouac's girlfriend. I didn't hesitate to say yes.

I was both flattered and intimidated. Soon Scheer was including me at the lively dinners he regularly held at his Forest Street home, introducing me to luminaries like Susan Sontag and Frances FitzGerald and Vivian Gornick, whose *The Romance of American Communism* was the book Scheer said I was destined to write but Gornick had got there first. These were writers and personalities whose gifts were obvious. Me, not so much. For a long while, I suffered from what is now called imposter syndrome. Whatever confidence I strove to show was anchored in the arrogance that is the birthright of youth. Privately, I tried to convince myself that any hubris I might harbor was merely a prerequisite to realizing ambition. In the sclerotic atmosphere of Berkeley during those years, you risked being accused by the comrades whose approbation you desperately sought of "careerism" and "individualism" if you couldn't find ways to throttle or conceal such disreputable sins. I envied those writers who seemed to have found their voice early on, and I often wondered how they came by it. Scheer was generous in his praise of my contribution to his book, writing in his acknowledgments that I "played a decisive role as researcher, editor, king of the footnotes, political foil, and constant energizer. He should go on to write better books than this one."

In the event, I never did. I did try to fail upward. I became an editor and a publisher, not a writer, despite the evidence on offer in this book—my first—which appears when my three score and ten are already two years in the rearview mirror of my life. Working as an editor is a form of midwifery. I helped birth ideas by others, smarter and more articulate than I could be on my best day. It relieved me of needing to have an opinion about everything. I do have opinions about everything, but most of them are unoriginal. The great conceit of being an editor is that you need only to write on those occasions when you think you might really have something to say. Prospecting as a publisher for writers who were more talented than myself, getting to be an author's first critic, helping to craft and hone arguments, to find ways to cut through the noise of the culture and get attention for deserving work, to advance public understanding and deepen civic conversation—all this became my life's passion.

I'm grateful to my colleagues at Heyday, who urged me to publish a selection of the best of my writings from the past several decades. I'm grateful to the editors at various publications in which many of these essays first appeared. I'm surprised that there are enough to make up a volume that I hope will both delight and provoke. The truth is, I'm a talker, not a writer. I don't like to be alone with my own thoughts. And I'm too lazy—writing is hard work. And, for many years, I didn't think I was smart enough. Or original enough. I didn't have the cheek that confers confidence, even entitlement, that some of my friends, like the late Christopher Hitchens, seemed to have in spades. I settled for something else: I found joy in learning from the many authors I came to know, engaged in a mutual dialectic of discovery, shaping and sharpening ideas that matter. If luck is the residue of design, then I have been a most fortunate man.

Tell Me Something,
Tell Me Anything,
Even If It's a Lie

Machine-Age Muse

THE STAGE IS BLACK save for a white platform on which several microphones and a violin rest. A tamboura leans against it. A small black box with blinking red lights stands near the lip of the stage. Two towers of black speakers flank the proscenium arch. A drum sits at stage right, an electronic synthesizer in front of it. Another keyboard instrument is at stage left. Several microphones are scattered about. Behind the white platform, dwarfing everything, is a movie screen. On it are projected two words—UNITED STATES—and four clocks (set at one, two, three, and four). They glimmer unevenly, as if caught in the headlights of a passing car, or the flashlight of a cop on patrol.

As the lights go down, a small figure clad entirely in black, except for the occasional flash of bright red socks, walks onto the stage, picks up the violin, and with back to the audience begins to play. The sound is thunderous, relentless, rhythmic, like the cries of large animals in a stampede. A red map of the world fills the screen. Continents begin to pulsate and sway. North America turns into a bird (an eagle?), its claws gripping Mexico and Latin America, which dangle helplessly. Africa rocks to the beat, as do India and Southeast Asia. Russia looks bloated. Suddenly a grid pattern (prison bars?) covers the world. The music stops. The figure in black turns round to face the audience. She is wearing white glasses as if blind. Her electric violin glows as if irradiated. Her name is Laurie Anderson, and she has, as she says in the show, "been baffling audiences for years with her special blend of music ... slides ... films ... tapes ... hand gestures, and more—Hey hey hey hey hey hey hey ... Much more."

United States: Parts I–IV, Anderson's ambitious five-hour attempt to examine America, its dreams and nightmares, as if it were a mental patient awaiting analysis, was given its premiere in February 1983 at the Brooklyn Academy of Music. Since then, she has performed an abridged version (lasting two and a half hours and including almost the whole of Parts III and IV) in sixteen American cities and several in Europe. In each version, *United States* is about an America gone awry, its people both liberated and lobotomized by the machines they have invented to assure prosperity. It is about our fascination with utopia, pastoral and industrial, about remembering and forgetting.

Fastening on the flotsam of urban America, Anderson manages the difficult feat of leavening her critique of industrial life with a sense of humor that disarms even as it disturbs. Her reflections on science, money, transportation, and love are saved from pretension by an absurdist wit and an ear for the non sequiturs of everyday talk. If her work sometimes seems riven by cliché, it is redeemed by her wry irony, her winking acknowledgment that this is so. Not the cliché of consciousness, but the consciousness of cliché informs her impish sensibility.

Anderson's dramatic methods are, as Greil Marcus has noted, largely derived from the avant-garde experiments of the Futurists. Her love of radical juxtaposition also owes much to Surrealist conceits. Marinetti's call for a "Futurist Synthetic

Theater" offers perhaps the best description of Anderson's dramatic techniques. He wanted a theater that "bombards us with squalls of fragments of interconnected events . . . since in daily life we nearly always encounter mere flashes of argument made momentary by our modern experience, in a tram, a café, a railway station, which remain cinematic in our minds like fragmentary dynamic symphonies of gestures, words, lights, and sounds." Unlike Marinetti, however, Anderson can't believe in the apotheosis of machines. Science seduces, but it too often feels like violation. She seasons her passion with a skeptic's pessimism. Indeed, it might be said that Laurie Anderson is America's first postutopian pop artist.

United States is a kind of multimedia séance, with Anderson as the medium through which spirits are summoned and through whom they speak. Her voice is often inflected in the somnolent manner of a sleepwalker. Electronic devices are used to alter its range and pitch. She wields her violin bow (which is strung with prerecorded magnetic tape, allowing the instrument to "speak" when drawn against the playback heads attached to the violin's bridge) as if it were a magician's rod, capable of conjuring up images of urban America (microchips, automobiles, skyscrapers), of evoking frightening apparitions of everyday life (a three-pronged electric wall socket, for example, is enlarged to look like a skull). Her show is about possession, spirits, voices.

"Our plan is to drop a lot of odd objects onto your country from the air," she declares. "And some of these objects will be useful. And some of them will just be odd. Proving that these oddities were produced by a people free enough to think of making them in the first place." Such objects include telephones, apple pie, Kennedy half dollars. They are blown up to immense, often grotesque proportions. The movie screen, the ever-present backdrop to Anderson's electronic cabaret, serves as a kind of illuminated dream screen onto which projections of such objects are cast. These images are frequently enigmatic, luminous, disquieting.

Anderson is an archaeologist of language and memory. Her work suggests that the past, however repressed, has a way of intruding on the present. It may fade from memory, but something lingers, waiting to be discovered and deciphered. She knows that the steady erosion of language is the first step in the destruction of thought. Without words, memory is impossible—thus her fascination with machines, with memories (the camera, the answering machine, the tape recorder). It is a considerable paradox, however, that as our means of preserving memory have grown ever more sophisticated, we seem increasingly to be a people without memory.

Among the most moving of her tales is the story of an elderly blind Cree Indian who is asked to sing traditional hunting songs for a documentary of his tribe. The video equipment is set up in a tin Quonset hut. The lights are turned on. The old man starts to sing, but soon falters as he gropes for the words to the songs he never learned. As Anderson tells it, "He just kept starting over and sweating and rocking back and forth. The only words he really seemed sure of were 'Hey ah . . . hey ah hey . . . hey hey hey ah hey . . . hey . . . .'" On the screen, while Anderson sings, the image of a red buffalo flickers, like the shadow of a forgotten ancestor. Words appear on the screen in a kind of simultaneous translation (confession?) of the old man's feeble chant: "I never went hunting . . . I never sang the songs . . . of my fathers . . . I am singing for this movie . . . I am doing this for money . . . I remember Grandfather. He lay on his back while he was dying . . . I think I am no one . . . ."

"After electricity," Mayakovsky once remarked, "I lost interest in nature. Too backward." The Russian poet was by no means the first to utter such sentiments. Americans have long been enrolled in the cult of the machine. Ever since Jacob Bigelow, a Harvard professor, coined the word "technology" in 1829, Americans have rushed to praise and promote the blessings of industrial invention. The doubts of Europeans like Thomas Carlyle (who regretfully dubbed the nineteenth century the "Age of Machinery") or Baudelaire (who dismissed America as a republic "of counting-house morality") were shunted aside. Men like Whitney and Edison, it was thought, held the keys that would unlock the door to the munificent future.

Emerson was among the more enthusiastic boosters of the new Machine Age. He looked forward to the day "when the whole land is a garden, and the people have grown up in the bowers of a paradise." He was sure America was "the country of the Future," that the pastoral paradise inherent in the American enterprise was made more certain as a result of technological progress. Only after a ten-month visit to England did he begin to have his doubts. In *English Traits*, Emerson's grim reflections on the sooty reality of the Industrial Revolution, he wrote, "Mines, forges, mills, breweries, railroads, steam-pump, steam-plough, drill of regiments, drill of police, rule of court and shop-rule have operated to give a mechanical regularity to all the habit and action of men. A terrible machine has possessed itself of the ground, the air, the men and women, and hardly even thought is free." The misery machines seemed to bring in their wake filled Emerson with despair. "I cannot think the most judicious tubing a compensation for metaphysical debility. . . . Machinery is good, but mother-wit is better." The industrial juggernaut was not to be so easily persuaded. Today, the atomic bomb stands poised to clinch the argument.

Anderson's work is precisely about the ghost in the machine, the nagging suspicion that something has gone terribly wrong. She longs for escape and solitude. She tells of a dream that takes place in the tropics: "I'm not a person in this realm. I'm a place . . . And I have no eyes, no hands . . . And there's no . . . no scale. Just a lot of details. Just a slow accumulation of details." She sings a song: *Days, I remember cities. Nights, I dream about a perfect place. Days, I dive by the wreck. Nights, I swim in the blue lagoon.*

For Anderson, Manhattan's skyscrapers can no longer be worshipped as benign totems of America's industrial destiny. Nor can they easily be seen, as Le Corbusier saw them, as "hot jazz in stone and steel." Instead, these ubiquitous monoliths of the modern metropolis recall Rousseau's warning that "Cities are the abyss of the human species." "There are ten million stories in the naked city," Anderson intones, "but nobody can remember which is theirs." The proliferation of machines designed to pierce the physiological barriers that separate people (airplanes, telephones, television) has ironically resulted in increased psychological estrangement. The telephone as prophylactic, as *conversation interruptus*, is the subject of an amusing satire in which Anderson is besieged by a barrage of calls from friends, associates, acquaintances. It ends with a friend urging Anderson to ring up any time she wants to talk—the answering machine will always be on.

Despite Anderson's misgivings, she isn't entirely willing to condemn helter-skelter science. Its sensuousness is too seductive. Besides, without machines she is mute. Nevertheless, a sense of doom pervades her work. (The torch clenched in the hand of the upraised arm of the Statue of Liberty, for example, is revealed as the blastoff of a nuclear warhead. The show climaxes with a prolonged film of exploding fireworks that burn incandescent arcs in the canvas of the night, while images of astronauts on the moon; Meteor Crater near Winslow, Arizona; and an advertisement for Coca-Cola in Russian swirl on the screen. The music is deafening.) Something more fundamental than the demise of the American dream is at stake in all this. Anderson's real achievement is her acknowledgment that the unfettered faith in the future made possible by science is no more.

Days after the show ended, I remained haunted by her final image: an airplane, tumbling over and over in the inky darkness of space, directionless, as if it were a ghost ship bereft of its pilot—the passengers, I imagine, strapped to their seats, bound together on a collective journey toward the unknown.

[1983]

Future Shock

NEARLY TWO WEEKS AFTER SEPTEMBER 11, rage is the order of the day. The avalanche of daily news provides riveting, if sketchy details, but the historical and contextual frame that might offer genuine insight is largely missing or shattered. Pundits offer sound-bite pronunciamentos, shedding little light; the politics of hysteria banish sobriety. Wisdom is scarce. The specter of war looms. Questions abound: Why was such slaughter visited upon us, by whom, and to what purpose? How did we come to this place? And where is it going to lead?

What is certain is that the end of the Cold War has unleashed a host of furies: renewed nationalisms, messianic cults, the need for scapegoats, deeper divisions between rich and poor. The old geopolitical order is vanished, supplanted by a still-inchoate new order that bears little resemblance to the familiar world of the last half of the twentieth century.

For years now, our best writers and reporters and thinkers have sought to understand the forces shaping this strange new world. They have tried to give us a more truthful sense of things, a more nuanced sense of the world we inhabit. They oppose simplification and mystification. They are interested in complex readings informed by history. Their books may help us to understand what, for many, eludes understanding.

Taken together, these works, written with an exceptional combination of erudition, intelligence, and empathy, but also with an abiding commitment to democratic values, may help to illuminate the present in a time of dizzying transformations, cynical manipulations, and malleable geopolitical realities. They offer both a theoretical template to apprehend the forces that give rise to rage, and an excavation of specific policies and alliances gone awry.

Benjamin R. Barber's *Jihad vs. McWorld*, first published in 1995, is a coruscating and lucid look at what he insists is the underlying conflict of our times: religious and tribal fundamentalism versus secular consumerist capitalism. It offers a lens through which to understand the chaotic events of the post–Cold War world.

Barber believes the world is simultaneously coming together and falling apart. On the one hand, corporate mergers are steadily weaving the globe into a single international market, challenging traditional notions of national sovereignty. On the other hand, the world is increasingly riven by fratricide, civil war, and the breakup of nations. He argues that what capitalism and fundamentalism have in common is a distaste for democracy. Both, in different ways, lay siege to the nation-state itself—until now the only guarantor of conditions that have permitted democracy to flourish.

Democracy, Barber suggests, may fall victim to a twin-pronged attack: by a global capitalism run rampant, whose essential driving force destroys traditional values as it seeks to maximize profit-taking at virtually any moral or religious or spiritual cost; and by religious, tribal, and ethnic fanatics whose various creeds are stamped by intolerance and a rage against the "other."

Barber gives us two scenarios, which he fleshes out in considerable detail. The first holds out the grim prospect of a retribalization of large parts of humanity by war and bloodshed, a threatened balkanization of nation-states in which culture is pitted against culture—"a Jihad in the name of a hundred narrowly conceived faiths against every kind of interdependence, every kind of artificial social cooperation and mutuality: against technology, against pop culture, against integrated markets; against modernity itself."

The second scenario paints the future in primary colors, a portrait of seemingly irresistible economic, technological, and corporate forces that demand integration and uniformity and that mesmerize people everywhere with "fast music, fast computers, and fast food—with MTV, Macintosh [computers], and McDonald's, pressing nations into one commercially homogenous theme park: one McWorld tied together by communications, information, entertainment, and commerce."

The paradox, Barber contends, is that the tendencies of both Jihad and McWorld are at work, both visible sometimes in the same country at the same instant. Jihad pursues a bloody politics of identity, while McWorld seeks a bloodless economics of profit. Belonging by default to McWorld, everyone is compelled to enroll in Jihad. But no one is any longer a citizen, and, without citizens, asks Barber, how can there be democracy?

In 1991, Jacques Attali, a French novelist, essayist, and former advisor to French President Francois Mitterrand, was president of the newly founded European Bank for Reconstruction and Development. He published a small and largely prescient book titled *Millennium: Winners and Losers in the Coming World Order*. While he badly misjudged how well the European Union would knit itself together, both politically and monetarily, and he sorely underestimated the ability of the United States to balance its budget and reduce its deficit, he judged all too well how the privileged preside, from the relative safety of their technological perches, over a world that has embraced a common ideology of consumerism but is divided between rich and poor, girdled by a dense network of airport metropolises for travel and commerce and wired for instant communication.

His vision is one in which, as he writes, "Marx's *Das Kapital* or Adam Smith's *Wealth of Nations* may be less useful than Ridley Scott's celluloid fantasy *Blade Runner*." It is a world of high-tech economies that render national borders irrelevant, in which privileged elites are surrounded by a sea of impoverished nomads—boat people on a planetary scale—who are condemned to ply the planet in search of sustenance and shelter. Desperately hoping to shift from what Alvin Toffler calls the slow world to the fast world, they will live, Attali predicts, the life of the living dead.

Attali worries over what he calls "millennial losers," those for whom the prosperity of the fast world will be both a permanent lure and a constant insult. Millions, he writes, will migrate, seeking a decent life elsewhere, perhaps to Paris or London or New York or Los Angeles, which for them "will be oases of hope, emerald cities of plenty and high-tech magic." Or, he concludes, they will "redefine hope in fundamentalist terms altogether outside modernity."

In particular, the Middle East will be a cauldron of resentment. After all, "the peoples of this region suffer from the terrible trauma of repeated defeats inflicted upon it by the West. These defeats have inspired both secular and religious fanaticism, characterized by paranoia and defiance, anxiety and frustration. . . . This dynamic threatens true world war of a new type, of terrorism that can suddenly rip the vulnerable fabric of complex systems."

Ahmed Rashid is a correspondent for the *Far Eastern Economic Review* and the *Daily Telegraph*. For more than twenty years, he has reported on Pakistan, Afghanistan, and Central Asia. His book, *Taliban: Militant Islam, Oil and Fundamentalism in Central Asia*, was published in 2000 by Yale University Press. It is virtually the only informed work on the men who, since 1994, have ruled almost all of Afghanistan. (The other necessary book is Michael Griffin's *Reaping the Whirlwind: The Taliban Movement in Afghanistan*, a meticulous dissection of the limits of power in a violently sectarian society.)

Rashid covered the ferocious civil war that ruined that already-ravaged nation. He traveled and lived with the Taliban and has interviewed most of their leaders. Their meteoric rise and rigid theocratic beliefs compelled him to write their story as another bloody chapter in the continuing saga of Afghanistan's long history of torment and turmoil.

How the Afghans and their country were historically turned into an object of power politics by the Persians, the Mongols, the British, the Soviets, and the Pakistanis is the subject of his indispensable book. Rashid also examines how American attitudes changed toward the Taliban, from early support to belated opposition. He does so against the backdrop of intense rivalry among Western countries and companies to build oil and gas pipelines from Central Asia to Western and

Asian markets. His chapter, "Global Jihad: The Arab-Afghans and Osama Bin Laden," is especially incisive, detailing how the United States enlisted thousands of foreign Muslim recruits to help end the 1979 Soviet invasion of Afghanistan.

The multiple contradictions inherent in American Cold War policy (which for decades saw the world split between the godless Evil Empire of Communism and the god-fearing Free World) is explored in two books published in 2000: Chalmers Johnson's *Blowback: The Costs and Consequences of American Empire* and John K. Cooley's *Unholy Wars: Afghanistan, America and International Terrorism.* Johnson is a highly regarded scholar of China, Japan, and East Asia, a former director of UC Berkeley's Center for Chinese Studies, and the author of the standard work on Japanese industrial policy. The book's title is a term used by the CIA to describe the often-unintended consequences of actions that the agency itself has committed. It refers to the reactions that its own skullduggery sparks in the form of protest, riots, violence, and terrorism in the nations it targets. A good example would be the Cubans trained and sent to overthrow Fidel Castro at the Bay of Pigs who, years later, would turn up implicated in the Watergate burglary. Johnson is persuaded that American global expansion—what is now known as "globalization"—has prompted an extraordinary backlash, much of it paradoxically impelled by US policies themselves. Blowback does not end at the nation's borders, he concludes; it reaches into America itself.

Few have more thoroughly plumbed the implications and consequences of these forlorn policies than John K. Cooley, whose firsthand familiarity with both the Middle East and Central Asia is nearly unrivaled. A reporter for the *Christian*

Science Monitor since 1965 and a longtime correspondent for ABC News, he is the author of numerous books, including the first biography of Kadafi and books on the rise of the PLO.

Unholy Wars tells the story of how three American administrations promoted a bipartisan policy that bankrolled and trained an estimated thirty-five thousand militants from forty Islamic countries to take part in what was commonly called the Afghan Jihad, or holy war, against the Soviets in the early 1980s that would eventually turn its wrath on its US paymasters. This legion of rogue mercenaries spread across a great arc, from the Russian Caucasus and the former Soviet republics in Central Asia southward to India's Kashmir province.

Cooley describes how these militants made common cause with disaffected Muslims in western China, Egypt, and Algeria. Across the sea in New York, the World Trade Center was bombed in 1993. Caught and convicted, the culprits proved to be adepts of Sheik Omar Abdel Rahman, a recent and celebrated visitor to Afghan training camps in Peshawar, whose US visa had been approved by the CIA. Cooley's book investigates what he calls "a strange love-affair that went disastrously wrong," the curious and largely unexamined alliance between America and "some of the most conservative and fanatical followers of Islam."

Americans suffer from a persistent collective historical amnesia. Our politics are hobbled by our refusal to understand the manifold ways in which history, as was once so famously said, weighs like a nightmare on the brain of the living. Americans have cleaved to the conceit that history, insofar as it was deemed important at all, was more hindrance than help in our presumed unstoppable march to the munificent future.

Optimistic, pragmatic, impatient, inventive, generous, Americans have refused to be held hostage to history, believing America to have burst its bounds. The cost of such myopia is large. It enfeebles understanding, promotes nostrums of all kinds, licenses the infantilization of public debate.

For too long we have let our romance with distance and escape and denial define our culture and our politics. As Michael Wood suggests in his stimulating book, *America in the Movies*, there is in our country "a dream of freedom which appears in many places and many forms, which lies somewhere at the back of several varieties of isolationism. . . . It is a dream of freedom from others; it is a fear . . . of entanglement. It is what we mean when we say, in our familiar phrase, that we don't want to get involved." There is, however, no hiatus from history, no reprieve from reality.

[2001]

Avenging Angel

ALL BOOKS ARE NEW until you've read them. *The Sabres of Paradise* by the late Lesley Blanch, published fifty years ago, is one such book. It is a remarkable story of resistance to empire, heroism and treachery, savagery and generosity, religious fanaticism and imperial ambition. Though the tale it tells occurred more than one hundred fifty years ago, its implications for our era are evident on nearly every page. If you want to understand something of the futility and hubris of the American effort to pacify Afghanistan and the unruly clans of Pakistan, or the forlorn and ruthless Russian war against Chechnya's murderous insurgents, you would do well to consider the story of Shamyl, imam of Daghestan.

Blanch, a nearly forgotten writer, died in the south of France three years ago, just one month shy of one hundred and three. She had been a features editor of *Vogue* in England from the mid-1930s through the mid-1940s and gained a considerable reputation as a book illustrator, columnist, war reporter, movie and drama critic, theatrical designer, and book reviewer. The author of more than a dozen books, she is perhaps best known for her international bestseller *The Wilder Shores of Love*, a compelling if overly romantic portrait of a quartet of intrepid nineteenth-century Englishwomen who were drawn to the seductions of what they imagined were the more

17

authentic passions of the East. Blanch admired these women as "realists of romance who broke with their century's dream, to live it, robustly."

She herself was always fascinated by Russia, her imagination inflamed by Tolstoy and Lermontov's imperishable stories set in the Caucasus—stories that vividly portray the effort by the czarist court of St. Petersburg to subdue the proud tribal peoples, mostly of the Islamic persuasion, who fought to preserve their rituals and traditional ways against the encroachments of a rapacious Russian empire. She loved the blood-curdling stories handed down from generation to generation. Atrocities excited her: she wrote in a characteristically empurpled passage that "it had been secretly every [Russian] woman's dream to be seized, flung over the saddle of a pure-bred Kabarda steed, and forced to submit to the advances of some darkling mountaineer." From the opening pages of *The Sabres of Paradise*, she breathlessly recounts the diabolical ways the tribes of the Caucasus went to battle, how they "wrote love-poems to their daggers, as to a mistress, and went to battle, as to a rendezvous." They were a hard and hardened people: "Vengeance was their creed, violence their climate." Collections of severed rebel heads were matters of competitive pride; a girl's dowry might be reckoned in such trophies. Caucasian warriors, she writes, would dress their saddlebows with the severed hands of their enemies, which dangled provocatively from the prize mounts they rode with enviable skill. Brutality was a way of life, the ability to suffer abuse without complaint a sign of virtue. Stoicism was synonymous with nobility.

The peoples of the Caucasus were legendary for their refusal to submit to would-be conquerors. Neither Alexander the Great nor successive invaders from the Roman legions to Attila the Hun and Genghis Khan, nor Tamerlane nor the shahs of Persia could crush these fierce tribes, secure in their nearly inaccessible mountain redoubts, mighty ranges that dwarfed the Alps. In Persia there was even a much-ignored proverb: "When a shah is a fool, he attacks Daghestan." Into this vortex of violence and stubbornness came Czar Nicholas I with his dream of extending St. Petersburg's writ. His nemesis was the towering figure of Shamyl of Daghestan, who strove tirelessly to unite the disparate Caucasian tribes to resist their Russian invaders. He issued a call for holy war and imposed Shariah law wherever he could. For twenty-five years, from 1839 until his surrender in 1864, Shamyl was an implacable foe of Russian ambitions, forging an army of religious fanatics "whose private feuds," Blanch writes, "were submerged in their common hatred of the Infidel invaders." His word was law. His four wives and several sons submitted to his least whim and every command. His fury knew no bounds. Osama bin Laden is his heir.

The quarter-century war Shamyl waged was unrelenting: an estimated half-million men would die, soldiers sent by the czar into the bloody, bottomless maw of Caucasian hatred. The Russians had greater resources, the backing of a mighty and expanding empire. But Shamyl's men were better able to withstand climatic extremes, to utilize the nimble and disciplined tactics of partisans who fought for their independence, for Allah, and for Allah's prophet, the indefatigable and unforgiving Shamyl. A single story from his remarkable career, wonderfully and indelibly recounted by Blanch, reveals something of the man's austere and rigid character and his charismatic power. (Blanch's book offers up a trove of such stories, rooted in her admirable research and excellent reporting on several continents.) It is a story that suggests the many ways "Shamyl dramatized himself, turning to his own advantage events which, less imaginatively treated, would have spelled disaster." In 1843, the tribes of Great and Little Chechnya are besieged by Russian troops. Shamyl's men are occupied elsewhere and can send no aid. The Chechen predicament is increasingly desperate, and rather than continue a futile resistance, they conclude that the better part of valor is to submit to the czar. Fear of Shamyl's wrath, however, prompts them to send a delegation to Dargo, then his mountain headquarters, to beg his permission. But no one has the courage to ask directly. Instead, they decide to ask Shamyl's aged mother to intercede on their behalf. She is known to exercise a considerable and moderating influence over her fanatic son. He is said to revere her and to confide in her as to no one else, apart from Fatimat, his first wife.

She listens to their entreaties and agrees to speak to her son on their behalf. At midnight, he emerges from her audience with him, his face inscrutable, and strides directly to the nearby mosque, where he remains alone for the rest of the night. His mother tells the trembling Chechens that the imam says it is for Allah to decide, and that therefore he has gone to the mosque, where, with prayer and fasting, he will await Allah's command.

For three days and three nights, he stays closeted in the mosque. Finally, he sends word that the entire population of Dargo, along with the delegation from Chechnya, is to assemble in the town's square to hear the divine decision. The people wait for Shamyl to emerge. They have been wailing and praying on their knees for hours. Suddenly the doors of the mosque are flung open and Shamyl appears, "livid pale, his half-closed cat's eyes glinting." He stands stock still, "as if turned to stone," expressionless. A silence descends; the streets and rooftops are empty; only the dogs prowl. Two of his executioners accompany his mother, who kneels before him. Shamyl raises his left hand and says,

> Mighty Prophet, thy will be done! Thy words are law to thy servant Shamyl. Inhabitants of Dargo! I bring you black news. Your brothers, the Chechen, have spoken shamefully of submission to the czar. But they knew their audacity, their lack of faith, their dishonour: they did not dare to face me themselves, but used my mother, through her womanly weakness, to approach me. For love of her, as proof of her persuasions, I laid their request before Mohammed, Allah's prophet. For three days and nights I have sought the Prophet's judgment. And now, at last, he has deigned to answer my prayers. . . . It is Allah's will that the first person who spoke to me of submission should be punished by a hundred lashes! *And this first person is my mother!*

The crowd gasps; his mother cries out and falls to the ground. The assemblage begins to wail. His henchmen bind his mother, and Shamyl seizes the whip from his executioners and begins to lash the shrieking woman. At the fifth blow she faints, and Shamyl flings himself across her body, sobbing uncontrollably. Suddenly, he springs to his feet, "his face now radiant, his eyes 'darting flames.'" "Allah is great!" he cries. "Mohammed is his first Prophet, and I am his second! My prayer is answered! He allows me to take upon myself the remainder of the punishment to which my wretched mother was condemned. I accept with joy! I welcome the lash! It is the sign of your favor, O Prophet!" He tears open his tunic and orders his executioners "to deliver the rest of the 95 lashes upon his own back, threatening them with death if they do not strike hard enough." He kneels beside his unconscious mother.

The blows begin to fall. He utters not a sound, and only the thwack of the lash upon his back can be heard. No grimace distorts his impassive face, nor is any grunt of pain permitted to escape his lips. At last, the final blow is delivered. Shamyl, his shoulders bleeding, rises to his feet: "Where are the Chechen traitors? Where is the deputation who brought this punishment upon Mother?"

The Chechnyans grovel; they lay in the dust, prostrate with fear. They await their fate, unable even to beg for mercy.

Shamyl orders them to stand, enjoins them to "take heart, to have courage and faith." He tells them, "Return to your homes. Tell your people what you have seen and heard here. Depart in peace. Hold fast to the rope of God. Farewell."

There was no further talk of submission. Shamyl's place as Allah's prophet upon earth was secure.

Until one day it wasn't. In the end, he would not be able to overcome the Russians' might, and he and his stalwart sons would be forced to surrender, his people decimated, the victims of a nearly genocidal policy pursued by a series of successive Russian generals who did not scruple to cut down whole forests to deny Shamyl's warriors the cover and refuge they needed to survive.

What happened next is utterly surprising, and it would be a sin to even hint at it in this review. Suffice it to say, the reader who spends time with *The Sabres of Paradise* will find instruction of a sort that will not soon be forgotten.

[2010]

Rage and Ruin

I N THE EARLY MORNING HOURS of April 1, 1967, in North
Richmond, California, a small, impoverished, all-Black town
near Oakland, Denzil Dowell lay dead in the street. The police
said that Dowell, a twenty-two-year-old construction worker,
had been killed by a single shotgun blast to the back and head;
they claimed that he had been caught burglarizing a liquor
store and, when ordered to halt, had failed to do so. The coro-
ner's report told a different story. His body bore six bullet holes,
and there was reason to believe Dowell had been shot while
surrendering with his hands raised high. His mother said, "I
believe the police murdered my son." An all-white jury found
that Dowell's death was "justifiable homicide." Many people in
North Richmond didn't agree.

Only six months before, Huey P. Newton and Bobby Seale,
brash upstarts from Oakland, had established the Black Panther Party for Self-Defense. They had quickly garnered a
reputation for their willingness to stand up to police harass-
ment and worse. They'd made a practice of shadowing the
cops, California Penal Code in one hand, twelve-gauge shotgun
in the other. Soon they were meeting with the Dowell family,
investigating the facts of the case, holding street-corner rallies,
confronting officials, arguing that only by taking up arms could
the Black community put a stop to police brutality. Newton and

Seale were fearless and cocky—even reckless, some felt—and itching for a fight. One Sunday, the police came knocking on Mrs. Dowell's door while Newton was there. When she opened the door, Newton later recalled, "a policeman pushed his way in, asking questions. I grabbed my shotgun and stepped in front of her, telling him either to produce a search warrant or leave. He stood for a minute, shocked, then ran out to his car and drove off." A new history of the Black Panther Party, *Black against Empire*, tells what happened next:

> The Panthers showed up armed and in uniform and closed off the street. Word had spread and almost four hundred people of all ages came. Many working-class and poor black people from North Richmond were there. They wanted to know how to get some measure of justice for Denzil Dowell and in turn how to protect themselves and their community from police attacks. People lined both sides of the block. Some elderly residents brought lawn chairs to sit in while they listened. Some of the younger generation climbed on cars.
>
> Several police cars arrived on the scene, but . . . kept their distance. A Contra Costa County helicopter patrolled above. According to a sheriff's spokesman, the department took no other action because the Panthers broke no laws and as required, displayed their weapons openly. . . . Neighbors showed up with their own guns. . . . One young woman who had been sitting in her car got out and held up her M-1 for everyone to see. The Panthers passed out applications to join their party, and over three hundred people filled them out. According to FBI

informant Earl Anthony, he "had never seen Black men command the respect of the people the way that Huey Newton and Bobby Seale did that day."

Several days after Dowell's death, alarmed by the Panthers' growing prominence, California legislator Donald Mulford introduced a bill to ban the carrying of loaded weapons in public. Newton responded by upping the ante and in early May dispatched thirty Panthers, most of them armed, to Sacramento, the state capital. They were to show up at the capitol building as the bill was being debated. The police confiscated their guns soon after they arrived but later returned them, as the Panthers had broken no laws. The Mulford Act passed. The Panthers were instantly notorious, and images of their armed foray were splashed across the nation's newspapers and shown on television. It was a PR coup. Soon thousands of young Blacks joined the party, and by the end of 1968 seventeen Panther chapters had opened across the country. One enthusiast, quoted in a major feature story in the *New York Times Magazine*, spoke for many when he said, "As far as I'm concerned, it's beautiful that we finally got an organization that don't walk around singing. I'm not for all this talking stuff. When things start happening, I'll be ready to die if that's necessary and it's important that we have somebody around to organize us."

The rise and fall of the Black Panther Party is a heartbreaking saga of heroism and hubris, which, in its full dimension and contradiction, has long awaited its ideal chronicler. The material is rich, some of it still radioactive. A good deal of it can be found in a clutch of memoirs, inevitably self-serving but valuable nonetheless, that have appeared sporadically over the years by ex-Panthers, including Bobby Seale, David Hilliard, and Elaine Brown among the better known, but also such lesser figures as William Lee Brent, Flores Forbes, and Jamal Joseph. There are also accounts by David Horowitz, Kate Coleman, and Hugh Pearson. All are to be read with care. The Panthers were controversial in their day and remain so. Their history is swaddled in propaganda, some of it promulgated by the party's enemies, who sought assiduously to destroy it, and some by its apologists and hagiographers, who, as often as not, have refused to acknowledge the party's crimes and misdemeanors, preferring to attribute its demise almost entirely to the machinations of others. Peopled by outsized characters—starting with its magnetic and headstrong founder, Huey P. Newton, eulogized at his 1989 funeral as "our Moses"—the party's complicated history, replete with Byzantine political schisms, murderous infighting, and a contested legacy, has eluded sober examination.

Now, two scholars—Waldo Martin Jr., a historian at the University of California, Berkeley, and Joshua Bloom, a doctoral candidate in sociology at UCLA—after more than a decade of work offer a corrective in their book, *Black against Empire*. They demolish the canard that the Panthers were anti-white. What distinguished Newton and Seale's approach was their refusal to go along with the narrow cultural nationalism that had appealed to so many African Americans. They fought tremendous battles, sometimes turning deadly, with those who thought, as the saying went, that political power grew out of the sleeve of a dashiki. Bloom and Martin rightly emphasize the Panthers' steady embrace of a class-based politics with an internationalist bent. The party was inspired by anti-imperialist struggles in

Africa, Latin America, and Asia. They began by emphasizing the local but soon went global, ultimately establishing an international section in Algiers. Their romance with the liberation movements of others would eventually become something of a fetish, reaching its nadir in the bizarre adulation of North Korea's dictator Kim Il-Sung and his watchword, *juche*, a term for the self-reliance that the Panthers deluded themselves into thinking might be the cornerstone of a revolutionary approach that would find an echo of enthusiasm in America.

In the beginning, little about the party was original. Even the iconic dress of black leather jackets and matching berets was inspired by earlier Oakland activists, like the now all-but-forgotten Mark Comfort, who, Bloom and Martin note, "had begun appealing to young African Americans with militant style." As early as February 1965, the month Malcolm X was assassinated, Comfort had launched a protest "to put a stop to police beating innocent people." Later that summer, Comfort and his supporters demanded that "the Oakland City Council keep white policemen out of Black neighborhoods" and took steps to organize "citizen patrols to monitor the actions of the police and document incidents of brutality." This wasn't enough for Newton and Seale. Inspired by Robert F. Williams's advocacy and practice of "armed self-reliance"—for which he'd had to flee the country in the early 1960s, seeking sanctuary in Castro's Cuba—Newton and Seale decided to break entirely with "armchair intellectualizing," as Seale would later call it. Propaganda of the deed, they believed, would arouse the admiration of, in Newton's words, the "brothers on the block." They'd had it with bended-knee politics. It was time, as a favored slogan of the party would later urge, "to pick up the gun."

Drawing up a ten-point program stuffed with demands for justice and self-determination, the Panthers represented a rupture with the reformist activism of the traditional civil rights movement. It wasn't long before the party saw itself as a "vanguard," capable of jump-starting a revolution. For some—and here I do not exempt myself—it was an intoxicating fever dream.

In early November 1969, I left Berkeley for a few days and went to Chicago to support the Chicago Eight, then on trial for the bloody police riot that had marred the anti–Vietnam War protests at the 1968 Democratic National Convention. I knew some of the defendants: Jerry Rubin, whom I'd met four years before while organizing one of the first junior high school protests against the Vietnam War; Tom Hayden, who'd taken an interest in my rabble-rousing posse at Berkeley High School during the battle for People's Park; and Bobby Seale, whom I'd encountered through my close friendship with schoolmates who'd joined the Panthers and let us use the party's typesetting machines in its Shattuck Avenue national headquarters to put together our underground newspaper, *Pack Rat*. Seale had been bound and gagged in the courtroom—a "neon oven," Abbie Hoffman had called it. The country was riveted by the appalling spectacle. I arrived at the apartment that Leonard Weinglass, one of the defense attorneys, had rented. It served as crash pad and general meeting place for the far-flung tribe of supporters and radical nomads unafraid to let their freak flags fly, who sought to muster support for the beleaguered defendants. I walked into a cloud of pot smoke and the sounds of "Here Comes the Sun" on the turntable, the Beatles' *Abbey Road* having just been released.

Sometime around midnight, Fred Hampton, clad in a long black leather coat and looking for all the world like a gunslinger bursting into a saloon, swept in with a couple of other Panthers in tow. You could feel the barometric pressure in the room fall with Hampton's entrance. At the time, the favored flick was Sam Peckinpah's *Wild Bunch*, an epic western revenge fantasy that inflamed the overheated imaginations of a number of unindicted coconspirators like my friend Stew Albert, a founder of the Yippies. Hampton was already in the crosshairs of the FBI and Mayor Daley's goons, to whom he'd been a taunting nemesis. He had an open face, and his eyes flashed intelligently. He had the Panther swagger down pat, yet his voice was soft, welcoming. He radiated charisma and humility. He seemed tired, and somehow you knew he was already thinking of himself as a dead man walking. He was famous for having proclaimed, "You can kill a revolutionary, but you can't kill the revolution." You could see how people could fall for him, and you could well imagine how his enemies hated and feared him. A month later he was murdered, shot dead by police while sleeping in his bed. He was twenty-one.

Hampton seemed destined for greatness, having already eclipsed in his seriousness Eldridge Cleaver, the party's minister of information and an ex-con who'd written the bestselling *Soul on Ice*. Cleaver was regarded by many of the younger recruits within the party as their Malcolm X. A strong advocate of working with progressive whites, Cleaver was a man of large appetites, an anarchic and ribald spirit who relished his outlaw status. After years in prison, he was hell-bent on making up for lost time and wasn't about to kowtow to anyone—neither Ronald Reagan, whom he mocked mercilessly, nor, as it would turn out, Huey Newton. He was the joker in the Panther deck and a hard act to follow. Like so many of the Panthers' leaders, he had killer looks, inhabiting his own skin with enviable ease. (The erotic aura that the Panthers presented was a not inconsiderable part of their appeal, as any of the many photographs that were taken of them show. And in this department, Huey was the Supreme Leader, and he never let you forget it.) Eldridge was the biggest mouth in a party of bigmouths. He especially loved invective and adored the sound of his own voice, delivered in a sly baritone drawl. He was a gifted practitioner of the rhetoric of denunciation, favoring such gems as "fascist mafioso" and given to vilifying the United States, at every turn, as "Babylon." He was a master of misogynist pith, uttering the imperishable "revolutionary power grows out of the lips of a pussy." He was fond of repeating, as if it were a personal mantra, "He could look his momma in the eye and lie." He was notorious in elite Bay Area movement circles for his many and persistent infidelities and for his physical abuse of his equally tough-talking and beautiful wife, Kathleen. About these failures, however, a curtain of silence was drawn. He was, all in all, a hustler who exuded charm and menace in equal measure.

Cleaver would ultimately flee the country, rightly fearing a return to prison following his bungled shootout with Oakland police in the immediate aftermath of Martin Luther King Jr.'s assassination in April 1968. The debacle had given the Panthers their first martyr, seventeen-year-old Bobby Hutton, the nascent party's first recruit, gunned down by the cops as he sought to surrender. His funeral was front-page news; Marlon

Brando was a featured speaker. Cleaver was arrested, released on bail, and then disappeared, heading first to Cuba and then to Algeria. Newton was still in prison, awaiting trial for killing an Oakland cop. Now Bobby Seale was fighting to avoid a similar fate in Chicago. David Hilliard, the party's chief of staff, was left to try to hold the group together. Hoover's FBI, sensing victory, ratcheted up its secret COINTELPRO campaign, in concert with local police departments across the country, to sow dissension in the party's ranks and to otherwise discredit and destroy its leaders. Hoover was a determined foe. He too had seemingly embraced Malcolm X's defiant slogan, "by any means necessary." He cared a lot about order and about the law not a whit. With King gone, he worried, not unreasonably, that the Panthers would widen their appeal and step into the breach.

The suppression of the urban rebellions that erupted in many of the nation's cities in the hinge year of 1968 underscored the Panthers' fear that the United States had entered a long night of fascism. Nonviolent protest struck a growing number of activists as having run its course in the face of unsentimental and overwhelming state power. The Vietnam War, despite the upwelling of the Tet Offensive, seemed endless. Richard Nixon's election on a platform of "law and order" made a generation of reform-minded progressives seem hopelessly naïve. Fires were being lit by a burgeoning and increasingly despairing discontent. For some time, Jim Morrison had been singing about "The End." Soon, Gil Scott-Heron would intone that "The Revolution Will Not Be Televised," and from his California prison cell, Huey P. Newton began to dream of "revolutionary suicide."

*

Bloom and Martin have written about as close to an official history as can be imagined. Cornel West has praised it as "definitive," and Tom Hayden thinks it "should become a standard historical work." It would be surprising if it did: Bloom and Martin have chosen, oddly for scholars, to adopt the world view and sometimes the language of their subjects. Empathy, for them, goes a long way—too far, I would argue. Objectivity, of course, is the fool's gold of historical writing, but, like perfection, it is a virtue worth pursuing. Bloom and Martin, however, are more activists than traditional historians, even dedicating their book to, among others, "young revolutionaries everywhere." When it comes to the Panthers, they are as close to their subject as lips are to teeth. In a note on how they went about writing the book, they trumpet their decision not to use material from the many conversations they had in the late 1990s with surviving former Panthers, including such luminaries as Seale, Hilliard, Elaine Brown, and Ericka Huggins, among many others. The authors say that they came to distrust such accounts as "highly contradictory" and so decided to avoid "using retrospective interviews as a principal source of evidence." They preferred to trust "many thousands of firsthand accounts of historical events offered by participants shortly after they occurred."

Did it not occur to them that contemporaneous accounts might be hostage to particular agendas and interests, thus reducing their usefulness as a reliable guide to the reality they purport to reflect? Bloom and Martin are proud to have "assembled the only near-complete collection of the Party's own newspaper, the *Black Panther*," an archive that includes 520 of the 537 issues published. This record, they assert, "offers the most comprehensive documentation of the ideas, actions, and projections of the Party day to day, week to week," and it is the foundation stone upon which the edifice of their history of the Black Panther Party is built. This is perverse. It's as if they had written the history of the Nation of Islam by mainly quoting *Muhammad Speaks* or assembled a serious history of the American Communist Party by relying on back issues of the *Daily Worker*. Do Bloom and Martin not realize that such unabashed organs of propaganda are deliberate exercises in spin, often pushing this or that favored political line while seeking to conceal intraparty squabbles, as well as fierce clashes, large and small, over personalities and politics?

Too often there is an airless quality to their prose, and the human factor, sadly, is sometimes lacking. Thus, the story's inherent drama is diminished, inert. Bloom and Martin have inexplicably chosen to ignore much that illuminates but which lies hidden in plain sight in the memoirs of several former Panthers, works they cite in the book's endnotes but whose most revelatory nuggets remain buried. For example, among the things you will not learn from *Black against Empire* but would from Elaine Brown's hair-raising account in her indispensable *Taste of Power* (1992) is how Newton viciously turned on Seale, his comrade and peerless organizer. You will not learn in detail from Bloom and Martin how Newton succumbed to his cocaine and cognac–fueled megalomania; how he ordered Big Bob Heard, his six-foot-eight, four-hundred-pound bodyguard, to beat Seale with a bullwhip, cracking twenty lashes across his bared back; nor how, when the ordeal was over,

Newton abruptly stripped Seale of his rank as party chairman and ordered him to pack up and get out of Oakland.
Hilliard, too, Newton's friend since they were thirteen, would
be expelled, as would his brother, June. As would Seale's brother,
John, deemed by Newton to be "untrustworthy as a blood relative of a counterrevolutionary." Newton became what he arguably had been from the start: a sawdust Stalin.

You won't learn from Bloom and Martin the hard truth
about Flores Forbes, a trusted enforcer for Newton, a stalwart
of the party's Orwellian "Board of Methods and Corrections,"
and a member of what Newton called his "Buddha Samurai,"
a praetorian guard made up of men willing to follow orders
unquestioningly and do the "stern stuff." Forbes joined the party
at fifteen and wasted no time becoming a zombie for Huey.
Forbes was bright and didn't have to be told; he knew when to
keep his mouth shut. He well understood the "right to initia-
tive," a term Forbes tells us "was derived from our reading and
interpretation of *The Wretched of the Earth* by Frantz Fanon."
What Forbes took Fanon to mean was "that it is the oppressed
people's right to believe that they should kill their oppressor in
order to obtain their freedom. We just modified it somewhat
to mean anyone who's in our way," like inconvenient witnesses
who might testify against Newton, or Panthers who'd run afoul
of Newton and needed to be "mud-holed"—battered and beaten
to a bloody pulp. Newton no longer favored Mao's *Little Red
Book*, preferring Mario Puzo's *The Godfather*, which he extolled
for its protagonists' Machiavellian cunning and ruthlessness.
Nor will you learn from Bloom and Martin how Newton admired Melvin van Peebles's *Sweet Sweetback's Baadasssss Song*,
the tale of a hustler who becomes a revolutionary. Military

regalia was out, swagger sticks were in. Newton dropped the rank of minister of defense. Some days he wanted to be called "Supreme Commander," other days "Servant of the People" or, usually, just "Servant." But to fully understand Huey's devolution, you'd have to run Peebles's picture backward, as the story of a revolutionary who becomes a hustler.

Several years ago, I spent an afternoon with Seale, renewing a conversation we'd begun some months before. He'd moved back to Oakland, living once again in his mother's house, and was contemplating writing a book—the truth, the whole truth, and nothing but the truth, as he put it to me, about the rise and fall of the Panthers—on the very dining room table where almost a half century ago he and Newton had drafted the Panthers' Ten-Point Program. No one was getting any younger, and he felt he owed it to a new generation to come clean. At his invitation, we jumped into his car and, with Bobby at the wheel, drove around Oakland, visiting all the neighborhood spots where history had been made: here was the corner where Newton had shot and killed Officer John Frey in October 1967; and there was the former lounge and bar, the notorious Lamp Post, where Newton had laundered money from drug deals and shakedowns; and over there were the steps of the Alameda County Courthouse, where thousands, including myself, had assembled in August 1970 to hail Newton's release from prison and where, beneath the blazing summer sun, Huey, basking in the embrace of the adoring crowd, had stripped off his shirt, revealing his cut and musclebound torso, honed by a punishing regimen of countless push-ups in the isolation cell of the prison where he'd done his time, a once slight Oakland kid now physically transformed into the very embodiment of the powerful animal he'd made the emblem of his ambitions.

As Seale spoke, mimicking with uncanny accuracy Huey's oddly high-pitched and breathless stutter, virtually channeling the man, now dead more than two decades—ignominiously gunned down at age forty-seven in a crack cocaine deal gone bad by a young punk half his age seeking to make his bones—it became clear that, despite everything he'd endured, Bobby Seale was a man with all the passions and unresolved resentments of a lover betrayed. There could be little doubt that, for Seale, the best years of his life were the years he spent devoted to Newton, who still, despite the passage of time, loomed large. Seale, like the party he gave birth to, still couldn't rid himself of Huey's shadow.

Among the challenges in grappling with the Panthers and their legacy is keeping in reasonable balance the multiple and often overlapping factors that combined to throttle the party. The temptation to overemphasize the role of the FBI is large. It should be avoided. There is no doubt about the evil that was done by Hoover's COINTELPRO: it exacerbated the worst tendencies among the Panthers and did much to deepen a politics of paranoia that would ultimately help hollow out what had been a steadily growing movement of opposition. It sowed the seeds of disunity. It cast doubt on the very idea of leadership. It promoted suspicion and distrust. It countenanced murder and betrayal. But the Panthers were not blameless. Newton, for his part, provided fertile ground for reckless extremism and outright criminality to grow and take root. Cockamamie offshoots like Donald DeFreeze's so-called Symbionese Liberation Army and even the lethal cult of Jim Jones's benighted People's Temple owed an unacknowledged debt to Newton's example. His responsibility for enfeebling his own and his party's best ambitions, gutting its achievements, and compromising its ability to appeal to the unconvinced majority of his fellow citizens is too often neglected in accounts of this kind. Yet it is precisely this sort of postmortem and historical reckoning that is necessary for any proper and just understanding of the party's politics and history. It is work that remains to be done.

Bloom and Martin barely concern themselves with the party's swift descent into thuggery, consigning only six paragraphs in the closing pages of their book to a section called "Unraveling." They prefer to dwell on the party's glory years from 1967 through 1971. They deny that the party's end was rooted in its undemocratic character, and instead attribute its defeat largely to what they believe was the deft way the political establishment undercut its base, by initiating reforms and awarding concessions that won over the Panthers' allies. "The costs of appeasing allies," they conclude, "thus made continued insurgency impossible, and the national organization defanged itself." While they allow that after 1971, the party "became increasingly cultish . . . with a mafioso bent," they blame the erosion of the party's image on journalists and critics like Kate Coleman and David Horowitz. They excoriate both as "right-wing activists," which in Coleman's case is calumny. In no instance do they dispute the accuracy of either Coleman's reporting or Horowitz's *cris de coeur*. Coleman, a veteran of the Free Speech Movement and a longtime muckraking reporter, published, together with Paul Avery, a scrupulously reported and damning indictment of the Panthers' criminal practices in *New Times* magazine in

1978. For this sin, she incurred death threats and castigation from former party stalwarts. Horowitz, a former editor of *Ramparts* magazine in its senescence, broke with Newton when he learned that the Panthers had very likely murdered Betty Van Patter, a white woman who had loyally served as the party's bookkeeper and had discovered suspicious irregularities in the accounting ledgers. Horowitz felt responsible, for it was he who had recommended Van Patter for the job. He has spent the years since atoning for the blood he feels still stains his hands.

But what matters most to Bloom and Martin, apparently, is not whether Coleman's reporting is accurate, or Horowitz's criticisms and self-flagellations are warranted. Rather, they are most exercised by the damage they believe was done to the party's image by Coleman and Horowitz in making the charges public. They concede that "retrospective accounts from a range of sources add some credence to these accusations," but insist that "few of the accusations have been verified." Bloom and Martin's research is impressive—yet somehow, they have missed or omitted accounts that might detract from or unduly complicate their overly generous portrayal. For example, the late Ken Kelley, a gifted and honest reporter, wrote courageously about Newton, whom he knew well and for whom he once worked. In a story published in the month following Newton's death, which appeared in the *East Bay Express*, Kelley revealed that Newton had admitted to him shooting seventeen-year-old Oakland prostitute Kathleen Smith and ordering the killing of Betty Van Patter for refusing to clean up the party's books. Van Patter's end was gruesome, according to Kelley: "They didn't just kill her. They kept her hostage, they raped her, they beat her up, then they killed her and threw her in the Bay."

*

It would be unjust to allow the supernovas of the Panther elite to overshadow the unsung heroes whose audacity and tenacious commitment to change was sparked by the party. That would miss the larger, less obvious story, which is one of persistent idealism. It owes almost everything to the wellspring of activism that the Panthers, at their best, summoned into being. Bloom and Martin are alive to this crucial point, and it is here that they make their strongest and most convincing contribution. The collapse and destruction of the party, occasioned by the unremitting enmity of the state as well as by its numerous self-inflicted wounds, should not be permitted to overwhelm the good work that it engendered in the many who enrolled in its cause.

I remember especially my old high school comrade Ronald Stevenson, who at sixteen joined the party, inspired by its program of resistance and empowerment. There were thousands like him across the country. With the party's encouragement, Ronnie organized a Black Student Union, going on to be elected its first chair. Together, we launched a campaign to establish a Black history course and department. Our only disagreement was whether the course should be elective or mandatory, he favoring the former, I the latter. I felt that if the class were voluntary, only the Black kids would be likely to enroll. I believed that such history was arguably even more important for white people to know in order to challenge racial stereotypes and to grasp the essential contribution that Black people had made to American history and culture. After all, how could you consider yourself an educated and serious person if, say, you only knew about Abraham Lincoln but not Frederick Douglass? Or about John Brown but not Nat Turner? All this may seem self-evident today. In 1968, it was not. We fought hard, mobilized fellow students and their parents, and issued our "nonnegotiable demands." We won, and the Berkeley Board of Education agreed to establish such a course. It was among the first in the nation to be offered in a high school, and Ronnie and I were eager to enroll. Forty-five years later, Lerone Bennett's *Before the Mayflower* and Basil Davidson's *The African Genius*, two of the books we were assigned to read, still have pride of place on my bookshelves.

A year later, seventeen-year-old Ronnie was on the run, accused of having shot and killed a former member of the Black Panther Party outside its Shattuck Avenue headquarters. For the next decade, I'd occasionally hear that he was in Cuba or Algeria. The truth was that he'd gone underground and changed his name, but instead of fleeing to Havana, he'd gone to Mahwah, New Jersey, where he'd gotten a job in an auto plant. There, ever the organizer, he'd become a member of the United Auto Workers, eventually elected to represent three hundred of his fellows as their district committee man. But after eight years in the plant, Ronnie and the other workers found themselves out of a job; the plant had closed. He told me all this when he showed up at our tenth-anniversary high school reunion, having decided to return to California and face the music. The charges against him were eventually dismissed, and he reenrolled at UC Berkeley in 1983, where he founded a program called Break the Cycle that hired undergraduates to tutor local at-risk elementary and middle school students, with an emphasis on mathematics. The program was a success, running for more than twenty years. Ronnie would graduate with a degree in African American studies in 1990 and became a lecturer in the department. He also started a community program that put kids from South Berkeley together with police officers each week to discuss racial profiling. He died in 2010 of a brain aneurysm. He was fifty-eight.

Postscriptum

At the time of Huey P. Newton's murder in August 1989, I was, briefly, Doubleday's executive editor. I had long wanted to publish the story of Newton's improbable and spectacular ascent, and now, with his equally spectacular if depressing demise, it was a tale, if told right, to put alongside Malcolm X's autobiography. But who could do it? You'd need a writer familiar with the quicksands and bogs of Bay Area left-wing politics, someone with empathy for the audacity that animated Newton and catapulted his party to international prominence but also someone who would approach the story with unflinching devotion to the truth, no matter where it led. Someone who could do for Newton what Taylor Branch had done for Martin Luther King Jr. Maybe such a writer didn't exist. But if anyone could do it, I thought, maybe Kate Coleman could. It wouldn't be easy, of course. After all, it might be all but impossible for her as a white woman who had already washed a good deal of the Panther's dirty laundry in the late 1970s to gain the cooperation and trust of the sources she'd doubtless need. But I was willing to give her a shot. Her reporting chops were impeccable, and as a veteran of the Free Speech Movement, she was as politically savvy as she was honest and driven.

Somehow David Hilliard, the former chief of staff of the Black Panther Party, learned that I was contemplating asking Coleman to write Huey's biography. We agreed to meet and talk about his concerns. I had known Hilliard slightly, having met him briefly while working at the Panthers' Berkeley headquarters on the underground high school newspaper I was helping to put out in 1969.

He arrived at my Upper West Side apartment in the company of Marty Kenner, a white commodities broker and a past financial adviser to the party. It quickly became plain that Hilliard intended to put the kibosh on the project. To put him at ease, my wife had put up a pot of coffee and had baked some muffins for us to share. The meeting began amicably enough but didn't end well when it became clear that I was willing to give Kate a chance and David wasn't.

David was adamant that no white person, much less Kate Coleman, could write Huey's story. I asked him what he thought of Taylor Branch's magisterial biography of Martin Luther King Jr.

"Fucking genius."

"I rest my case," I said.

Here's what I can promise, I told him: "If Kate turns in a book as good as Branch's, I'll publish it. If not, I won't."

David swore that no way, no how would he permit Coleman to write such a biography. Soon he was shouting, and my wife was cowering in the kitchen.

He stood up abruptly, muttering threats, turned on his heel, and made for the door. Kenner followed. Then, just before storming out, he said, "But tell your wife she makes some goddamn motherfucking great blueberry muffins."

[2013]

44

Exit Stage Left

B ERKELEY IN THE YEARS THAT I came of age was heady
with the scent of night jasmine and tear gas. It whipsawed,
sometimes violently, between clichés, from the Age of Aquar-
ius to the Age of Apocalypse and back. I especially recall the
evening in February 1969 when hundreds of us, exhausted from
a day of battling cops seeking to break the Third World Liberation Strike at the University of California's campus, trooped
down to the Berkeley Community Theatre, where we hoped to
find relief in the much-ballyhooed provocations of Julian Beck
and Judith Malina's Living Theatre.

Much to our surprise, the production of *Paradise Now*
was a bust. What was an outrage to bourgeois sensibilities
elsewhere—nearly nude members of the troupe intoning
mantras of prohibition against smoking pot and sexing it up
in public—was greeted by the solemn radicals and spirited anarchists of Berkeley as feeble and largely empty gestures. Joel Tornabene aka "Super Joel," one of the town's
more colorful and ubiquitous characters, stood up and loud-
ly denounced Beck and Malina for their faux radicalism,
then lit a joint and began to disrobe. Others quickly followed. Hundreds surrounded the couple, angrily demanding that their tickets be refunded. Dozens of debates erupted
all around—over the nature of drama and the character of

revolution. The show did not go on. The audience stormed the stage. Finally, at midnight, the fire marshals arrived and kicked us out. Beck and Malina had inadvertently achieved what had previously eluded them: goading the audience into taking collective action, seizing the moment, arguing over whether to remain passive spectators or become actors in a drama of their own making. It was unforgettable. I also remember the denouement: no sooner had the Living Theatre departed than the next day, a furious Governor Reagan arrived and threatened to deploy the National Guard, in addition to the hundreds of police from throughout Northern California that filled the streets.

Bedazzled as we were by the spectacle of our own high ideals and the intoxications of making history, we perhaps might be forgiven for mistaking the theater in the streets as the main event, while failing to tumble to another high drama taking place, as it were, offstage. We were deaf, alas, to the malign fugue that was being played within the inner circles of the old order. It is the welcome and signal contribution of Seth Rosenfeld's important, if flawed, tome *Subversives: The FBI's War on Student Radicals, and Reagan's Rise to Power*, to provide a necessary threnody to an era whose many tumults and contradictions still lie buried beneath a carapace of cliché. Rosenfeld, a former longtime, prize-winning investigative reporter for the *San Francisco Chronicle*, aspires to tell how, in one small American hamlet whose recalcitrant students had won for it an outsize international reputation as a magnetic pole of rebellion, the state waged a two-front struggle—one open and without apology, and the other often invisible and illegal— to stamp out opponents, real and imagined, to its rule.

Berkeley called itself the "Athens of the West," a moniker meant to summon its origins and promise as the mid-nineteenth-century site of the fabled first campus of the University of California. The conceit suggested the agora of ancient Greece, where citizens would freely debate the issues of the day, and Socratic dialogues would occur about the meaning and purpose of life. Educating citizens to build and manage the expanding American imperium was at the center of this great project, born of the lofty ambitions of California progressivism. This publicly funded university and its eight (now ten) other campuses throughout the state, which any qualified high school student could attend for a paltry annual cost, were the pride of California. The University of California had, by almost any measure, quickly joined the ranks of the private Ivy League institutions that had dominated the higher tiers of elite American education. Its students counted themselves among America's best and brightest. They were also renowned for their political activism. Robert McNamara would remember, with not a little nostalgia, the protests he participated in as an undergraduate during the 1930s—protests he would have occasion to recall decades later when, as a principal architect of the Vietnam War, he would be condemned as a war criminal by students at his alma mater (and not only there).

From the militant longshoremen's strikes and upheavals of the Great Depression through efforts by Communist spies in the late 1940s and 1950s to steal the nation's atomic secrets at Berkeley's Lawrence Radiation Laboratory, to the forcing of loyalty oaths on the campus's professoriat, Berkeley—and San Francisco—had long been regarded by the grim men in Sacramento and Washington as swamps of subversion. For years, J. Edgar Hoover and his Federal Bureau of Investigation had sought to drain them of suspected traitors. By the midsixties, the FBI's San Francisco Bay Area offices boasted several hundred agents. Hoover's obsessions would keep the hive humming.

The Bay Area was engulfed by multiple and successive student protests. The most notable included the anti-HUAC protests of 1960; the great civil rights sit-ins of the spring of 1964 at the Sheraton-Palace Hotel in San Francisco, along with the Auto Row demonstrations seeking an end to racial discrimination, which began in late 1963 and continued through the spring of 1964; the Free Speech Movement in the fall of 1964, followed by one of the nation's first teach-ins, organized by the Vietnam Day Committee in May 1965; and, three months later, the efforts to prevent the passage of troop trains through Berkeley. Then came the founding of the Black Panther Party in 1966 and the riotous antidraft demonstrations in Oakland in 1967, the Third World Liberation strike at UC Berkeley in February 1969, culminating in the violent suppression of People's Park protesters in May 1969, which saw the death of one onlooker and the blinding of another by shotgun-wielding Alameda County deputy sheriffs, the indiscriminate gassing of the campus by a National Guard helicopter, the imposition of martial law, and the monthlong occupation of the entire city by thousands of armed troops. These traumatic irruptions form the epic backdrop to *Subversives*.

It is Rosenfeld's achievement, after a twenty-seven-year legal battle, to have compelled the FBI to make public some three hundred thousand pages of its secret files—files the bureau was so loath to see the light of day that it spent more than $1 million of the taxpayers' money to prevent their release. Those documents would provide, Rosenfeld hoped, the Rosetta stone that would crack the bureau's greatest secret: the record of its hidden war against Berkeley's student radicals and the heretofore unacknowledged alliance between Reagan and Hoover. And indeed, Rosenfeld's labors help to deepen our understanding of those years of hope and rage.

The story is, at first blush, straightforward: a tale of dirty high jinks pursued by a rogue institution—the FBI—dominated by an aging despot at its helm, unwilling to let go the delusions that had so successfully made him one of America's most powerful and feared men. Rosenfeld builds his narrative around four figures: Mario Savio, the brilliant and emotionally tormented avatar of the Free Speech Movement; Clark Kerr, the hapless liberal anti-Communist head of UC Berkeley, much reviled as a soulless toady by the students whose protests he ineffectively sought to contain (for which services he would incur the enduring enmity of his minders); Ronald Reagan, the demagogic former actor whose landslide election in 1966 as California's governor would later catapult him into the White House; and J. Edgar Hoover, the notorious scourge of all things pinko, who had long worked to enlist Reagan's vaulting political ambitions and willing acquiescence in Hoover's crusade against Communism. It is through their interactions that Rosenfeld weaves the threads he has teased out from the welter of FBI documents.

What embarrassments did the bureau so desperately want to conceal? According to Rosenfeld, the documents detail the extraordinary lengths—often duplicitous and sometimes criminal—that Hoover and his men went to in their decades-long effort to demonize and marginalize citizens suspected to be of an oppositional bent. The trove, writes Rosenfeld, "is the most complete record of FBI activities at any college ever released. The documents reveal that FBI agents amassed dossiers on hundreds of students and professors and on members of the [university's] Board of Regents; established informers within student groups, the faculty, and the highest levels of the university's administration; and gathered intelligence from wiretaps, mail openings, and searches of Berkeley homes and offices in the dead of night." More: "FBI documents show that bureau officials misled a president by sending the White House information the bureau knew to be false; mounted a covert campaign to manipulate public opinion about campus events and embarrass university officials; collaborated with the head of the CIA to harass students; ran a secret program to fire professors whose political views were deemed unacceptable." Rosenfeld claims that "these documents show that during the Cold War, FBI officials sought to change the course of history by secretly interceding in events, manipulating public opinion, and taking sides in partisan politics."

This isn't exactly news. Can anyone at this late date, after the COINTELPRO revelations and Church Committee reports of the mid-1970s and numerous other subsequent journalistic scoops of government skullduggery over the past four decades, affect to be shocked? Almost everything we had long suspected turns out to be true, only more so. Were telephones tapped? Routinely. Were *agents provocateurs* planted? Every chance the government got. Rosenfeld reveals, for example, that one of

the early and influential members of the Black Panther Party—
not unexpectedly one of the few who knew most about how to
use guns—was very likely a longtime government informant.
But is anyone other than Bobby Seale, who publicly praised
the man as a stalwart hero of the revolution on the occasion of
his funeral several years ago, entirely surprised?

Rosenfeld has spent too long in the archives. Entranced by pages
upon pages of redacted documents, redolent of the patina of
official authority, he has made a category error, regarding as
holy writ the effluvia of careerists and spies while remaining
largely blind to the multiple and often self-serving agendas at
work by the documents' dirty tricksters. Assessing these desic-
cated documents requires caution. Weighing statements and
testimonies as evidence of the actual beliefs and practices of
the alleged "subversives" under surveillance demands a nearly
forensic care. Conspiracy is a rare commodity, much sought
after by true believers. The FBI rarely found it among those
that the bureau deemed enemies or potential enemies of the
state; but neither is conspiracy in the precincts of the powerful to be much found among these often inherently dubious
documents. Instead, what they evidence is mostly blunder and
unintentional comedy. Rosenfeld's often admirable dedication to flushing out the darker designs of the powerful renders
him insufficiently attentive to other, arguably more significant,
factors. Irony isn't his strong suit.

A single example makes the point. A few years after the
bureau established its Berkeley office in 1957, two senior agents
secreted themselves in the crawlspace beneath the floorboards

of the aristo ex-Communist Jessica Mitford and her husband Bob Treuhaft's Oakland home, keen to collect any pearls of subversion that could be gleaned from the meeting of comrades taking place above their heads. But so dull was the gathering that one agent dozed off and began to snore, panicking his partner—and so, fearing discovery, they fled. Another agent, Rosenfeld informs us, after spending hours tapping Mitford's phone, learned only that Decca's preferred toothpaste was Ipana. Such, such were the goods.

Hoover, infamously, had made a fetish of finding Communists under every bed. His agents strained to tell him what they thought he wanted to hear. Often, they could not. When in doubt, they tried to fail upward. What surprises is how often their dutiful investigations and wiretaps forced the more honest of the G-men to confess that, try as they might to catch them, actual Communists were elusive game, members of an endangered species. The suspicion gradually arose within the bureau's ranks that by the late 1950s and early 1960s, they were largely a phantom of Hoover's perfervid imagination, a thick gumbo whose ingredients were spiced in the early years of his efforts to break the back of radical strivings, out of which he had made his bones and to which he would remain unswervingly if stupidly loyal.

In 1968, for example, Hoover ordered his men to use every means to "neutralize" several of the more prominent leaders of the Bay Area New Left. The head of his San Francisco office pushed back, patiently pointing out that none of Hoover's targets (which included Savio and Robert Scheer, an editor of the radical slick *Ramparts*, closely affiliated with the New Left) were "members of any known subversive organizations. . . .

They are independent free thinkers and do not appear to be answerable to any one person or any group or organization." Hoover was undeterred. He believed that the stigma of bureau investigation would be sufficient to frighten his targets into submission. After all, such tactics had worked on an earlier generation of radicals. Now, however, they were all but useless. The new radicals didn't remotely resemble the cautious Communists he was used to intimidating. Jerry Rubin could never be mistaken for Gus Hall. They didn't want society's traditional jobs and spurned its blandishments. The culture had slipped Hoover's grasp. But still he was convinced that by planting stories with compliant reporters exposing such radicals' allegedly aberrant lifestyles, he could tarnish their public reputation. His man in San Francisco knew better, telling Hoover, "They are not embarrassed by this coverage. In fact, they seem to enjoy it and thrive on it." Hoover refused to listen. He ratcheted up his efforts. Surveillance programs proliferated. Secret budgets ballooned. But little worked as intended. If the war on radicals was, at least in Hoover's head, a war without end, it was a war largely without significant result, as Rosenfeld inadvertently makes clear.

A story, possibly apocryphal, that Rosenfeld doesn't include contains a larger dollop of truth than the hundreds of thousands of FBI documents that he insists reveal government conspiracies run amok. It was a favorite of Warren Hinckle, the author of *If You Have a Lemon, Make Lemonade* (1974), his unjustly neglected memoir of his years presiding over *Ramparts*. The bureau was beside itself with the exposés the magazine regularly published, in particular by Scheer, Hinckle's comrade in muckraking. And so it came to pass that the magazine's North

Beach lair was burglarized. Suspicion was strong that Hoover's men were responsible. Scheer was possessed of a mind as startlingly lucid as his desk was invariably disheveled, covered with a mad shambles of telephone numbers and notes scrawled higgledy-piggledy on the backs of envelopes and scraps of paper. His "runic scribble," as Hinckle called it, was the bane of the magazine's copy editors. And so it proved to Hoover's black bag men, who were unable to decipher Scheer's poison penmanship. Hoover's FBI, increasingly irrelevant, was more and more a spent force.

Rosenfeld seems not to understand this, however, convinced that he's found in these documents a veritable Pentagon Papers. Rosenfeld argues that the FBI's refusal to give up its secrets was rooted in a desire to keep hidden its decades-long effort to bend and often to break the law in pursuit of suspected "subversives," fearing that revelation of its misdeeds might arouse the public's ire. Another, more compelling reason suggests itself: on the evidence of the Everest of documents that the bureau sought to conceal, what Hoover and his successors were at pains to cover up was its thoroughgoing incompetence. As the bureau knew, few "subversives" were there to be found. Far from the model of a modern and relentlessly efficient intelligence-gathering machine, Hoover had instead created a massive and costly bureaucracy whose actual workings reveal a startling gap between its fearsome public image and its shabby, inept inner reality. What these hundreds of thousands of FBI documents show is how little the bureau accomplished for all its fevered exertions.

Rosenfeld thinks the tale he's telling is one of unbridled abuse of government power seeking by hook or by crook to dislodge and demolish a corpuscular and burgeoning movement of discontent. And it is, up to a point. The more sinister drama, however, is the one that unfolds in the shadow play of the backstage efforts to get rid of Clark Kerr, deemed by establishment figures to his right to be no longer trustworthy: naïve at best and an unwitting, pusillanimous comsymp at worst. Kerr's sin was to have betrayed his class—an even greater crime, as far as his overseers were concerned, than the obstreperous bleatings of a young malcontent like Savio. Suspicious of his Quaker convictions, his fieldwork as a young graduate student studying the plight of striking farmworkers in the 1930s in the harvests of sorrow that formed California's San Joaquin Valley, and his years as a labor negotiator, Kerr's critics within the corporate boardrooms and private clubs to which the men who ran the state belonged assiduously sought his ouster. He was, they felt, invertebrate. Harder, more ruthless, and more cynical men were needed. With Hoover's connivance, they plotted Kerr's removal. They were confident that the ever-pliant Reagan would do their bidding. After all, he always had, as Hoover had known ever since Reagan's stoolie days for the bureau, when the second-rate star, as head of the Screen Actors Guild during Hollywood's long night of redbaiting, yearned for Hoover's recognition and approbation. The FBI documents on this count are convincing. When the fateful day came, just weeks after Reagan's inauguration, Kerr was stunned. His sacking, he recalled, felt "like a whip across my face."

Though it is heresy to say so, Kerr was, in a strange way, Savio's doppelgänger. Who doesn't remember Savio's imperishable exhortation, one of the most eloquent remarks ever made in the history of modern American radicalism, uttered extemporaneously at the height of the Free Speech Movement? "There is a time when the operation of the machine becomes so odious, makes you so sick at heart, that you can't take part, you can't even passively take part; and you've got to put your bodies upon the gears and upon the wheels, upon the levers, upon all the apparatus and you've got to make it stop. And you've got to indicate to the people who run it, to the people who own it, that unless you're free, the machine will be prevented from working at all!"

One wonders whether this striking bit of oratory may have evoked in Savio's nemesis a sense of déjà vu, for it recalled the spirit and almost the very words of Kerr's own profound distress more than thirty years before at seeing a pregnant mother and her ailing infant evicted from a one-room hovel in Pasadena. The sight had filled him with a barely contained anger. He knew to do the right thing. In an anecdote he all but buries, Rosenfeld tells how Kerr, in his own words, had joined with others to "break the law and move the family back in" by smashing the lock that police had placed on the shack's door to bar their return. As Kerr later wrote to his father, "This country has come to a place where one must break the law in order to insure [sic] that the people may have the privilege of 'life, liberty and the pursuit of happiness.'" Kerr never entirely succeeded at ridding himself of the bleeding-heart cells that fitfully coursed through his veins, though he spent years trying. His masters, however, were experts at sniffing out such misplaced sympathies.

Kerr is Rosenfeld's most tragic and misunderstood figure. One wishes that *Subversives* had made more of this dimension of the drama and explored the larger implications of Kerr's unhappy end. His ouster as president of the University of California was the new governor's first real political victory—a victory initially applauded by Savio and his comrades, who had come to detest Kerr nearly as much as did Hoover and Reagan. Kerr's firing was a body blow to the hallowed and heretofore largely sacrosanct notion that the university and its campus ought properly to be a protected zone of discourse, free of state intervention. It was a principle that Kerr had fought to uphold. His defeat would have lasting consequences and was a rare victory for Hoover, whose machinations were often ineffective where they weren't counterproductive.

Did the bureau, despite its legal, extralegal, and often criminal manipulations, actually bend history's arrow? For all its provocations, did it really derail or significantly disrupt the New Left? Did it truly succeed in putting the kibosh on student protest? Was it an important factor in propelling Reagan to the pinnacle of power—a summit to which he somehow might not, on the strength of his own political genius, have risen?

The answer, *contra* Rosenfeld, is no. The FBI's antics were a sideshow. The main drama was elsewhere. The war against radical students was, in several crucial respects, something like the thirteenth-century war against the Cathars, when the Catholic Church persistently denounced heresy in repeated inquisitions and crusades seeking to identify and stamp out beliefs that departed from the true religion. These persecutions were often campaigns of convenience against imagined communities of opposition. Often, they masked rivalries within the Church that rent the outwardly coherent fabric of elite power. A similar dynamic seems to have animated Hoover and the FBI, Reagan and his henchmen. Their fiercest combat was as much against radical zealots as it was against reformers within their own ranks, against honorable do-gooders like Clark Kerr. Of course, cudgeling students played well with a public who saw Savio and his cohorts as little more than petulant brats who ought no longer to be indulged by hardworking taxpayers. The strategy worked, and so began the successful effort to return an unruly campus to the more controlling orbit of the state—and, ultimately, to launch the long counterrevolution to undo the achievements of the New Deal.

As for the wounds suffered by the New Left, they were largely self-inflicted. Did the FBI seek to take advantage of our weaknesses, to exploit our missteps, and to use our naïveté as a noose by which to hang an entire movement? Sure it did. Rosenfeld adds nuance and appalling detail to a familiar story of suppression: police attacks on peaceful demonstrators, the secret (and often successful) efforts to encourage extremism in order to isolate dissenters, and the open campaign to crush resistance by wielding the state's powerful legal truncheon, thus draining the left's always meager treasury and depriving it of its most able leaders. Such tactics encouraged the politics of paranoia. The result, as Christopher Lasch so clearly understood, "imprisoned the left in a politics of theater, of dramatic gestures, of style without substance—a mirror image of the politics of unreality which it should have been the purpose of the left to unmask." But we did not need Hoover's hooligans to prompt us to embrace the terrible logic of politics as a total art form. We came all on our own to believe that only by increasingly provocative spectacle could the veil of public apathy be pierced. It is we who elevated extremism to the level of strategy. It was a dialectic of defeat.

[2012]

American Berserk

PEOPLE NEVER FIND IT EASY to confront the past; they generally prefer to consign it to oblivion. Today, the model citizen is too often one without memory. Complex events are simplified; history is coarsened and turned into a species of exorcism and kitsch. This is especially true whenever one hears talk about the radical upheavals of the 1960s and their afterglow in the 1970s. Pundits prefer turning those overoxygenated years into a kind of exotic folklore: Twiggy, the Beatles, Timothy Leary, Godard, Vietnam, Huey Newton, the Weather Underground, Patty Hearst. The mosaic of moods and movements that colored and shaped that period are flattened and made safe for our collective consumption. The many divisions and differences, inherent in any time of social dislocation, are ignored. Thus is the hegemony of particular experiences created (Woodstock Nation, say, or Altamont), a hegemony that neglects or diminishes the importance of others (the so-called Silent Majority, for instance). It is worth recalling that there was much political conservatism and quietism in the 1960s and 1970s.

There also was what Philip Roth would memorably call in his 1997 novel *American Pastoral* "the indigenous American berserk," the decision by some young Americans to take up arms against the regnant order. What happened to them, what they actually did, the web of conceits they wove then and later to justify their revulsion, and the efforts by the authorities, largely unsuccessful and often illegal, to catch and crush them is the subject of Bryan Burrough's *Days of Rage: America's Radical Underground, the FBI, and the Forgotten Age of Revolutionary Violence.*

A former business reporter for the *Wall Street Journal* and since 1993 a star writer for *Vanity Fair*, Burrough is justly admired for his meticulously researched *Barbarians at the Gate*, written with John Helyar, a bestselling epic of the avarice that led to the $25 billion leveraged buyout of the RJR Nabisco Corporation, a book that caught something of the zeitgeist of Wall Street's go-go years in the late twentieth century. Struck by the disparity between today's overheated response to the specter of terrorism and the relative complacency that Burrough believes greeted the bombings carried out in the 1970s by what he calls "apocalyptic revolutionaries," he decided to take a closer look, to perform a kind of autopsy on the corpse of a past that, he says, is all but forgotten. He had a lot to choose from, for a bewildering array of groups and grouplets had declared war on the American imperium. They included the Weatherman, the militant faction that arose in June of 1969 from the breakup of Students for a Democratic Society (SDS); the Symbionese Liberation Army, the brainchild of ex-con Donald DeFreeze, which grabbed headlines with its killing of Marcus Foster, Oakland's Black school superintendent, and kidnapping of heiress Patty Hearst; the Black Liberation Army, a violent cabal, based largely in New York City, that rejected Huey Newton's Black Panther Party for its alleged timidity and soon embarked on a shakedown of drug dealers and bank heists, a gang which, aided by a number of white radicals, successfully executed the spectacular jailbreak and flight into Cuban exile of Assata

Shakur; and the FALN, a deadly serious clandestine group devoted to the cause of Puerto Rican independence, whose bomb-maker would prove to be among the more skilled of the radical pyrotechnicians until the day something went terribly awry in his Queens flat, blowing off nine of his fingers and shredding most of his face.

Who were these people and what did they want and why did they do the things they did? Very largely they emerged from the despair and perceived defeats of the New Left, a term created to mark the difference between the dull apologists for the Soviet Union that had so compromised the Old Left and the fresher, less ideological voices that had been forged in the crucible of the civil rights movement. Like much of the postwar generation it reflected, the New Left was rooted in utopian romanticism. It was often tainted, especially in the late 1960s and early 1970s, with a disturbing streak of intolerance and messianism. It was frequently intemperate, unreasonable, arrogant—that is to say, it was a movement of the young. It was, in the words of Al Haber, a founder in 1962 of SDS, a mixture of "mysticism, humanism, innocent idealism, and moral urgency."

In its early years, the New Left declared its belief in reason, in persuasion, in moral sobriety. It opposed the use of violence. It set in motion an unwieldy and diverse movement of vigorous dissent that helped to end the American intervention in Indochina, improve the lot of the poor and the disenfranchised, and spark a cultural upheaval felt all over the world. For a time, the New Left advanced seemingly from victory to victory, from strength to strength. That it would falter (even collapse) at the moment of its greatest triumph—the US withdrawal from

Vietnam—is an enduring irony. That it finally splintered into dozens of squabbling sects whose critique of American society was derived largely from a bad conscience peculiar to the privileges of the upper-middle class cannot be denied. Why and how some of those sects became cults for zealots willing to countenance murder is the subject of Burrough's inquiry.

No one who lived through that turbulent era ever forgot it. Burrough's assertion that its intoxications, crimes, and misdemeanors have been neglected is inaccurate. He concedes that over the past four decades there have been "thousands of words written about Weatherman . . . including six memoirs, three other books, two films, and countless news articles." The spectacle of the sons and daughters of the American middle class renouncing their spoiled patrimony by embracing violent methods of rejection has been over the decades a mesmeric subject for some of our most gifted writers. Fiction often yields more insight than nonfiction. A short list of the indispensable novels on the temptations of terrorism would include Don DeLillo's *Players* (1977), Joan Didion's *A Book of Common Prayer* (1977), Marge Piercy's *Vida* (1979), Walter Abish's *How German Is It* (1980), Henry Bean's *False Match* (1982), Philip Roth's *American Pastoral* (1997), Robert Hellenga's *The Fall of a Sparrow* (1998), Neil Gordon's *The Company You Keep* (2003), Susan Choi's *American Woman* (2003), Russell Banks's *The Darling* (2004), Dana Spiotta's *Eat the Document* (2006), Christopher Sorrentino's *Trance* (2006), and Rachel Kushner's *The Flamethrowers* (2013).

Burrough's neglect of this literature is unfortunate, for it enfeebles the story he wants to tell. He is strikingly deaf to the

ambiguities that are at the heart of any exploration of character, whatever the ostensible and usually self-serving political
rationales. It's too bad Burrough omits this dimension since
such an approach might have helped vivify his story with an
irony and an empathy otherwise lacking in the way he's chosen
to tell his tale. As a result, the drama he tries to convey is mostly
stillborn.

The book is both bloated and thin. Burrough's style gives the
game away, his writing marred throughout by lazy sentences.
The potted history he uses to set his scenes is of the *Information Please* almanac variety. Doubts deepen when he confesses
his MO in a brief, altogether inadequate "Note on Sources":
most of his information is derived from "previously published
books, contemporary interviews, and personal interviews." In
addition, "Documents generated by the FBI and the NYPD,
along with an oral history or two, were also used." Yet he says
that the "highly redacted" FBI files "are almost useless . . .
almost all of it is dreck."

His endnotes are embarrassingly unhelpful. Whole chapters are given just one or two notes; others a half dozen or so.
Mostly the reader is forced to take Burrough on faith. He is an
unapologetic stitchmeister. His book isn't so much written as
it is knitted together from the yarns of others. The pixie dust
of the clutch of interviews with ex-radicals he obtained (others
refused to speak to him) isn't enough to save his book from the
suspicion that the real story is elsewhere.

To be sure, clandestine activity is inherently murky stuff,
but for all of Burrough's self-congratulatory huffing and
puffing, he hasn't come up with much. Sure, he's put a name
to the one guy who was probably the sole expert bomb-maker

for the Weatherman, now living free and unrepentant in Brooklyn. As for his other "scoops," it's hardly news that the strongest motivation for Weather's actions wasn't so much it wanting to hasten an American defeat in Vietnam but rather its desire to become a fifth column of modern-day John Browns aiding Black resistance to racism. Such vaulting ambition was declared at the time by the Weather people, who were at pains to spurn what they condemned as "white-skin privilege." Burrough's big discovery: that in the ninety days between Weather's going underground in January 1970 and the shocking explosion of March 1970, which demolished a Greenwich Village townhouse—killing the three people who were as-sembling an antipersonnel bomb in the basement, apparently intended to be detonated at an officers' dance at Fort Dix—Weather stalwarts had contemplated attacks that would actu-ally kill and maim people.

They wanted, as the slogan du jour then proclaimed, to "bring the war home." No bystanders were innocent. You were either part of the problem or part of the solution. They aimed at giving Americans, whether in uniform or not, a taste of the undiscriminating terror that was being visited upon the Viet-namese. In the event, whatever their intentions, they were about as inept as they were deluded.

Yet Burrough can't help but hype the story. He quotes a retired FBI agent who claims that in 1972 there were over "nineteen hundred domestic bombings. . . . Buildings getting bombed, policemen getting killed. It was commonplace." But was it? Or was this J. Edgar Hoover pushing his campaign to expose the reds he was convinced were under every bed, reds who had to be rooted out by any means necessary, however illegal? Burrough is not unsympathetic to Hoover's obsession; he seems to believe that had the FBI not been constrained by the revelations of the bureau's skullduggery, Hoover's G-men could have put a full nelson on the crazies who had gone to ground. That can hardly have been the case, however, as the long-running secret FBI campaign to identify and suppress suspected dissenters, COINTELPRO, preceded by many years its exposure by the daring radicals who burgled the FBI field office in Media, Pennsylvania, in 1971 and the subsequent Church Committee hearings on intelligence, held in 1975. Burrough makes plain his disagreement with the retired agent who told him that "some of us felt that what the Bureau did constituted a far greater danger to society than what the Weatherman ever did."

Burrough claims that in all of 1969 there were about a hundred bombings. The following year, the number trebled. Then, in "an eighteen-month period in 1971 and 1972, the FBI reported more than 2,500 bombings on US soil," a period which, he tells us, saw a precipitous decline in Weatherman's membership, especially after the townhouse debacle. By January 1971, Burrough reports, the group likely consisted "of a core group of barely a dozen people," and he quotes the band's chief bomb-maker admitting that the "the ones who did things, was ten or twelve people, no more than fifteen." By then Weatherman had publicly abandoned its romance with violence as a "military error," acknowledging that "the town-house forever destroyed our belief that armed struggle is the only real revolutionary struggle."

A year later the group was all but finished. Burrough notes that "in 1972, for example, the Los Angeles collective consisted of six or seven people who never participated in a single bombing." He concludes that "less than one percent of the 1970s-era bombings led to a fatality," and in fact, "the single deadliest radical-underground attack of the decade killed four people." The bombs "basically functioned as exploding press releases." Weather's largely ineffectual attempts at armed propaganda may well have prompted others to imitate them, however, and Burrough believes that almost all the bombings the FBI recorded were "the work of 'one-off' student rage." The real story lay elsewhere, but Burrough tosses it away in a single sidelong sentence: according to the Associated Press, by 1971 "three thousand communes had opened, taking in three million people," but he's evidently uninterested by this remarkable statistic and what it suggests about America and its discontents.

Burrough prefers dynamite and sex. He affects a hard-boiled prose when, cribbing from Jane Alpert's memoir of radical wilding, he opens his book by describing Sam Melville, Alpert's lover and an aspiring bomber, removing the yogurt and salad from their refrigerator to make room for the boxes of red dynamite sticks he'd stolen and how, afterward, they'd made love, "the most tender and passionate in a long time," as Alpert recalled. Burrough's use of Alpert's solipsistic book gives him the curtain-raiser to his tale of feckless ambition and radical derangement, but in truth there's nothing in his approving and uncritical acceptance of her pomposities that causes one to revise the unsentimental view advanced by the altogether sober Murray Kempton, who reviewed the book when it was published more than thirty years ago. Kempton saw that

Alpert's "memories abound with occasions that might have been moments of revelation, and yet her account of them reads like transcriptions from a parrot." As for Melville, Kempton's characterization sticks: his "only credential was the air of command." Yet for Burrough, Alpert's book is "excellent."

For Burrough, Bernardine Dohrn, a principal organizer and leader of Weatherman, is "the glamorous leading lady of the American underground, unquestionably brilliant, cool, focused, militant, and highly sexual." The heavy breathing is unmistakable. He's transfixed by her "tight miniskirt and knee-high Italian boots." He quotes approvingly one anonymous former member of SDS as remembering, "Every guy I knew at Columbia, every single one, wanted to fuck her." He is well pleased to recycle David Horowitz and Peter Collier's *Rolling Stone* article of more than thirty years ago quoting Mark Rudd as having once remarked that "power doesn't flow out of the barrel of a gun, power flows out of Bernardine's cunt." The salaciousness is relentless. Burrough tells that when Dohrn was underground, living on a Sausalito houseboat, she liked to clamber to the roof and sunbathe, "sometimes topless." Burrough can't resist a flourish: "Overhead, seagulls swooped to and fro." He breathlessly repeats an oft-quoted characterization by Timothy Leary, whom Weatherman broke out of a California prison, engineering his escape into exile in Algeria, where Eldridge Cleaver, already on the lam, welcomed him with less than open arms. Leary recalled Dohrn as having had "unforgettable sex appeal" and "the most amazing legs."

*

With the implosion of Weatherman, Burrough turns to the psychopathology of ever-smaller cults. He tells of the forlorn "New World Liberation Front," which the FBI tied to "sixteen bombings and attempted bombings between 1973 and their final attack in 1978." He admits the full story "will never be known," yet asserts that the mysterious NWLF detonated more explosive devices than any other radical group, nearly twice as many as the Weather Underground. Most of the bombs, he informs us, were the work of a nutcase named Ronald Huffman, described by Burrough as a "small-time marijuana dealer in the San Jose area, a balding radical typically adorned in biker regalia; his customers called him 'Revolutionary Ron.'" Huffman was in cahoots with a girlfriend who is described as "a quiet hippie girl" who "graduated with honors from Berkeley." Burrough's source: the FBI, which estimated Huffman's group as consisting of maybe six or seven people. Huffman would eventually murder his lover and chief follower, ordering her to kneel and then splitting her skull with an axe. He pled not guilty by reason of insanity; a jury disagreed, and he was convicted of second-degree murder and sentenced to California state prison, where he would die in 1999.

Burrough is a serial exaggerator. He claims that the saga of Joanne Chesimard, aka Assata Shakur, "was a singular moment in underground history, the first time the press was obliged to introduce and attempt to explain a Black revolutionary—and an attractive woman at that—to a mainstream audience." Really? What happened to Malcolm X and Stokely Carmichael and H. Rap Brown and Huey P. Newton and Eldridge Cleaver, all of whom had earlier transfixed the white national media with their angry rhetoric, all of whom seemed to raise the specter of Nat Turner? And what, one is obliged to ask, was Angela Davis, chopped liver? He calls the Patty Hearst kidnapping "after Watergate, probably the greatest media event of the 1970s." Bigger than the 1978 People's Temple cyanide "revolutionary suicides" of more than nine hundred acolytes (and the murder of US Congressman Leo Ryan) at the behest of the Reverend Jim Jones? Bigger than the assassinations of Harvey Milk and San Francisco's Mayor George Moscone at the hands of Dan White, a disgruntled former supervisor? Bigger than the partial meltdown in 1979 of Three Mile Island's nuclear reactor?

There isn't an honest-to-God, flesh-and-blood character in the whole book. Everyone and nearly everything is reduced to cliché and caricature. For example, George Jackson is "a thug with a fountain pen." His attorney and lover, Fay Stender, is a "plain woman with a smoldering sexuality," who Burrough says was "utterly entranced" by the prospect of sexual congress with the "black inmates she represented." She was, he writes, "a genius" at public relations and "under Stender's guidance, George Jackson emerged as the living symbol of everything the Bay Area Left yearned for: strong, black, prideful, masculine, and undeniably sexual."

(Curiously, Burrough neglects to tell what happened to Stender, perhaps because it both bolsters and complicates his story. She would ultimately be branded an "enemy of the people" for having betrayed Jackson by refusing to slip him the gun he needed to escape San Quentin. For this sin, she incurred the wrath of the so-called Black Guerrilla Family, a California prison gang. She would be grievously attacked by an ex-convict, shot multiple times in her home in Berkeley, leaving her paralyzed from the waist down. She spent her remaining years in agony before taking her life in a Hong Kong hotel room.)

A Harlem squad of the Black Liberation Army boasts a "lean, charismatic thug" and a "squat, muscled gangbanger." Detectives are "cigar-chomping," and veterans are "square-jawed." White radicals are almost always "shaggy" or "stringy-haired" or "aging" or "prematurely gray" or, worse, "balding." Burrough sneers that by 1973 Berkeley was a "bizarre bazaar" chockablock "with radicals devoted to every conceivable cause" but which "now ran less to the brainy Ivy Leaguers of the Weather Underground than to the escaped convicts, janitors, runaways, and angry lesbians." Whoa, angry lesbians. Steady, man, steady.

Purple prose is everywhere: New York in the 1970s is "a city that seemed to be entering its death throes. Gotham's financial crisis had devolved into a new ring of urban hell.... Between bombings, riots, blackouts, and serial killers, the last shreds of civilization appeared to be disintegrating ... a dying city, a softly throbbing bass line deep in the rhythms of a funeral dirge."

Or how about second-rate James M. Cain: "When he stepped inside, he could feel hatred radiating from the prisoners like bad cologne." Or the Vietnam vet who read Che Guevara's diary and "downed it like a starving dog." To say that he "was an angry young man is like saying Mozart could play the piano." Or take Burrough's description of Mayor Ed Koch closing a detox program run by radicals at a Bronx hospital, smashing them "like a clove of garlic."

Odd errors, trivial in themselves, crop up. A single example will suffice: "Tania," Che Guevara's sidekick in his doomed

Bolivian adventure, is described as "a noted Cuban revolutionary" when, in point of fact, she was of East German origin.

The truth of the matter, as Burrough well knows, was that the actual threat to the public posed by these American Narodniks was minuscule; the reality was that most of the wounds were self-inflicted. The violence that occurred, born of desperate delusions and accompanied by ideological fevers, was committed by renegades who were drawn to a world that placed a premium on secrecy and duplicitous behavior. The public was indifferent. Most of the left was appalled. All in all, it's a sad story whose tragic and misbegotten essence was understood and denounced at the time. Robert Scheer, former editor of the muckraking *Ramparts*, nailed it when he condemned "movements that aim to create zombies in the name of establishing some social utopia. . . . What the crazies do have in common is their distortion of ideas, and indeed history, in order to leave themselves at the center of our attention. They have a contempt for ordinary life, for the right and ability of individuals to make rational decisions. They become humorless, fanatical 'saviors' of our souls.'"

There was at the heart of these "apocalyptic revolutionaries" a hoary notion that revolved around the idea of authenticity: an end to estrangement and the construction of community were constant refrains. The injection of moral passion, with the concomitant suggestion that direct action and the willingness to embrace violent means is the best barometer by which commitment is measured and authenticity confirmed, proved a disaster, as dangerous as it was naïve. These ideas embodied a terrible logic: only by ever grander gestures could the veil of apathy be pierced in an America whose citizens' political sensibilities had been dulled by the narcotic of consumerism and the relative prosperity derived from being beneficiaries of an imperial behemoth. Politics thus became a form of gestalt, a species of social psychoanalysis. Its aim was not merely revolution but catharsis.

Burrough, alas, is neither the writer nor the thinker talented enough to tackle this subject with the seriousness and insight it deserves. In truth, the more dangerous terrorists were elsewhere, hiding in plain sight, living large in the nation's capital, relentlessly pursuing a punishing war against the Indochinese, backed by the lethal power of the mightiest war machine the world had ever known. Millions would die, hundreds of thousands maimed, combatants and noncombatants alike, leaving an open wound that has yet to heal. About this forgotten horror, however, Burrough has nothing to say.

[2015]

Commie Camp

"*G*OOD MORNING EVERYBODY / *Get up for exercise / You need a healthy body / To fight the parasites.*" So went the morning song at Camp Kinderland. The parasites referred to were fascists, capitalists, and revisionists—and the sleepy young socialists from the Bronx who stumbled out of bed to begin their morning jumping jacks to sing this immortal verse to greet the day were all summer campers at a remarkable secular Jewish camp in upstate New York called Kinderland.

The first reunion since Kinderland was founded in 1923 was held the summer of 1979 in the exhibition rotunda of Madison Square Garden's Felt Forum, attracting nearly two thousand middle-aged and elderly men and women from all over the United States. Two years were spent planning the event— gathering testimonials, documents, and photographs for inclusion in a commemorative journal. An afternoon photographic exhibit and an evening presentation chronicled Camp Kinderland's precarious survival since the 1920s.

Greeting each other with affectionate embraces and kisses, former Kinderland campers—hardly a shy group—eagerly engaged one another in rapid-fire conversations. The crowd grew until it appeared that at least a thousand people, from near and far, had made the trek. Everyone seemed to have a nickname: Whitey, Velvel, Blackie, Talkie, Lefty, Blisters,

75

Pajamas, Aba Daba, Stretch. As more and more people drifted into the Forum, renewing friendships of some ten, twenty, and even thirty years, the volume of the crowd's excited babble grew louder until all that could be heard was a happy roar.

What brought them together was not only nostalgia for a shared past but also a certain loyalty to the ideals of *Yiddishkeit*—that special brand of Jewish humanism and intellectual passion—and to the radical political commitment that was the secular faith of their Eastern European immigrant parents. The reunion was a celebration of the rich culture and values that their parents had instilled in them through a once-flourishing network of Yiddish choruses, reading circles, orchestras, dramatic societies, and summer camps.

The many summer camps mirrored the political persuasions of the Jewish labor movement, which was divided into Labor-Zionists, social democrats, socialists, and Communists. Kinderland, sponsored by the Jewish People's Fraternal Order, a part of the International Workers Order, was the most popular—and most left-wing—of the half dozen or so such retreats located at Hopewell Junction, on the shores of Sylvan Lake. Kinderlanders were warned of the "enemies" at the Workmen's Circle camp, located on the opposite shore. Some survivors still remember the scandal that was caused when one of the Kinderland counselors went to work for the rival camp. (He was promptly dubbed a traitor and a revisionist.) The rivalry heightened when Workmen's Circle campers raided Kinderland and hoisted a red flag above the canteen because they used "Communist" (Red Circle brand) syrup in the soda fountain. Ideological animosity, however, did not prevent the camps from sharing rescue equipment.

Founded by radical Jewish garment-industry workers in 1923, Kinderland was more than a country refuge from the cramped conditions of tenement life; it was, above all else, a place for the preservation and perpetuation of the socialist ideals that were so much a part of Jewish life in the sweatshops and factories of New York.

At Kinderland the sons and daughters of Jewish workers were protected from the notion that their parents' world of ideological squabbling was peculiar or that their parents' ideas were taboo. The camp offered an opportunity for fishing, swimming, hiking—the usual summer fare—but it was also a place where campers declared a hunger strike to protest the execution of Sacco and Vanzetti, where cabins were named after Paul Robeson, Henry Wallace, and Ana Pauker (former foreign minister of Romania), and where sports teams were divided between "Communist" and "Fascist." (Of course, no one ever wanted to be on the "Fascist" team, and 1936 was the only year that anyone can remember the "Fascists" winning.) At Kinderland, it was not at all unusual for budding thirteen- and fourteen-year-old Marxists to stay up half the night discussing sex and Stalinism (after Khrushchev's speech at the Twentieth Party Congress in 1956) and acceptable standards of moral behavior.

Some camps, presumably to combat homesickness among their young charges, try to supply campers with all the comforts of home: hot showers, soft mattresses, heated swimming pools. Kinderland was and remains different. Kinderland's campsite was purchased with the savings of Jewish garment workers. Its price tag of $50,000 in 1923 represented some five million hems sewed. There was little money left over to construct an elaborate camp.

Always a slapdash affair, the camp had crumbling washrooms, rickety cabins, a wobbly dock that stretched out into Sylvan Lake (in 1971, rising property taxes forced the camp to relocate; it is now in Tolland, Massachusetts), an overgrown sports field that had been a cow pasture, an enormous social hall, dining room, and a library stocked with all the Yiddish classics. Compositions and poems written in Yiddish by the campers were regularly posted on bulletin boards hanging on the sides of each ramshackle bungalow.

During their stay at the camp (usually between two and ten weeks, depending on how much parents could afford— I went, for example, at age ten for just fourteen days in 1962; my parents had worked as counselors in the 1940s), Kinderlanders would attend Yiddish language classes, participate in dances and dramas in the manner of social realism, and gather around campfires at night to sing Yiddish working-class songs whose haunting melodies would drift across the lake. On Sundays, visiting parents would watch as their children, dressed in neatly pressed white uniforms and wearing red bandanas around their necks, paraded before them. Especially conscientious campers were awarded banners for marching and cleaning, and if they were talented enough, were chosen to participate in the camp's elite drum and bugle corps.

Of course, not everyone who went to Kinderland did so to receive a political education or, as its critics charged, an indoctrination. One former camper remembers getting a job as a nightwatchman in order to seduce a young girl he had had his eye on back in the Bronx. She thwarted his designs by going to the Workman's Circle camp.

Kinderlanders were a contentious lot, always questioning authority. Each summer the camp's waiters and busboys threatened to strike for higher wages. Finally, it came. At a general meeting in the dining hall, the camp's management granted a pay increase of fifty percent—from six dollars to nine dollars a summer. However, the director immediately announced that all salary increases would be donated to the Yiddish school fund drive.

Harriet Holtzman, who first attended Camp Kinderland in 1938 at the age of eight and returned every summer for many years, recalled Kinderland as "a place where I had no fear of discussing politics, where my friends understood about *shule* [Yiddish secular school] and about May Day." For most of the camp's alumni, the reunion was an occasion to relive the camaraderie of an experience that deeply marked their lives, a chance to remember the byzantine world of left-wing politics in the hothouse of New York City during the 1920s, 1930s, and 1940s. "How nice it was to learn the 'Internationale' in Yiddish and feel part of a worldwide 'family' when I marched singing with clenched fist raised into the dining room," Holtzman recalled.

The close personal ties Kinderlanders share is something most outsiders find remarkable. Even those who attended the camp for only a few weeks, as I did, feel an extremely strong bond with fellow former campers. Lifelong friendships took root; and many marriages were made at the camp, as was the case with my own parents. Richard Flacks, now emeritus professor of sociology at the University of California at Santa Barbara and a founder of SDS, met his wife, Mickey Hartman, when he was a Kinderland counselor in the mid-1950s. "It was a great place for rapid intimacy," he said with a smile. "The test was if you kept seeing each other in the city when one lived in Brooklyn and the other lived in the Bronx."

While interest in Kinderland remains high among former campers, many of whose children and grandchildren now attend the camp, both the Communist movement and the Yiddish milieu that gave rise to Kinderland no longer exist. The Hitler-Stalin Pact of 1939, the revelations of Stalin's crimes, the Soviet invasions of Hungary and Czechoslovakia, and the persistence of anti-Semitism in Lenin's homeland spawned disillusionment within the radical movements that had nurtured and sustained Kinderland in its heyday. McCarthyism also took its toll on leftist activism. But the desire to organize on behalf of workers' rights, to fight racism, to enfranchise women, to end war, gave rise in the 1960s, and down the decades since, to causes from the civil rights movement to the protests to end the Vietnam War, all of which gave Kinderland a new vigor. Then came the effort to end apartheid, the wars in Central America, the struggle for gay rights, and, more recently, Occupy Wall Street, among other issues. Kinderlanders have thrown themselves into the heart of these struggles.

Most Kinderlanders refuse to accept the idea that a lack of proficiency in Yiddish necessarily means the weakening of the spirit of *Yiddishkeit*. Nor do they believe that the increasing affluence and rapid upward mobility of many Jews must necessarily mean a weakening of the radical ideals that were so much a part of their youth. Joe Dorinson, a Kinderlander of the 1950s, insisted that most campers have remained true to the essential beliefs of their parents. "Though we have deviated, we embody certain core values," he said. "Social justice, enduring friendships, compassion, commitment, community, elemental decency inform our lives; they inspire our actions. Even as we became doctors, lawyers, professors, teachers, writers, and, pardon the expression, businessmen, we could never forget."

[1979]

Tom Hayden: Troublemaker

A WEEK BEFORE HE DIED IN LOS ANGELES at age seventy-six in October 2016, I went to say farewell to Tom Hayden. I'd known him ever since we met in Berkeley in 1969 during the tumult of People's Park, when he was twenty-nine and I was sixteen. I knew he was gravely ill, debilitated by the stroke he'd suffered the year before, just three weeks after he'd agreed to write a book I'd been urging him to undertake for Yale University Press. For the next eighteen months, we would work closely together on a modest book-length essay about the legacy of the Vietnam protest movement. I had suggested he write it as a natural outgrowth of the conference he and other antiwar veterans had organized in Washington, DC, to protest the Pentagon's plan to sanitize an official commemoration of America's Vietnam veterans. That plan had conveniently omitted to mention those courageous vets who protested the war, the brave young men who resisted the draft, or the many millions of patriotic citizens who had come together in an unprecedented movement of opposition.

Tom was appalled that our legacy of protest was in danger of being forgotten. As he wrote, "One can only guess why so many elites want to forget the Vietnam peace movement by history cleansing, why public memories have atrophied, and why there are few if any memorials to peace." We talked about how efforts to end an unjust war had been whitewashed and stricken from mainstream memories, and what to do about it. He felt that "the steady denial of our impact, the persistent caricatures of who we really were, the constant questioning of our patriotism, the snide suggestions that we offered no alternative but surrender to the Communist threat have cast a pall of illegitimacy over our memory and had a chilling effect on many journalists, peace dissenters, and the current generation of students today. Of course, one reason for this forgetting is that the Vietnam War was lost, a historical fact that representatives of a self-proclaimed superpower can never acknowledge. Accepting defeat is simply not permissible." We agreed that if truth is famously war's first casualty, memory is its second. Tom's book would be a necessary intervention in the ongoing conflict between empire and democracy.

That the book got written at all is something of a miracle. I was shocked to receive an email from him just days after he'd signed the contract with Yale, telling me he'd suffered a serious stroke. "I am the victim of my own reckless character," he wrote:

I was photographing a toxic pit of fracking wastewater out in the land of the devil, Kern County. It was hot, the air full of dust, the black ooze sinking into the aquifer below and evaporating into the air above. I threw myself into the cave of the devil and the devil blew back into my heaving lungs. It was something like Ginsberg staring into the eye of Moloch. And so in the course of an exhausting day and night my breathing worsened and I eventually fell into a stroke and was rushed twice to emergency rooms, doctors and nurses, and the MRI machine where I experienced life and loved ones passing before my eyes. The man at the MRI was named Jesus. When it was over and I asked him how his day was going, he said with an upbeat shout, "You survived, everybody's gonna survive in this place today."

Tom went on to say that while he would "need therapy to help recover my brain over the next little while," he assured me that "if you call me, and I hope you will, it will seem that I am my old self, slicing and chopping words into sentences and arguments, living again in the immanent world that I nearly left behind." Yes, he'd have "new medicines, a different diet, and will be banned from driving," but, he declared, "the *New York Times* will be on my bed every morning, and I will read the latest on the Pope and the [California] Senate will pass a resolution I drafted just days ago mandating all state officials to read and consider the papal encyclical on the climate, and I guess I will be a miracle incarnate and a devoted student of the human brain."

He closed his missive, which he'd written from his hospital bed at five in the morning, with "I am wide awake in the unforgettable present moment, and now I must try to sleep."

Tom always did live in the unforgettable present moment, and he refused an easy, self-aggrandizing nostalgia for his rebel past. As much as he had a profound respect for the ways that history, as was once so famously observed, weighs upon the brain of the living like a nightmare, he spent his life trying to write it by making it in the here and now. He never lost his capacity for outrage at the way things are. It kept him young. He was ever ardent, with a deep faith in the capacity of people to change. His constant efforts over many decades to reach out to others, to build alliances, to combat injustice, overcome racism, and deepen democracy, are widely known.

I loved Tom as much as I admired him. When I met him in that spring of 1969, he and a couple of comrades were taking a break from the exertions of resisting the violent police suppression of People's Park to wander down to the campus of Berkeley High School, where I and several hundred other students had organized a "sleep-in," refusing to leave the school grounds while the city was occupied by police and the National Guard. Because Berkeley had been a magnetic pole of rebellion, I enjoyed a precocious adolescence. I was familiar with the Port Huron Statement and was aware of Hayden's antiwar activism, having read his account of his visit to North Vietnam, and followed his writings in various journals, including the *Nation*.

That summer, as Tom prepared for his upcoming trial in Chicago to defend himself against charges that he'd organized violent riots to protest the Vietnam War at the 1968 Democratic National Convention, he agreed to conduct what amounted to a graduate seminar in sociology for me and my radical high school posse. We met twice a week in the backyard of the Berkeley stucco home at 2917 Ashby Avenue he was renting with Stew Albert and Stew's partner, Judy Gumbo. We read our way through a daunting stack of books, including C. Wright Mills's *The Power Elite*. I was enthralled by how Tom led our discussions, often taking a Socratic approach, asking questions, prompting us to delve deeper and think more rigorously and never to check our critical faculties at the title page. He had the habit of letting everyone in the group have their say and then, at the end, succinctly and often, as it seemed to me, brilliantly summarizing the various views. Even better, he had the knack of being able to tease out of apparently contending and contradictory positions a path forward that might braid together the salient aspects of different ideas while enrolling them in a more coherent and plausible synthesis. I saw him do this at countless meetings to chart political strategy in Berkeley. This talent was perhaps rooted in his Catholic upbringing and Jesuitical turn of mind. He had a way of breaking down complex arguments, often offering up an analytical taxonomy that almost always had three components, out of which he'd forge some more compelling approach. And it was all delivered in a voice that evinced the deliberate, rather flat affect of his Midwestern origins. A southpaw, he held his ubiquitous coffee mug in a wraparound embrace which, for reasons that elude me, was utterly captivating.

His critics suspected that beneath the apparently objective delivery was a hidden agenda whose aims were almost never publicly disclosed. Some regarded Tom's supple political turn of mind and gift for adroit and deft navigation of the currents of sectarian squabbles as evidence of a Machiavellian temperament and, what was worse, the sort of careerist ambitions and lust for power that were condemned as the unexamined birthright of the alpha male. Tom, for his part, after surviving the Procrustean suffocations of Berkeley in the late 1960s and early 1970s, found himself expelled by his former comrades and forced into a kind of internal exile in Venice, California. He would ultimately shed the provincial precincts of political correctness for a return to the politics of coalition, a politics that wouldn't permit a purity of principle to subvert a more pragmatic, if messier, pursuit of real-life change. For all his idealism, Hayden never wanted to live in a world of delusion. He had a more unsentimental view of making history.

Tom's half decade in Berkeley coincided with a growing intoxication with ideology and a mounting sense that apocalypse was at hand. With Nixon triumphant and the Vietnam War continuing, some in their despair grew desperate. Tom was not immune to such feelings. Berkeley in those years contained less a politics than a collection of seductive moral sympathies. A taste for extremism was shared by almost everyone we knew. My high school mates cut each other with knives in order to practice sewing up the wounds we were sure would be inflicted upon us as we mounted the barricades. We went to nearby rifle ranges to practice with the M-1 carbines and shotguns we thought we would need to defend ourselves against the savageries of the nation's police and *agents provocateurs*.

I remember vividly the day Neil Armstrong landed on the moon. I had accompanied Tom and Stew Albert to the United Front Against Fascism Conference in Oakland that had been chiefly organized by the Black Panther Party. Afterward, we repaired to the Ashby house to watch the historic landing. While Walter Cronkite was nearly overcome narrating the descent, Stew smoked a joint, Tom steadily drank cheap red wine, and I spotted in an open closet door Stew's .30-06 rifle.

Ultimately, Tom, though tormented by the way some of his compatriots had helped fuel the fires of fanaticism, would embrace a steadier politics of reform, based on a thoroughgoing sense that real change comes from grassroots activism combined with persistent efforts to win concessions from within the citadels of power. His years working as an elected state legislator while simultaneously seeking to arouse disaffected citizens to organize on behalf of their own—and others'—interests would put paid to the canard that he was a bomb-throwing revolutionary. In truth, Tom was an exemplary reformer, ever stalwart, in the best American tradition. He drew strength from the battle to make history. The destination was important, of course, but truly the journey was the crucible that forged character. Birthing the new was always at the heart of his love of life.

When my daughter Mira was born, Tom and his wife, Barbara, made a gift to us of the crib their son Liam had once used and a pillow bearing the likeness of Alice in Wonderland, as drawn by the great Sir John Tenniel. It was as if Tom had said that the point of it all was to turn yourself inside out and see the world with new eyes.

[2016]

A Nervous Nellie for Scheer

ROBERT SCHEER FIRST CAME INTO my life in 1966, in Berkeley. He was editor of *Ramparts* magazine and running hard to topple the incumbent Jeffrey Cohelan, a Cold War apologist for Johnson's war in Vietnam, from his perch in the House of Representatives in the Seventh Congressional District. Bob's campaign was built around two pillars: ending the war in Vietnam and ending poverty in Oakland. LBJ had branded dissenters "Nervous Nellies." I still possess the campaign button, which we wore with pride, declaring that we were "Nervous Nellies for Scheer." I enrolled myself in the campaign and went door-to-door, urging people to vote. In the event, Bob nearly won, garnering forty-five percent of the vote, paving the way just four years later for the election of Ron Dellums. The campaign was rightly seen by such commentators as Tom Wicker of the *New York Times* as a harbinger of things to come.

I was just fourteen but already, like so many, in thrall to Bob's supple turn of mind and his seemingly inexhaustible capacity for moral and political outrage. Years later, I would come across a line in André Gide's journals that captured Bob to a T. Gide wrote: "I know I shall have entered old age when I awake and no longer find myself filled with outrage at the way things are." By that measure, Bob has remained forever young.

Scheer had a gift for stump oratory, honed at City College of New York and sharpened by street-moxie lessons learned in the hardscrabble years growing up in the Bronx. His devotion to his working-class roots was as admirable as it was rare. He was obsessed with who had power and who didn't, or, as he would later put it, "who got screwed and who did the screwing." He wanted to know how things worked, who said what to whom, and was driven by an overwhelming sense that the great taboo in America's political culture was the notion of class. He was at pains, always, to speak truth to power. He seemed fearless. He was—and is—possessed of a fierce intelligence, insatiable curiosity, and, like almost no one else I had ever met, an ability to read the newspaper and connect the dots.

Eight years later, we came together to work on a book he wrote called *America after Nixon*. I marveled at his openness and generosity when he turned to me with sincerity and trust, not only hiring me as a researcher to spend hours in Cal's Doe Library exploring the corruptions of multinational corporations who sought to slip the noose of civic obligation in favor of something that would later be called "globalization," but also introducing me to the delights of a world beyond politics. We spent the summer of 1974 finishing work on the book in New York City, he bunking with his old friend Jules Feiffer, me with Susan Sontag, whom I had met thanks to Bob at a dinner party he hosted at his home in Berkeley in April.

I remember with affection the weekends up in Inverness at Manka's Lodge, Scheer typing away furiously and as a section or chapter would be completed handing me the draft, insisting I tell him where I thought he'd gotten things right and where, perhaps, he'd gotten things wrong or omitted parts of the argument that ought to be given more weight. How and why he thought I was up to the job, I don't know. But I was enormously flattered, and I intuited then what I know now: If you want to get smart, surround yourself with people who are smarter than you. Scheer was the smartest person I knew.

He also taught me how to cook Chinese, for which I shall forever be grateful: how to pick out a hand-wrought cast-iron wok in San Francisco's Chinatown, how to season it with Crisco, and how to cut flank steak thin across the grain after it had been partially frozen in the freezer, and then stir fry with broccoli smothered in hot chili peppers and garlic in peanut oil.

I shall never forget strolling down Telegraph Avenue with Scheer and dropping into Grodin's, one of Berkeley's few upscale men's clothing stores. Bob was to pick up a Pierre Cardin suit, which he was looking forward to wearing to the interviews he'd been asked to do for *Playboy* magazine by Barry Golson and *Esquire* by Don Erickson. He was eager to write for them, as the assignments came after some years of de facto blacklisting during the Nixon administration. Those were sometimes strict and unforgiving days in Berkeley. Many of the comrades were dubious about such sartorial affectations, regarding them as evidence of a lingering bourgeois taint. The suit was swell. We emerged from the store. I turned to Bob and asked whether he was worried that he'd be condemned as "bourgeois" by sporting so fashionable and fine a garment. "Wasserman," he said,

all my life I've heard such castigations, some even going so far as to condemn various rights as "bourgeois." But what did Marx mean when he used the term? What's wrong with the right to assemble or the right of free speech or the right to be secure in one's home against the intrusions of the state? Or the right to be adequately clothed and to have shelter? Are those bourgeois rights? What Marx opposed was that it was only the bourgeoisie that got to exercise them. He wanted a world in which the rights of the few would be extended to the many.

Many years later, reading Robert Walser's *The Walk*, his novella published in 1917, I came upon a similar sentiment. In a passage that tells of his encounter with a "peacock" of a wealthy gentleman, the narrator wonders if the man does not "feel in any way whatsoever concerned when he sees stained, disheveled youth? How can mature men want to walk about adorned while there are children who have no finery to wear at all?" And then Walser adds "But one might perhaps have just as much right to say that nobody ought to go to concerts, or visit the theater, or enjoy any other kind of amusement as long as there are places of punishment in the world with unhappy prisoners in them. This is of course asking too much; for if anyone were to postpone contentment until he were to find no more poverty or misery anywhere, then he would be waiting until the impenetrable end of all time, and until the gray, ice-cold empty end of the world, and by then all joie de vivre would in all probability be utterly gone from him."

Perhaps, more than anything else, I admired Bob's refusal to succumb to nostalgia. I never heard him speak of the "good old days" of the upstart years of the sixties. Bob lives in the present and always surrounded himself with younger people, giving them a chance, learning from them. That disposition has kept him young.

People are too often like wonderful planets whose orbits never cross. I'm glad ours did.

[2023]

The Heresy of Daniel Ellsberg

O N THE FIFTIETH ANNIVERSARY of Daniel Ellsberg's leak of the Pentagon Papers to the *New York Times*, there is a question that lingers unasked: How did the *New York Times* and the *Washington Post* find their vertebrae? How was it that they found the strength and the courage to resist the attempt of the government to suppress and restrain them from publishing the Pentagon Papers? I submit that they found their vertebrae quite late in the day.

It was no surprise to those of us who had been reading *I. F. Stone's Weekly* for many years that the Pentagon Papers confirmed what had been hiding in plain sight for a decade. I submit that both the decision by then Secretary of Defense Robert S. McNamara to even order such a study of the war's origins and Daniel Ellsberg's courage in leaking the documents had everything to do, by their own admissions in subsequent writings and interviews, with a rising, vociferous, and intensifying antiwar movement.

We know, for example, exactly when McNamara decided to commission the Pentagon Papers. In his book *In Retrospect*, released in 1995, McNamara tells us it was on November 7, 1966, in the aftermath of an appearance at Harvard University where he refused to debate Robert Scheer (who in 1965 had published, after several New York houses had turned it down, a little pamphlet called *How the United States Got Involved in Vietnam*, which could have been the introduction to the more than seven thousand pages of the Pentagon Papers).

McNamara's car was surrounded by hundreds of chanting Harvard students insisting he debate Scheer. As he was taken through an underground tunnel to give a lecture at another building—at Henry Kissinger's class—he was escorted by then student Barney Frank, who would decades later become a distinguished congressman. That evening McNamara found himself at dinner with Richard Neustadt, a Harvard professor. McNamara confessed he was deeply troubled by the intensity of the protesting students and their opposition to the war, and he began to think: How the heck did we get into this goddamn mess?

On June 17, 1967, he ordered that the Pentagon Papers project start. It was originally to have taken three to six months, maybe six people writing it. In the event, it would take eighteen months and involve thirty-six people. Four years later, on June 13, 1971, the *New York Times*—the papers having been leaked to it by Daniel Ellsberg—published the first part of what they did. It is important to understand what was going on in the events surrounding this scoop:

A year before, there was a widening of the war and the invasion in Cambodia, and the killing of students at Kent State and Jackson State amidst the largest student strike in US history.

Just a few weeks before the *New York Times* went to press, there had been a demonstration on April 20 and 24: more than a thousand Vietnam veterans tossed their medals onto the steps of the Congress, and a then young man named John

Kerry testified memorably, "How do you ask a man to be the last man to die for a mistake?"

Half a million people showed up to demonstrate in Washington, and the first week of May saw thirteen thousand people arrested protesting the war under the slogan, "If the government won't end the war, we'll stop the government."

The context of that time is important to remember because, of course, the temptation to read history backward is always a category error—history is famously lived forward—and no one knew then what would take place the next day.

I also submit that both the *New York Times* and the *Washington Post*, among other newspapers, did have the notion— it was in the air—that scrappy upstart publications like *Ramparts*, what was then called the alternative press, had already embarrassed them on major stories using leaked documents. And they didn't want to be humiliated anymore. The rising tide of the antiwar movement lifted all boats and helped stiffen their spines.

One of the questions that cries out to be asked today, especially in an era when technology has democratized the means of leaking and publication, when everyone with an iPhone and a computer potentially has the ability to get information to an even wider audience than ever before, an era in which geography itself has been banished and time zones mean nothing and are porous: Why haven't there been more Ellsbergs? Why has Ellsberg's example been so little emulated?

I suggest that Ellsberg's great crime, the one that made Henry Kissinger so mad and caused him to condemn Ellsberg as the "most dangerous man in America" even as Kissinger called him a son of a bitch and the most brilliant man he'd ever met, was that he broke ranks with his caste and class: He betrayed the Harvard tie. This was an intolerable thing for the national security state to permit, and it explains why Ellsberg had to be made an example of, and this is why they threw the book at him, why he was going to suffer, if he'd been convicted on espionage charges, one hundred fifteen years in prison, and why Anthony Russo, his coconspirator, faced thirty-five years.

What's so extraordinary is that two weeks after the *New York Times* published and the *Washington Post* began publishing, the Nixon White House created the so-called Plumbers Unit in the basement of the Executive Office Building to plug those leaks. On September 3, 1971, E. Howard Hunt and the other bagmen broke into Ellsberg's psychiatrist's office in Beverly Hills to try to get dope on him to smear him. The country was launched on the slippery slope that led to Watergate, the unraveling of the Nixon administration, and the president's ignominious resignation on August 9, 1974.

While some may argue that the Pentagon Papers didn't have much impact on anybody, I can tell you that for those of us in the antiwar movement, they emboldened us because they suggested that the radical critique of the war was the correct critique, that we didn't have it wrong. And we knew this now from the government's own documents.

I went to the 1973 Ellsberg-Russo trial in Los Angeles. I only attended one day. It was a startling day because there, testifying for the defense, was McGeorge Bundy, Kennedy's former national security advisor and a chief architect of the war. I could hardly believe it: Mac Bundy, testifying on Ellsberg's behalf.

I'll never forget Leonard Weinglass, who was Tony Russo's attorney, asking him: Mr. Bundy, if you were a spy working for a foreign power, engaged in espionage, how would you go about your business? He replied, "Well, the first thing I would do is take out a subscription to the *New York Times* and the second thing I'd do would be to take out a subscription to the *Congressional Quarterly*, and the third thing I would do is make sure that my library card was up to date. All that would give me ninety-eight percent of everything I would need to know."

The Pentagon Papers was merely the confirmation of the two percent that made legitimate everything else we knew or had long suspected about the government's duplicity and long-standing mendacity.

[2021]

Barbra Bows Out

I MET BARBRA STREISAND in 1994 through our mutual friend, Bob Scheer. I was well aware of Streisand's passionate and sterling accomplishments as a singer, actor, and director. I also admired her political engagement and activism. I vividly remember the concert that she and Liza Minnelli had given at the Dorothy Chandler Music Pavilion to raise needed funds to defend Daniel Ellsberg and Tony Russo during the Pentagon Papers Trial in the early 1970s. I was in L.A. organizing around the trial, and Stanley Sheinbaum, the chief fundraiser, had invited me to attend the concert.

Decades later, making my way in New York publishing, I was ever on the lookout for good books to acquire that might sell well. Streisand had yet to write a memoir, and when Scheer talked me up to Barbra, I jumped at the chance to meet her. And so I flew out to Los Angeles in the fall of 1994, hooked up with Scheer in the late afternoon, and together we made our way to Streisand's Beverly Hills home.

We rang the bell, were ushered into a foyer, and after cooling our heels were summoned to her bedroom. There, surrounded by stacks of books, curled up on her bed, was Barbra.

She was then the object of a right-wing hate campaign both because of her friendship with Bill Clinton and, more generally, because of her outspoken support for a wide range of progressive causes. The reactionary rap on Streisand amounted to alarm that she—an actor, of all things—was using her celebrity to advance her politics, which the nabobs of the right believed was somehow a betrayal of the American way. She was demonized and excoriated by the Rush Limbaughs and others of his ilk, twenty-four/seven.

The JFK School of Government at Harvard had invited her to deliver a lecture about the obligations of artists in a time when notions of citizenship were under siege and sorely contested. Barbra had never gone to college and was riven by deep insecurities. After all, as she explained, why should the erudite professors of Harvard listen to her? If they'd wanted to know about how to sing a song, fine, but she was no scholar.

She then told a story on herself: She was about to graduate at the top of her class at Brooklyn's Erasmus High School. It came to the attention of the principal that Barbra hadn't bothered to apply to college. Her mother was called to find out why, and Barbra's mother vented, "I can't talk to her. You talk to her." And so, Barbra was summoned to the principal's office.

He told Barbra that with her grades she could get into any college in the country. You don't understand, Barbra said. For what I want to do, you don't go to college; you go to Manhattan.

And that is what she did. As a result, she'd spent a good deal of her life playing catchup and wrestling with her perfectionism. She had been working on her Harvard lecture for months, consulting (at all hours of the day and night) an entire solar system of friends and acquaintances, including Peter Jennings, Scheer, and now, apparently, even me.

Why, she wanted to know, had actors aroused persistent antipathy down the centuries? Why had Plato banned poets from his ideal republic? Why had the theater been attacked not only by straitlaced moralists but by philosophers—Saint Augustine, Rousseau, Nietzsche? Why did actors on their deathbeds have to renounce their profession or risk excommunication by the Catholic Church? And why was this distemper so much a feature of the modern and seemingly implacable hatred of Hollywood by an enraged portion of both the public and the punditocracy?

We were off to the races. The discussion was wide ranging. I recommended she read Jonas Barish's learned *Anti-Theatrical Prejudice*. She scribbled it down on a pad of paper.

An hour went by. Then another. Food was ordered in. The talk was nonstop. I nearly missed my redeye back to New York.

More months went by. The phone would ring, usually in the middle of the night. It was Barbra. The conversation would pick up where it had left off. The date for her lecture loomed. She was going to be in New York at her duplex apartment, bought when she first came into money from the success of *Funny Girl*. As it happened, her building on Central Park West at Ninety-First Street was only a few blocks from where I lived on West Ninety-Second and Broadway. She needed a wingman to accompany her to Cambridge, and she insisted I was the one.

And so on February 3, 1995, I found myself in Cambridge at the Charles Hotel. Barbra's talk was scheduled for 5:00 p.m. at the JFK School of Government and was to be followed by a lavish dinner in her honor at the President's House at 17 Quincy Street, hosted by the acting president, Albert Carnesale, subbing for the unfortunate Neil Rudenstine, who'd apparently suffered a nervous breakdown some months before.

I joined Barbra in the green room just before she went on. Never had I seen someone so nervous. She was shaking with stage fright. I tried my best to assure her everything would be all right. She didn't seem convinced. I then went out into the front of the house and took my seat.

She appeared at the podium. After a shaky start, she gained palpable confidence, and by the end looked the picture of self-possession. The talk was rapturously received by a full house of adoring students and professors. She opened it up to questions.

A young woman in the balcony asked, "You are so wonderful, beautiful, accomplished, and smart . . ." Before she could finish, Barbra leaned over the lectern, her hands with their impossibly long and manicured nails gleaming in the spotlight, and said, "If I'm so smart and I'm so this and I'm so that, how come I can't get a guy?" (This was before James Brolin entered her life.) The audience collapsed in laughter. Her speech was greeted with a standing ovation.

I joined her backstage in the green room. She made a beeline for me and gripping my forearm asked, "How'd I do?"

"What? You want a grade?"

"Yes, yes," she said, "what's the grade?"

"A minus."

"Why the minus?" she demanded.

"For nervousness," I ventured.

Then we hightailed it to the dinner. And it was at that dinner that I saw the most astonishing faux pas it has ever been my unfortunate privilege to witness.

The President's House was kitted out as if for royalty. Round tables enough to seat scores of Harvard mucky-mucks, including such distinguished professors as John Kenneth Galbraith, were beautifully arranged and decorated with abundant floral displays.

Barbra was the guest of honor, and as we entered the room, she was greeted by Carnesale, whose academic specialty was nuclear arms control and nuclear nonproliferation. He was bursting with excitement at his proximity to Streisand, so much so that he blurted, "You were fantastic. You had them eating out of your hand. You could have popped out naked from a cake, you were that good."

The color drained from Barbra's face. "*What?*" she said.

And then Carnesale repeated, "You could have jumped out of a cake naked . . ."

"I could have jumped out of a cake—naked??!? I don't think you understand," she said, "I worked for months on this speech, I did my homework, I took it seriously, and you're telling me all I had to do was jump out of a cake naked?"

Carnesale looked like he was about to have a stroke.

Streisand turned on her heel and headed to her table, clutching my hand. Salad was served. She picked up her fork, then, putting it down, turned to me and said, "I can't stay here another minute. Let's go."

I couldn't bring myself to look at the clueless Carnesale, but I imagined his face was rearranging itself like a Cubist painting.

[2023]

Tell Me Something,
Tell Me Anything,
Even If It's a Lie

MORE THAN FIFTY YEARS AGO, I went to Cuba with nearly seven hundred other young Americans to cut sugarcane and to travel about the island on an eight-week tour. We did so to show solidarity with the beleaguered Cuban Revolution, to break the US blockade of Cuba, and to insist on our constitutional right as American citizens to travel unimpeded to any country in the world. It was to be the first of ten trips I would take to Cuba as, variously, activist, journalist, and publisher over the next five decades. On the most recent, in June 2019, I spent ten days in Havana, in part to say farewell to Pablo Armando Fernández, a wonderful poet, then ninety and in failing health—a kind of Cuban uncle to me—whom I met when he was forty and I just seventeen. I can never forget his remark all those years ago, when, after a great deal of rum, he turned to me and said, "Tell me something, tell me anything, even if it's a lie."

In 1970, having just graduated Berkeley High School, I, like most of those visiting Cuba then, tended to romanticize the Cuban Revolution. The very idea of Cuba—this rebel nation that had stood up to the Colossus of the North—was seductive. Cuba's revolution seemed relatively untainted by the sort of repressiveness that East European communism displayed. At times, Fidel Castro's leadership appeared almost flamboyant. He was given to unorthodox social experiments—such as schools in the countryside that combined work and study— and was apparently blessed with an admirable spontaneity of spirit. He was a welcome alternative to representatives of the drab bureaucracy and stale ideology of the sclerotic Soviet Union. Cuba had a glamor that many of my generation—me included—found irresistible.

Castro's quest to topple Cuba's strongman, Fulgencio Batista, captured the imagination of millions all over the world. Victory, secured on January 1, 1959, after only two years of urban insurrection and guerrilla warfare, catapulted the thirty-two-year-old former lawyer and son of a wealthy landowner into the ranks of revolutionary stardom. After the catastrophes and crimes that had befallen and sullied the 1917 Bolshevik project, Castro seemed to herald something new. His was the first socialist revolution, after all, to have been made without the central participation of the Communist Party (and even, it appeared, against the party, although there were always some militants who were in sympathy with Castro's upstarts and who would assume prominent positions after the triumph of the revolution). On July 26, 1953, five years before Batista fled the country on New Year's Eve 1958, Castro mounted an audacious and, in the event, disastrous attack on the military barracks of Moncada in Santiago de Cuba. Cuba's Communists promptly denounced him as a "putschist" and an "adventurist." By the end of the decade, Fidel stood at the head of a multilayered movement seeking to topple the dictator and to remake Cuban society from top to bottom. Where all previous socialist revolutionaries had seemed grimly puritanical, Castro's *barbudos* appeared almost to be bohemians with guns. Democracy and radical reform were poised to replace dictatorship and social misery.

The world watched agog. Ten years later, Castro had survived repeated attempts by the CIA to assassinate him; the revolution, though besieged by a relentless American embargo and efforts to make tight a diplomatic noose to cut off Havana's ties to other nations, stood strong and defiant. At that time, the moral landscape of the United States seemed to many of us to have been shattered beyond repair—an unconscionable war was in progress in Indochina, class and racial divisions were increasing in the country, and our economic system seemed intent on plundering the world's resources as fast as its multinational companies could devour them. A single statistic told the tale: Americans were just six percent of the world's population while consuming something on the order of sixty percent of the world's resources. To all this, the American experiment offered neither a new vision nor fundamental solutions.

While power in the United States—and in the Soviet Union—was in the hands of the old, in Cuba it was wielded by the young. By 1970, nearly half of Cuba's almost ten million people were born after the revolution. Cuba had a history worth admiring and a future worth building, apparently having renounced materialism for Spartan idealism. For many like me in the New Left, visiting Cuba was an opportunity to glimpse the liberated future and then return to the battlelines morally and politically replenished.

It is perhaps hard, from this remove, to apprehend the exhilaration that we felt when we thought of Cuba. Nevertheless, the hundreds of photographs taken of Fidel and his guerrillas as they made their five-hundred-mile-long victory march up the island's Central Highway from Santiago de Cuba to Havana capture something of the excitement that electrified people the world over. They show Castro and his men, weary with fatigue and near disbelief stamped on their youthful faces, being met by a thronging populace beside itself with ardor, as they rolled through province after province, city after city, en route to the nation's capital to proclaim their mastery of the island. Eyes dance with hope; the radiant future beckons.

History is on the move, bursting with possibility and promise. The tyrant is gone, and revolutionary idealism has yet to curdle into cynicism. Nor has the effort to survive soured into despotism. Today, it is all but impossible to gaze at these pictures of armed campesinos, many of them still boys barely able to boast peach fuzz on their cheeks, as they sprawl about the lobby of the newly occupied (and recently built) Hilton Hotel, promptly dubbed the Havana Libre (by which name it is still known), without thinking of the heartbreak that was to come in the years ahead. These early and heady days, preserved in innumerable photographs, are filled with Sunday patriots, city girls flirting with shy peasants who had M-1 carbines strapped to their backs, a general, if happy, chaos engulfing a people in almost libidinous tumult even as Fidel seeks to hold a disparate movement together by the sheer force of his leonine personality and his demonstrated and widely admired willingness to risk his life in the fight against the dictatorship. Vast numbers of people assembled in every city he entered, chanting, "Fi-del! Fi-del!" The crowds, according to one witness, "parting before him and closing behind him like Moses passing through the

Red Sea." Castro seemed "the incarnation of a legendary hero surrounded by an aura of magic, a bearded Parsifal who had brought miraculous deliverance to an ailing Cuba."

It was, of course, Castro's extraordinary eloquence, strength of character, and unyielding commitment to action that drew men and women alike to his side. Personality trumped politics. It was this striking element—an element that still infuses many of the pictures of the young Fidel with a nearly radioactive charge palpable after all these years—that caused many observers to regard him as a dangerous extremist even as they acknowledged the man's magnetism. Others, like the Argentine Ernesto Che Guevara, were drawn to him, although Guevara originally viewed Castro's movement as bourgeois, even while conceding that it was led by a man whose "image is enhanced by personal qualities of extraordinary brilliance." Later, Castro's willingness to embrace more radical solutions when necessary would continually surprise and please Che, as much as it dismayed the movement's moderates.

To understand Cuba's appeal, we need to summon up the Eros, the sheer vitality, of the revolution that he made. The seduction of his leadership was almost impossible to resist. He was virile, glamorous, in a word, sexy. He relied less on Marxist dogma than on photogenesis to capture the minds and hearts of millions. He was, as one observer later wrote, "an almost Tolstoyan figure in the profusion of his exuberance and imagination. Among all the premiers and statesmen over the globe, he was at least the one figure who seemed unquestionably, tumultuously alive." Not only were Castro and his *barbudos* better looking than the corrupt politicians and gangsters they overthrew, they knew it, and it is easy to see, on the evidence of the many iconic photographs of the period, how it was that a golden legend arose.

The history of every revolution is always a contest of clichés, and in Cuba's case the commonly accepted narrative reduces the Cuban Revolution to a romantic fable of the charismatic Castro and his twelve apostles, whose numbers multiplied faster than players in a pyramid scheme and who, having survived the rigors of guerrilla warfare, broke the back of a regime as brutal as it was corrupt. This myth was, in part, of Castro's own making. What is indisputable is that by December 1958, Castro's rebel army of four hundred armed guerrillas had defeated a government that fielded a vastly superior military force of forty thousand troops. Or, perhaps more precisely, in the face of mounting civil strife—Batista's feared secret police murdered and tortured an estimated twenty thousand people while Castro's rural army suffered a minuscule number of dead and wounded—Batista's political support vanished, Washington's confidence in him crumbled, and his will to power collapsed. And so, in time-honored fashion, the despot fled his suffering island in the middle of the night, stuffing his suitcases with millions of stolen dollars to live out the remainder of his life in the baronial manner to which he had long been accustomed. He died in Portugal in 1973.

By contrast, Castro appeared to be an authentic reformer, determined to break with the discredited lineage of caudillos who battened on the miseries of ordinary Cubans while kowtowing to US interests. Fidel was keen to radically transform Cuba—to rid it of the corruptions of the past, to diversify the economy by breaking the stranglehold of sugar and tobacco and restore the 1940 constitution. His zeal to remake Cuba was seen by sympathizers as a patriotic project, less to do with Karl Marx than with José Martí, the founding father of the country and the apostle of its quest for independence. It was a posture that won him many adherents, especially among the men and women of Cuba's middle and upper-middle class, whose political aspirations had been thwarted by Batista's March 10, 1952, coup. As for Fidel's anti-Yankee sentiments, he came by them honestly. The US-made bombs that Batista used against him would harden his attitude. In a letter from his redoubt in the Sierra Maestra to Celia Sánchez, the daughter of a dentist and his chief courier between the rebel army and the city underground, Castro wrote of his anger toward the United States: "When I saw the rockets that they fired on Mario's house, I swore that the Americans are going to pay dearly for what they are doing. When this war is over, I'll start a much longer and bigger war of my own: the war I'm going to fight against them."

The long, near-Talmudic debate over when and how Castro became a Communist is largely beside the point. What was clear from the start was the man's radical disposition and his refusal to be cowed into a complacent reformism. His defining ideological characteristic was his implacable anti-imperialism. His sympathies were plain. As a college student, he bought "most of the classics of Marxist literature" in the Cuban Communist Party's Havana bookstore on Calle Carlos III. While he found himself in accord with many of the party's goals, he despaired of its rampant sectarianism and what he condemned as its "ghetto mentality." In addition, the party was tainted in the eyes of many Cubans by its willingness to collaborate with Batista and to serve in his government.

He was careful not to prematurely proclaim the socialist character of his ultimate goal. He was cunning, confessing years later to Lee Lockwood, the gifted American photojournalist and one of his most perceptive interlocutors, that "To have said that our program was Marxist-Leninist or Communist would have awakened many prejudices. . . . It is possible that there was some moment when I appeared less radical than I really was. It is possible too that I was more radical than even I myself knew." More: "If you ask me whether I considered myself a revolutionary at the time I was in the mountains, I would answer yes. If you asked me, did I consider myself a Marxist-Leninist, I would say no."

Castro had not only to be certain of the support of a majority of the island's people but also of a majority of his comrades. He later recalled having "to do some heavy arguing, even among the militants of the 26th of July Movement." It couldn't have been easy. As Fidel said: "There was also competition, rivalry, among the leadership, and you had to keep your eye on all that."

It was a rare admission of the difficulty of keeping together the many, often-conflicting strands of the various factions that made up the opposition to Batista while constantly demanding fealty to his personal leadership. For in addition to the clash of personalities and the differences in temperament of the various men who vied to head the movement to oust Batista, it was also riven by ideological differences—differences that had their origin in the diverging strategies and priorities of those who fought in the mountains and in the cities. The seeds of future conflicts (and defections) after Castro's triumph are in the contradictions of class, which to a very considerable extent would mark both the struggle against Batista and the years following his overthrow during which Castro consolidated his power. Many who helped to make the revolution would later break with him. The list of ex-Fidelistas is long. It includes Huber Matos, Aníbal Escalante, David Salvador, Eloy Guitérrez Menoyo, Pedro Díaz Lanz, Carlos Franqui, Guillermo Cabrera Infante, Heberto Padilla, Ernesto Betancourt. Some would flee; others would be expelled; still others would be imprisoned.

The anti-Batista resistance was made up of men as diverse as Che Guevara, who insisted that "the solution of the world's problems lies behind the so-called iron curtain," and René Ramos Latour, a leader of the movement's urban underground, who castigated Guevara for thinking it possible "to free ourselves from the noxious 'Yankee' domination by means of a no less noxious 'Soviet' domination." The urban wing was composed mostly of middle-class moderates, many of whom would feel betrayed by Castro when he explicitly embraced socialism in 1961 following the victory in the US-backed Bay of Pigs invasion. The guerrilla army, on the other hand, drew upon the peasantry, the revolution's chief beneficiaries and most vigorous defenders.

The old debate over whether Castro was an opportunist with a hidden socialist agenda or a social democrat and Cuban patriot forced by the enmity of the United States into accepting the Soviet Union's help as the price of the revolution's survival hardly matters at this remove. It is clear from the abundant public and private record (only some of which has come to light) that Castro always regarded himself as a radical visionary and nationalist whose politics were shaped more by the writings of

Martí and Bolivar than by Marx and Lenin. Even though he would proclaim the revolution's ideology as Marxist-Leninist, in a speech delivered in East Berlin in 1977, Castro embarrassed his more orthodox Communist hosts by declaring "I still don't know to what extent I'm still a utopian and to what extent I've become a Marxist-Leninist—perhaps I may even be a bit of a dreamer."

Castro, of course, was familiar with and admired Marx and Lenin. In letters Castro wrote while in prison in the Isle of Pines, serving a fifteen-year sentence for his failed attack on the Moncada—Batista would grant him amnesty after less than two years in jail—he wrote, "Marx and Lenin each had a weighty polemical spirit, and I have to laugh. It is fun, and I have a good time reading them. They would not give an inch and they were dreaded by their enemies." Castro was enthralled by "the magnificent spectacle offered by the great revolutions of history: they have always meant the victory of the huge majority's aspirations for a decent life and happiness over the interests of a small group." He longed, as he wrote, to revolutionize Cuba "from one end to the other." He relished the prospect, vowing "I would not be stopped by the hatred and ill will of a few thousand people, including some of my relatives, half the people I know, two-thirds of my fellow professionals, and four-fifths of my schoolmates."

He read voraciously and was particularly taken with the life of Napoleon and Robespierre, whom he considered an honest idealist: "The French Revolution was in danger, the frontiers surrounded by enemies on all sides, traitors ready to plunge a dagger into one's back, the fence-sitters were blocking the way—one had to be harsh, inflexible, tough—it was better to go too far than not go far enough, because everything might have been lost. The few months of the Terror were necessary to do away with a terror that had lasted for centuries. In Cuba, we need more Robespierres."

But Castro was never a terrorist. He disavowed terrorism as a tactic of revolutionary war. In this he remained consistent all his long life. In point of fact, Cuba was the first country to condemn the 9/11 attackers and to express sympathy and solidarity with the citizens of the United States. Castro said at the time that "no war is ever won through terrorism. . . . Neither the theorists of our wars of independence nor any Marxist-Leninist that I know of advocated assassination or terrorist-style acts, acts in which innocent people might be killed. That's not contemplated in any revolutionary doctrine. . . . Ethics is not simply a moral issue—if ethics is sincere, it produces results."

The Cuban Revolution harbored huge ambitions: it sought not merely to overthrow a single dictator, but to alter the habits of a nation's entire cultural and political economy. Fidel and his comrades knew they would have to vanquish a notion of Cuba that had lodged itself firmly in the American imagination. This would prove to be a Herculean task. Cuba, for Americans, had long been a location of fantasy, of escape and reinvention. After the economic panic of 1893 plunged the United States into widespread depression, thousands of jobless men emigrated to Cuba to seek their fortune, seeing in Cuba, as the advertising campaigns of the time proclaimed, a "virgin land," "a new California," a "veritable Klondike of wealth."

By 1898, having won its bloody contest with Spain, Cuba was prostrate, its treasury depleted, its countryside devastated, its people destitute. The United States, which had helped deliver the coup de grâce to Spain, quickly moved to take advantage of the island's desperate plight. America's market reach and economic clout proved irresistible. Already, in the early 1850s, Americans had completed the first gasworks in Havana; in the 1860s, Cuban students returning from American colleges and universities brought baseball to the island, a game that was quickly embraced by Cubans as a way to dissociate themselves from the Spanish obsession with the bullfight; in the 1880s, Americans built the first ice factory in Havana and inaugurated a telephone service, then introduced electricity, changing the city's nightlife forever. Everyday objects of US origin came to be ubiquitous in Cuban life: woven wire mattresses, clocks, cameras, plated cookware, lamps, pianos and organs, pepper mills, cutlery, coffeepots, sewing machines, and furniture. Even a tool so quintessentially Cuban as the machete was not of Cuban manufacture, but was supplied by the Collins Company of Hartford, Connecticut. For many Cubans at the turn of the century, America was the future—modern, prosperous, democratic—in whose cause they eagerly enrolled.

For many Americans, Cuba quickly became a place of retreat and refuge, a resort for the smart set and the socially prominent, attracting trendsetters and celebrities such as Gloria Vanderbilt, Charles Lindbergh, Amelia Earhart, Irving Berlin, Will Rogers, and Errol Flynn. Cuba offered access to the exotic with minimum exposure to risk, a place where, as one writer said approvingly, "conscience takes a holiday." Havana, wrote Graham Greene, was an "extraordinary city where every vice was permissible and every trade possible." Ernest Hemingway put it more bluntly: it had "both fishing and fucking."

Many Cubans welcomed the American presence, as it promised the transformation of Cuban life from poverty to prosperity, from backwardness to modernity. To be sure, the price of success might well require Cubans to adapt to American values and tastes. But it was a price some Cubans were willing to pay. This was especially true of Habaneros. Increasingly, Havana's inhabitants were living beyond their means, imagining themselves as de facto citizens of the wealthy and paternal colossus ninety miles away even as they bridled at American presumption and swagger. By the mid-1950s, the sugar and tobacco economy began to sputter; prices on the world market for these unessential commodities plummeted, the island's economy contracted, and opportunities diminished. The cost of living began to soar, the cities flared into violence, Batista fled, and Castro came to power.

Castro imagined a different future. His true calling, he felt, was to do everything in his power to escape the American orbit. He would end decades of humiliation by fulfilling Martí's dream of having Cuba play David to America's Goliath. Cuba, he declared, would break with the past and renounce the blandishments of the profligate American way of life: "How could we import rice and buy Cadillacs? That is what we did before. Is that not madness? The act of a disoriented country. . . . Why were we buying Cadillacs when what we needed were tractors?" From now on, Cubans would have to tighten their belts, forgo the goods that they had for decades taken for granted. Castro sought to remake the Cuban personality, to construct what Che hailed as the "new man," purged of egotism and selfishness, motivated more by moral incentives and economic sobriety than material rewards, an ascetic revolutionary who would shun the gleaming goods on display in the seductive windows of El Encanto, once Havana's most elegant department store.

Fifty years before Castro's victory, expressing nationalism for many Cubans meant replacing Spanish customs with American ones. Now, with Castro at the helm, everything American was suspect. It was a political and cultural shock from which the Cuban middle class would never recover (and which Washington policymakers would never forgive). Most of them would prefer voluntary exile and prosperity in Miami to enforced equality and privation in Havana. The proximity of the United States made it possible for Castro to rid himself of the very class that had done so much to help him during the hard fight against Batista—and which suffered the greatest number of casualties at the hands of Batista's torturers—and now was outraged that Castro was bent on denying it the privileges that it had long enjoyed. To their astonishment, he refused to return to business as usual. The middle class's contribution to defeating Batista was largely written out of the official story of the revolution's triumph.

Soon the exiles would form a base where, with the constant encouragement and support of successive American administrations, they could launch a thousand conspiracies and attempts to subvert Castro and his regime. Castro would thwart more than five hundred attempts to assassinate him over the long decades of his rule. When Castro took power, Cuba's population was six million; nearly a million, or one out of six Cubans, would flee to the United States.

It was both Castro's curse as well as his blessing that the United States was so near. He was able to banish his opposition and send it packing across the Florida Straits. Having the

United States provide a haven for his opposition meant that Castro could favor expulsion over extermination. This was particularly true after the Missile Crisis of October 1962, which ended in a secret understanding between the United States and the Soviet Union: In exchange for the withdrawal of Soviet nuclear missiles, Washington agreed to stop its violent efforts to overthrow or otherwise end the Castro regime. Of course, this was a shift in policy honored more in the breach than in practice, and it did nothing to weaken the economic embargo that Washington had imposed on Cuba—an embargo that remains in force to the present day. But Castro's revolution had won a degree of security.

Castro, with the indispensable subvention of the Soviet Union, began to enforce an ethic of self-denial and unremitting labor. But the disobliging truth is, that despite unrelenting effort, neither incessant moral hectoring nor harsh laws against absenteeism worked. Cubans, despite the many years of being enjoined to "be like Che," remained firmly attached to the pleasure principle, with an undiminished affection for American movies, music, and sport. It didn't seem to matter whether they were workers or peasants, lived in the city or toiled in the countryside. The Russian Lada never had a chance against the American Ford. After years of wearing Arrow shirts, riding in Otis elevators, and repairing their clothes with Singer sewing machines, Cubans found it all but impossible to accept the inferior goods produced in the Soviet bloc. Ideology succumbed to aesthetics.

Nor could the Cuban Revolution be exported, as Castro hoped, even if its example proved an inspiration to aspiring peoples everywhere. Neither the debacle of Che's doomed effort in Bolivia to ignite a continental rebellion nor, in recent decades, the exemplary work of tens of thousands of doctors and teachers in a score of countries worked. The one commodity that Cuba had in abundance and could successfully export all over the world was music. Only music could travel unimpeded, and the music that sold best was the prerevolutionary music of an older, nearly forgotten Cuba whose representatives had become the invisible men of a decaying, melancholic Havana.

As early as 1920, RCA Victor began advertising what one critic would later call "the languorous appeal of native melodies." By 1925, hundreds of Cuban songs had been recorded and broadcast across America on the burgeoning commercial national radio network. The fusion of Spanish melody and African rhythm, the varied forms of Cuban music—son, danzón, guajira, rumba, mambo—proved spectacularly seductive. Its erotic appeal was explicit. Miami was deliberately created in the 1920s as a faux Havana, developers going to extraordinary lengths to achieve verisimilitude, in one instance importing more than two million old clay barrel roof tiles from Havana to give Miami the kind of weathered patina only time can bestow.

It is perhaps a further irony that for all the efforts made to fashion a new music that would promote the revolution's political ideals—and in this my old junior high school chum, Pablo Menéndez, the son of Barbara Dane, would play a leading role as a charter member of the Nuevo Trova movement, along with Silvio Rodrigues and Pablo Milanes—the music that triumphed the world over was the prerevolutionary music that antedated the arrival of Fidel. The varied and traditional forms of Cuban music proved astonishingly seductive and enduring, largely impervious to the periodic attempts to annex them to the revolution's agenda. The best representatives of this music were, after 1959, shunted aside. They were the embodiment and a reminder of the irrepressible libido that resisted being enrolled in the service of the revolution. These musicians were often regarded with suspicion by the revolution's cultural powerbrokers as untrustworthy custodians of fantasies of indulgence and abandon. All this was clear from Ry Cooder and Wim Wenders's rediscovery of the Buena Vista Social Club. What, after all, did these musicians have to do with the Fidelista upheaval? The truth is that, the revolution notwithstanding, they and their art had always been a defining feature of Cuba's culture, a feature that proved tremendously influential all over the world.

Today, for Cuba's youth, however, this is music for tourists; even salsa seems to belong more to the past than to the present. What commands the ears of the young is reggaeton, which has swept the Latinx world. Rooted in a robotic beat crafted from a relentless algorithm, reggaeton has conquered the international market. It is ubiquitous, an admixture of rap and the insistent beat more of the boom box era than the lilting songs of work and longing that were the guarijos' lament. The lyrics are often explicitly sexist, full of macho posturing, at pains to worship at the altar of consumerism. As Nancy Morejón, one of Cuba's leading poets, now seventy-five and a past president of the writers' section of UNEAC, the artists and writers union, told me, "For this we made a revolution?"

In 1999, I attended, along with more than two thousand other Americans, a sold-out concert of the Buena Vista Social Club, making their debut in Los Angeles at the art deco

Wiltern Theatre. With the legendary Cachaito López on bass, the elegant silver-haired Rubén González at the piano, the silky Ibrahim Ferrer and the sexy Omara Portuondo at the microphone, and a dozen other virtuoso musicians, including Eliades Ochoa, the entire ensemble seemed a miracle, indeed, a resurrection. Effortlessly gliding from ballad to ballad, the trombonist suddenly broke into a languorous Cuban-inflected melody whose familiar strains were greeted with an audible gasp of recognition from the delighted audience: he was playing, lyrically and lovingly, "Somewhere over the Rainbow." The audience began to sing, wistfully at first and then with gathering conviction, the lyrics of one of America's best-known tunes. Whatever else might be said about Cuba and the United States, one thing was certain: it was not yet the end of the affair.

During Castro's sunset years, in an effort to resuscitate the ailing Cuban economy, hard hit after the collapse of the Soviet Union, Havana turned to tourism in a big way, especially as the international market for sugar continued to contract. But the island's revolutionary luster had dimmed. The market for tourists of the revolution had all but vanished, and now, once again, Cuba sought to present itself as an exotic location for fantasies of indulgence and abandon—the very thing the revolution had been at pains to renounce. A new generation of Western movie stars, rock musicians, and supermodels—from Robert Redford to Ry Cooder to Naomi Campbell—parachuted into the island, seeking renewal and rejuvenation at the fount of its irrepressible libido. Havana, founded five hundred years ago in 1519, once again became a magnet for outsiders after years of deliberate neglect. The magnificently restored buildings dating from the sixteenth, seventeenth, eighteenth, and nineteenth centuries all jostle for space in a 350-acre section of Old Havana.

A Cuban friend of fifty years standing, a former ambassador, said to me, "Thank God for the people who convinced Fidel that we should invest in the rehabilitation of our architectural heritage. Otherwise, these precious artifacts of our history would have collapsed and disappeared, bulldozed into oblivion." Credit largely goes to the indefatigable Eusebio Leal Spengler, the city's official historian. He was able to wield considerable clout as a member of Cuba's National Assembly, the Communist Party's Central Committee, and the powerful Council of State. Castro's decision to restore Old Havana required overcoming one of his deepest prejudices that had long shaped the revolution's priorities. In the past, Havana was regarded, not wrongly, as a leech sucking a disproportionate share of the country's scarce resources. Havana was the opulent playground of gamblers and corrupt politicians, home to the rich battening off the immiseration of the campesinos laboring for centavos in the countryside. Castro was determined to carry out a sweeping reversal. And so, for decades, Havana, a city of one million inhabitants in 1959—now a metropolis of two million—was intentionally neglected as a matter of state policy in favor of devoting more resources to the overwhelming majority of impoverished Cubans who lived outside the capital.

The decision to abandon that policy, taken in the early 1980s, has paid off: today, tourism accounts for an estimated forty percent of all Cuba's foreign exchange earnings. (To give you a sense of scale, Cuba's economy is just under ten percent of the Netherlands's, $90 billion against the Dutch economy of $900 billion. The Netherlands has a population of seventeen million people, only six million more than Cuba.) But there is an irony: my friend, the former diplomat, is convinced that one hundred percent of all foreigners visiting Havana come not to admire or examine the achievements of the revolution, but rather to wonder and marvel at the edifices—Morro Castle, for example—built by slave labor under colonial Spanish rule and now preserved by a revolution that regards itself as the inheritor of the heroes of Cuban independence who fought to throw off the shackles first of Spanish colonialism and then the corrupting constraints and suffocations of US neocolonialism and its Cuban puppets.

When the Soviet Union fell, Cuba was bereft. Fidel said, "We lost all our markets for sugar, we stopped receiving foodstuffs, fuel, even the wood to bury our dead in. From one day to the next, we found ourselves without fuel, without raw materials, without food, without soap, without everything." The feverish attempts to diversify the country's economy had largely failed. Even today, Cuba is vulnerable. Trump's zombie foreign policy, despite Castro's demise and the end of the Cold War and just a scant thirty-six months after the Obama rapprochement, seeks to humiliate Cuba and punish its leaders and people for the sin of refusing to bow to Washington's interests. Under pressure from Trump, Brazil's new leader cut off all exports of chickens to Cuba, an indispensable part of the Cuban diet and the source of the country's entire supply.

Cubans I spoke to are stunned by both the suddenness and pettiness, not to mention the criminality, of Trump's efforts to throttle the revolution—a revolution that the ghoulish John Bolton and Elliot Abrams are convinced (mistakenly) has sunk into senescence. The months before my visit saw the US withdrawing of diplomatic personnel from its embassy, leaving just a skeletal janitorial staff and a Marine guard; expelling Cuban diplomats from their embassy in Washington; curtailing business travel; cutting off people-to-people, large-scale tourism by eliminating a subcategory for approved travel; levying some of the largest blockade violation fines ever; triggering the clauses of the punitive Helms-Burton law, permitting lawsuits against third-party investors in Cuba who seek to build on land claimed by long-ago owners; denying visas that had formerly been routinely granted to scholars, artists, writers, and musicians; putting Cuba on an international terrorist watch list, condemning it as a pariah state; enjoining international banks not to do business in the country; successfully pressuring Pay-Pal to withdraw its use by the US-based and US-operated Center for Cuban Studies; and ramping up an increasingly bellicose rhetoric, reminiscent of the darkest days of the Cold War.

A hurricane of high-tech, turbocharged capitalism swirls about this lonely socialist Erewhon as the generation that fought the revolution passes from the scene and the generation of kids who were fifteen and sixteen in 1969—kids who enrolled themselves in the great Literacy Campaign that fanned out across the country to teach peasants to read and write in the flush of its first fevered decade and a half—is itself entering old age. The future is passing into the hands of the generation that was born during the 1980s and 1990s, the years of the so-called Special Period after the fall of the Soviet Union, a generation for whom the slogans of their grandfathers, whose achievement seemed almost superhuman and who cast a very long shadow indeed, carry less and less weight. There is a palpable contest now unfolding in Cuba for the hearts and minds of the young. My old friend Miguel Barnet, poet and ethnographer, the editor of the remarkable *Autobiography of a Runaway Slave*, and the outgoing two-term president of the Union of Writers and Artists, who will be eighty in January, delivered a candid and sober speech at the end of June at the union's ninth congress. He worried aloud over what he called "the impact of the global colonizing wave on Cuban society." He acknowledged that, despite six decades of ceaseless effort, Cuba's government faces "a daily battle against bureaucracy, corruption, routine," and decried what he called "insensibility." He condemned attempts by "Cuba's enemies to create an intellectual fifth column," urged his fellow writers and artists to "combat passivity, accommodation, and mediocrity," and derided the persistence in Cuba of "vulgar materialism, marginal behavior, self-interest, discrimination, and intolerance." He was more succinct when I spoke with him on the eve of my departure. I asked him what was the greatest cultural challenge facing Cuban society. He replied without a hint of irony, "Bad taste."

It would, however, be a grave mistake to underestimate the enduring appeal of the largest legacy of Fidel's triumph: standing up for the right of small states to resist the bullying domination of large powers. Fidel was not willing to submit to the dictates of Washington, nor was he always a reliable cat's paw for Moscow. One has only to examine the roots of Castro's Africa policies, which antedated his coziness with the Soviets and were carried out independently of Soviet desires throughout much of the 1960s, to know that he often refused to follow Kremlin orthodoxy, despite his inexplicable and appalling endorsement of the August 1968 Soviet invasion of Czechoslovakia and the overthrow of Alexander Dubček. Whatever else might be said of this most complicated and audacious figure—and the revolution he created in his own remarkable image—he strode the world's stage as if his island were a continental power, raising a prophetic voice, decrying the unequal relations between North and South, upholding the right of rebellion and human solidarity, denouncing the despoilment of the environment, and excoriating what he called "the profligate, egotistical, and insatiable consumerism of the developed countries."

There is, of course, a great if largely unacknowledged irony: Had Fidel died shortly after overthrowing Batista, his unsullied place in Cuba's history would have been assured. His work as a revolutionary might have been regarded as fruitful up to the moment when he failed to recognize that it was time to step aside. He was unable to do so. His lust for power and a sense of messianic mission prevented him. Nations, it has been said, which do not have the opportunity of getting rid of their geniuses are sometimes liable to pay dearly for the privilege of being led by them. Or, as Brecht put it, "Unhappy the nation that needs heroes."

As for the United States, Washington's obstinate and shameful refusal to award Cuba the relations it is willing to accord other Communist countries, like China and Vietnam, is petulance raised to the level of policy. Cuba's heresy does not rest on the revolution's ideological conceits. Rather, it rests on its unwillingness to accept America's hemispheric hegemony. Cuba is neither the revolutionary specter of its most fervent supporters nor the subversive hobgoblin of White House propagandists. Havana's continuing threat does not lie in its fealty to Marxist dogma, but rather in the delusions suffered by planners in the Pentagon, and in its stiff-necked resistance to American hubris. For in the eyes of Washington's imperial overlords, yesterday and today, Cuba's greatest sin is its pride, and that they can never forgive.

Over my five decades of visiting the island and thinking deeply about the relations between the United States and the Pearl of the Antilles, I've become more and more convinced that the story that best explains our intimate and complex entanglements is that of a love affair gone bad—a love affair between two peoples thrown together by geography and history. Neither the United States nor Cuba has ever fully acknowledged how irrevocably they are lodged in each other's imagination. Or, to put it another way, understanding Cuba-US relations may well be more a matter for a psychiatrist's couch than for a political scientist's classroom.

I, like many others, went to Cuba because I was inspired by the promise of the revolution, and by the internationalism and martyrdom of Che Guevara, whose murder at the hands of the CIA in Bolivia in October of 1967 I can never forget. I wanted to understand better and experience firsthand the remarkable social experiments that seemed to open a window on a better, more just future, especially for those in what was then called the Third World who suffered the sharp end of the American stick. In the end, I fell in love with the Cuban people. To what extent are the character and culture of the Cuban people today a result of the revolution or a reflection of a temperament forged in the blast furnace of the island's unique history? Most likely an admixture of the two, braided together by serendipity and fate.

I was also drawn to the unprecedented cultural outpouring, especially in the visual arts and in the cinema, that the revolution unleashed. That creative explosion also engendered a backlash of censorious apparatchiks—most of them opportunistic hacks from the pre-Castro Communist Party, notorious for its timidity and its devotion to dogma, looking to ride to power on the backs of the victorious *barbudos* of the 26th of July Movement—who were determined to reign in the more anarchic spirits of Cuban intellectual life, leading to the so-called gray years of the early to mid-1970s. It's a depressing tale, one that starts with the suppression of *Lunes de Revolución*, the feisty, eclectic literary weekly, and concludes with the ascendancy of *Verde Olivio*, the chief journal of the armed forces, as arbiter of the country's cultural policies. Whatever the wafflings and uncertainties and aesthetic and political ambiguities and contradictions of the early 1960s, there occurred by the late 1960s what might reasonably be called an internal putsch with respect to the revolution's cultural policies. Even so informed and close an observer as Rebecca Gordon-Nesbitt concluded that by the end of that remarkable decade, the Cuban "armed forces exerted 'visible and sustained' control over the 'cultural life of the country.' In this way, the connection between the cultural leadership and the artistic vanguard was severed, with disastrous results." The Cuban art historian and curator Gerardo Mosquera agreed, rendering an unsparing verdict that "the basic result for culture was the closure of the plural, intense, and quite autonomous scene that had prevailed. No official style was dictated, but a practice of culture as ideological propaganda was imposed, along with a stereotyped nationalism." Journals were closed, editors fired, professors lost their jobs and were banished to factories far from Havana. Prominent cultural figures left the country. Cultural life stagnated. Boldness was out and timidity was in. The price of survival was keeping your head down.

A surpassing irony was obvious if little remarked upon: despite all the effort expended on denouncing the neocolonial imposition of cultural forms from elsewhere, despite all the attempts to secure and promote nativist and folkloric cultural expressions as somehow more authentic and representative of Cuba's indigenous culture, the Revolution seemed never to have any misgivings about embracing Alicia Alonso's classical ballet, derived from an aristocratic French tradition, nor was the Revolution troubled by Cubans' love for baseball, with its American origins. The whole notion of "culture" and what it is for and who gets to make it and how it affects people is always fraught and complicated.

Three stories by way of conclusion:

Thirty years ago, in 1989, I spent a considerable amount of time in the company of José "Pepe" Rodríguez Feo. Four years later, he would die, age seventy-three. As a young man, he was the founder of the literary quarterly *Orígenes*. He invited me over to his apartment in Vedado, not far from the Havana Libre. Across the hall in his building had lived his good friend, the poet Virgilio Piñera. Pepe, the scion of a wealthy sugar baron, had attended Harvard in the 1940s and had befriended the poet Wallace Stevens, with whom he carried on a ten-year correspondence. Their exchange was published in 1986 by Duke University Press in a volume called *Secretaries of the Moon*.

In 1959, Pepe was the only one of his family to cast his lot with the Revolution. He refused to flee the country, instead renouncing his inheritance and enrolling himself in the service of the new dispensation. He was among those, born before the Revolution, who came to be regarded after 1959 as one of the "men in transition," not likely to become a "new man," the ideal Che did so much to encourage. We met in his apartment for a modest dinner, which he'd gone to considerable lengths to prepare. What I mostly remember is drinking rum steadily with him until about 3:00 a.m., when I finally took my leave and stumbled back to my hotel. He asked how I had spent my day. I'd been wandering the city, and just before coming over to him, I'd killed a couple hours in the bookstore catty-corner from the Havana Libre. He doubted I'd found anything of interest, aside from the dusty volumes of the selected writings of Enver Hoxha, the leader of Communist Albania. I said, on the contrary, I had: Erich Auerbach's magnificent *Mimesis: The Representation of Reality in Western Literature*. He was astonished. That, he said, was good news and bad news. The good news was that such a book could be found in today's Cuba and that, thanks to the Revolution, the country was one hundred percent literate. The bad news was that you'd be hard-pressed to find a single person born after the Revolution who could understand even a tenth of the book's references or argument.

In 2010, through the magic of the internet, I met up with Wilfredo Marshall, my old cane-cutting partner in the great and doomed ten-million-ton *zafra* of 1970 (which nearly destroyed the Cuban economy) whom I hadn't seen in four decades. Black as anthracite, the son of a longshoreman, he'd come from a dirt-poor family of twelve brothers and sisters. When I met him, he was a twenty-two-year-old agronomy student at the University of Havana; I was a newly minted Berkeley High School graduate of seventeen, hell-bent on making history. Wilfredo went on to found the University of Camagüey and became dean of its school of agronomy. All his brothers and sisters became doctors and professional people, and all still live in Cuba. "I know all the problems of this revolution," he told me. "I have lived through every one of them, but there is one thing my family knew from the start: we didn't need Castro or Marx to tell us we needed a revolution and that it would be good for me and my family."

And, finally, Pablo Armando Fernández, the chief reason for my most recent trip to Cuba. He was ninety, and I had been told he was bedridden and dying. I needed to say good-bye. One of the original editors of the literary supplement *Lunes*, which enjoyed a brief eighteen-month run as the freewheeling arts and culture section to the newspaper *Revolución*, Pablo is a survivor. He was among that band of mischief-makers that included such brash writers and poets as Heberto Padilla, Guillermo Cabrera Infante, Edmundo Desnoes, and Carlos Franqui, who put out a publication that became the target of a bruising battle. It was a battle he lost. A notorious meeting was held in the National Library, where Fidel, whose moral authority as head of the victorious rebel army was unchallenged, castigated the assembled scribblers and eggheads and issued a striking and chilling commandment: "Within the Revolution, everything;

against the Revolution, nothing." *Lunes* was closed. It was a shattering blow. The unruly bohemianism of the *barbudos* was soon gone. A Stalinist starch was ironed into the criollo insouciance. The radiant future became luminous with casualties. Cabrera Infante, appointed cultural attaché in Belgium, would defect to the UK in 1965. Padilla, despite winning a prestigious Casa de las Americas prize for his poetry, would be forced in the early 1970s to publicly confess his thought crimes in a scandal that recalled the ugly years of Stalin's show trials. Ultimately, he would leave the island for the United States and would die in an Alabama hotel room, where he'd been staying to deliver talks at a minor Southern college.

As for Pablo Armando, he morphed into the Ilya Ehrenburg of the Cuban Revolution, making his peace with the often-capricious whims of the Maximum Leader, whose approbation he constantly sought and whose love he craved. God knows what public stratagems of self-protection he'd had to devise, possibly balanced by private interventions on behalf of writers more reckless or heedless than him, to retain his perch as point man of Cuba's official intellectual culture. For a half century, he'd been for most foreigners the go-to guy for introductions to Cuba's most savvy and gifted writers and poets. It hadn't been easy. For more than a decade, after his stint as Cuba's cultural attaché in London just after the Revolution's triumph in 1959, he was prevented from publishing. Work was scarce. He was shunted aside, banished to the margins, given work as a translator for UNESCO. He stuck it out, however, never denouncing the regime or allying himself with oppositionists like his former comrade Cabrera Infante, whose tart tongue and outspoken mockery of Fidel and refusal to shut up meant permanent exile from his beloved Havana, which he so memorably evoked in his wicked and furious novels and punning polemics. By contrast, a framed photograph of Gabriel García Márquez, Pablo Armando, and Fidel taken on the occasion of Pablo Armando's seventieth birthday, when Fidel graced Pablo Armando with a visit at his home, stands prominently on his mantelpiece.

A dead ringer for Trotsky, Pablo Armando had soft green eyes, full of intelligence, possessed of a gaze designed by his nature to seduce; an engaging rasp to his sonorous voice; a full head of snow-white hair, which he wore long; and was capable of uttering in at least two languages sentences almost Jamesian in their dependent clauses and compelling interpolations. His fingers were graceful, and he deployed them with the confidence of an experienced and passionate orchestra conductor. He was not tall, but his large and handsome head, which resembled Rodin's Balzac, was perched atop a barrel chest, which, in turn, rested on a foreshortened trunk to which were appended a pair of rather spindly legs. He radiated charm and was hostage, as were all who fell into his orbit, to an intoxicating loquaciousness. How could I forget his dulcet command: "Tell me something, tell me anything, even if it's a lie."

I well remember my visit, in 2010, in the company of one of my sons, then seventeen, the same age I was when I first visited Cuba. I had called Pablo Armando to make an appointment. His sweet voice crooned, "Yes, my child, I have been waiting for you, always, every day. Come soon, I shall be here."

We arrived at his two-story stately home in Miramar, in an upscale neighborhood full of embassies. I almost didn't recognize the house, obscured as it now was by a chest-high concrete wall and iron gate put up some years before to prevent burglars. Crime, almost unknown in revolutionary Havana, had become something of a problem. Pablo Armando had more than one hundred paintings, many by world-famous artists from all over the world, hanging on his walls, including two Picassos, which the artist had given him following Castro's victory. Years later, when they were stolen, he was forced to take measures to secure the house, which he has lived in since 1962, no longer trusting even ostensible friends to stay the night. An alarm system was installed. Another hundred paintings were stored elsewhere. Upstairs the walls of his study were lined with six thousand books, their pages rumpled from Cuba's persistent humidity; another four thousand were in storage, two-thirds of them, he liked to boast, signed first editions.

Pablo Armando, despite a heart bypass a few years ago and the death of Maruja, his beautiful wife, looked remarkably well. His memory was intact, and he still traveled widely and frequently, to New York and California, to Spain and Italy and Colombia. He and his family had prospered, his four children now grown, one son a former ambassador from Cuba to India and then posted to Colombia.

He greeted my son, Isaac, with open arms, telling us he had every day been looking upon us. I thought he was speaking metaphorically, in his usual florid way, but was stopped short when, up in his book-lined study, he pointed to a Polaroid snapshot of my son and me. I must have given it to him in the midnineties, when my son was about three years old.

Now, nine years later, I am again standing in front of Pablo Armando's home. The night before, when I called, his daughter Barbara asked me to arrive precisely between four thirty and five fifteen. From the second-floor balcony, a woman emerges, hair pulled back in a tight ponytail. She waves. The gate buzzes and I enter and walk to the gracious portico—a portico on which several comfortable rocking chairs rest—chairs that, in their time, hosted innumerable dignitaries and fellow travelers from all over the world, who made pilgrimage to the revolutionary Mecca for which Pablo Armando served as unofficial cultural ambassador.

The house is as I remembered it. Cool marble tiles bifurcate the home, dark dining room to the right, shuttered against the heat of the day, living room to the left, the walls covered with the paintings—scores of them—given to Pablo by artist-admirers down the decades, many portraits of Pablo himself, along with nudes and abstracts, many bearing personal dedications and loving inscriptions.

Barbara comes down the staircase of the central hallway and beckons. I follow and up the staircase we go and then down the upstairs hallway, where, facing open French doors, the rain falling steadily off the eaves of the house and pooling on the tiles of the balcony, is Pablo Armando, sitting in a wheelchair, a caretaker seated on a nearby bench. Clad in a t-shirt, a bib-like towel around his neck, wearing shorts, he seems much diminished, though his face, largely unlined, evinces the disturbing serenity of a man whose mind has begun to vanish. Barbara says, "Pappy, Steve is here, you remember, Steve Wasserman." His eyes are vacant, unblinking. The caretaker uses a corner of the towel bib that hangs around his neck to wipe some spittle collecting at the corners of his mouth. I stand next to him and lean over and kiss him on his forehead. I tell him I love him, that I always loved him and always will.

He seems, or so I like to think, to awaken at that moment from a stillness that was remote and inaccessible. I cannot say with any certainty—either then or in the next hour that I spent by his side—that he truly recognizes me. I ask Barbara for permission to take a photograph. She takes my iPhone. Just as she snaps the pic, his jaw slackens and something resembling a smile creases his face. Perhaps it is only the muscle memory of the well-practiced diplomat. His face is otherwise a rictus of incomprehension.

I take my leave. The rain has stopped. A rainbow arches over the glistening city.

[2019]

Susan Sontag: Critic and Crusader

I FIRST MET SUSAN SONTAG in the spring of 1974 at a dinner
in Berkeley given by Robert Scheer, former editor of *Ramparts*, for which Susan had written in the late 1960s. I especially
remember a fifteen-thousand-word "Letter from Sweden,"
which began with a sentence I never forgot: "The experience
of any new country unfolds as a battle of clichés." I was then
a senior at the University of California and was moonlighting
as Scheer's researcher on a book he was writing on multinational corporations and a growing phenomenon that years
later would be called "globalism," but which at the time was
more familiarly known to those on the left as "imperialism."
I was to graduate in June, and Scheer and I planned to go to
New York to finish our work on the book. Scheer was to stay
with his old pal Jules Feiffer, the gifted cartoonist for the
Village Voice, and I would repair, at her invitation, to Sontag's
penthouse, Jasper Johns's former studio, located on the Upper
West Side at 340 Riverside Drive.

I remember the apartment well. Flooded with sunlight,
surrounded by a generous terrace overlooking the Hudson
River, it was spartan: hardwood floors, white walls, high ceil-
ings; in the living room a single Eames chair, an original Andy
Warhol of Chairman Mao; in the dining room a long monk's
table made of oak with a brace of narrow benches on either

side; in the kitchen's cupboards a stack of plates, a few glasses, and row after row of back issues of *Partisan Review*; leaning against one wall of Susan's bedroom a curious stained-glass window from Italy of a spooky death's head, a kind of memento mori; and, perhaps most impressive, by her bedside atop a low nightstand a twenty-four-hour clock featuring time zones spanning the globe. Most important, of course, were the walls that bore the weight of her eight thousand books, a library that Susan would later call her "personal retrieval system." (By the time of her death thirty years later, the library had grown to twenty-five thousand volumes.)

I spent the summer nearly getting a crick in my neck from perusing the books, and I remember thinking that—though I had just finished four years of college—my real education had just begun. I discovered scores of writers I'd never heard of, as well as writers I distantly knew but had never read. For reasons wholly mysterious, I found myself drawn to four blue-backed volumes: *The Journals of André Gide*. These, like others in Susan's library, were filled with her lightly penciled underlinings and marginal notes.

For my twenty-second birthday in early August, Susan took me to see Waylon Jennings at the Bottom Line, the hot new club that had opened to great success six months earlier. (Five years later, I would return the favor by taking her to see Graham Parker and the Rumour at the Roxy in Los Angeles.) Her son, David Rieff, my age exactly, had long been besotted with country music and boasted a dazzling collection of bespoke cowboy boots, and we spent many humid evenings walking his dog, Nu-nu, an Alaskan husky with Paul Newman eyes, through the streets of the neighborhood while talking politics and literature and the higher gossip over endless cups of espresso and smoking Picayunes, the strong unfiltered cigarettes he then favored but would later give up. Thus was a lifelong friendship forged.

Six days later, President Richard Nixon resigned in disgrace. Scheer's book had to be retitled—now it was to be called *America after Nixon: The Age of the Multinationals*. Those were the days before computers, of course, and it fell to me to comb through the page proofs, meticulously changing all the present tenses to past, as in "Nixon was." Nothing so tedious was ever so pleasurable.

Susan and I kept up our friendship, and during the near decade that I edited the *Los Angeles Times Book Review*, she was a cherished contributor. She was something of an Auntie Mame figure for me. We spent years haunting secondhand bookstores in Berkeley, Los Angeles, and New York, talking for hours over ever-more bizarre dishes of Chinese Hakka cuisine in Yuet Lee, a hole-in-the-wall eatery at Stockton and Broadway in San Francisco, watching Kenneth Anger flicks and the surrealistic stop-motion puppet masterpieces of Ladislas Starevich, which Tom Luddy would screen for us at the Pacific Film Archive over and over again until our eyeballs nearly fell out.

When she fell sick in the spring of 2004, I feared it would prove to be her final illness, despite having successfully survived two previous cancers. I last saw her in April 2004. She was in Los Angeles to receive a lifetime achievement award from the city's Library Foundation. We met at her downtown hotel. She looked, as ever, full of life, ardent as always. She drew me aside and confided the grim diagnosis she'd just received from her doctors. She said, "Three strikes and you're out."

Months before she died in December, I began to draft her obituary, which, in the event, would be front-page news. Twenty-five years before, I had clipped from the pages of *Rolling Stone* what I thought was the best interview she'd ever given: a passionate and far-ranging conversation with Jonathan Cott, an original and longtime contributor to the magazine. I quoted generously from it in my obituary for the *Los Angeles Times*.

Years went by, and it came to pass that Cott discovered in his apparently bottomless closet the tapes he'd used to record his interview. It turned out that *Rolling Stone* had only used a third of their twelve hours of talk. And since Susan spoke in complete sentences and paragraphs, we decided to publish the entire conversation at Yale University Press, where I was now an editor.

Aside from the personal loss for those lucky enough to count Susan as a comrade and friend and ally, why should her death matter? What did her work stand for? And, ten years on, does it hold up?

She was, of course, one of America's most influential intellectuals, internationally renowned for the passionate engagement and breadth of her critical intelligence and her ceaseless efforts to promote the cause of human rights. She was, as a writer and as a citizen of the world, a critic and a crusader. The author of seventeen books translated into more than thirty languages, she vaulted to public attention and critical acclaim with the publication a half century ago, in 1964, of "Notes on 'Camp'," written for *Partisan Review* and included in *Against Interpretation*, her first collection of essays published two years later, in 1966.

Susan wrote about subjects as diverse as pornography and photography, the aesthetics of silence and the aesthetics of fascism, Bunraku puppet theater and the choreography of Balanchine, the uses and abuses of language and illness, as well as admiring portraits of such writers and filmmakers as Antonin Artaud, Walter Benjamin, Roland Barthes, Elias Canetti, Kenneth Anger, Ingmar Bergman, Robert Bresson, Carl Dreyer, Rainer Werner Fassbinder, Hans-Jürgen Syberberg, Jean-Luc Godard, Robert Walser, Marina Tsvetaeva, and Alice James. She was always hungry for more. All her life she aspired to live up to Goethe's injunction that "you must know everything." She wanted, as Wayne Koestenbaum has astutely observed, to devour the world. There were never enough hours in the day or the night. She stole from sleep the hours she spent reading and rereading, reading and rereading. She was an insomniac omnivore, insatiable, driven, endlessly curious, obsessed collector of enthusiasms and passions.

She was a fervent believer in the capacity of art to delight, to inform, to transform. She was hungry for aesthetic pleasures but haunted by the burden of a moral tradition for which purely aesthetic delights were a guilty pastime. She strained mightily to rid herself of its suffocations, even going so far as to turn a personal predicament into a general condition, famously urging in her 1964 essay "Against Interpretation" that "in place of a hermeneutics we need an erotics of art."

She was distressed by the way her earlier championing of popular culture had been used as a cudgel by her critics to beat down the very idea of high culture, accusing it of snobbery and elitism, calling into question the necessity of artistic or literary or cultural discrimination. She didn't believe, as she would later write, that her praise of contemporary work somehow reduced or detracted from the glories of the high culture she admired far more. Or as she put it,

> Enjoying the impertinent energy and wit of a species of performance called Happenings did not make me care less about Aristotle and Shakespeare. I was—I am—for a pluralistic, polymorphous culture. No hierarchy, then? Certainly, there's a hierarchy. If I had to choose between the Doors and Dostoyevsky, then—of course—I'd choose Dostoyevsky. But do I have to choose?

In no sense, as she insisted, did she ever mean when she called for an "erotics of art" to repudiate high culture and its complexities. When she denounced, as she put it, "certain kinds of facile moralism, it was in the name of a more alert, less complacent seriousness." She was appalled by the perverse populism that increasingly deforms our culture, elevating box office appeal and click meters to authoritative arbiters. She was alarmed by how, in the name of democracy, the tyranny of mass appeal had tightened its grip on the culture. She was repelled by the cultural hegemony imposed by the rise of the entertainment-industrial complex. Indeed, she feared, toward the end of her life, that a terrible sea change had occurred in the whole culture, and that at the dawn of the twenty-first century, we had entered—to use Nietzsche's term—the age of nihilism, as she wrote in the afterword she appended to a reissue of *Against Interpretation* thirty years after it was first published.

She was, as ever, drawn to art that upends assumptions and challenges prejudices. She was not afraid of deep thinking or the delights to be had from its rigors. She had many heroes of the mind—Elias Canetti, Roland Barthes, and, not least, Theodor Adorno, whose love of the aphoristic paradox, eclectic curiosities, and commitment to critical thinking were a model for Sontag's own aspirations. She didn't think that the pleasures of critical thinking ought to belong only to a cultural elite. Such pleasures were the birthright of every citizen. Yet she knew, as she said, that "we live in a culture in which intelligence is denied relevance altogether, in a search for radical innocence, or is defended as an instrument of authority and repression. In my view, the only intelligence worth defending is critical, dialectical, skeptical, desimplifying." She was a paladin of seriousness.

Unfortunately, Sontag's actual writings and ideas interest her critics rather less than what they imagine having been her private life. Her critics are transfixed by the halo of celebrity that seemed to hover above Sontag during her life and which, even after her death, continues to glow. A good example is the documentary *Regarding Susan Sontag*, which had its premiere on HBO in the United States and made the rounds of international film festivals. It is strikingly coarse and prurient, mocking and condescending even as it pretends to an unearned seriousness of purpose, accompanied by an overheated musical score designed to tell viewers what to think and feel. Several of the talking heads in the film—Wayne Koestenbaum and Terry Castle, among others—accuse Sontag of being a coward about her sexuality, a narcissistic diva, a person whose efforts to transform herself are derided as comic. As her son David Rieff has pointed out, suppose they are right—what does this have to do with the work—her writings—which is, after all, why we ought to care, if we care at all, about Susan Sontag? If people think the work is no good, or at least that it's wildly overrated, fine, then they should say so.

But if the work has any true and lasting merit, then this rather voyeuristic emphasis on celebrity and careerism is, to say the least, misplaced, not to mention that it seeks to have it both ways, and exploits the very fame it so condescends to. But then condescending to Sontag while fixating on her, even when she was alive, is something so commonplace as to be tediously familiar. Paying any attention to Sontag, especially now, a decade after her demise, matters only if her work matters. Everything else amounts to gossip about a person who was famous in her lifetime or is grist for the most trivial sort of social and cultural history. Sontag's critics seem to believe that what matters most about Sontag was her effect on her contemporaries, not her work. This view is a disservice to and a caricature of the woman and writer I knew.

Jonathan Cott has aptly characterized Sontag as a writer who was

> continually examining and testing out her notion that supposed oppositions like thinking and feeling, consciousness and sensuousness, morality and aesthetics can in fact simply be looked at as aspects of each other—

much like the pile on the velvet that, upon reversing one's touch, provides two textures and two ways of feeling, two shades and two ways of perceiving.

Here, nicely put by Cott, is the key that unlocks the whole of her work, including a hint of why, over time, the form of the essay exhausted itself, and why, increasingly, she was drawn to fiction.

A self-described "besotted aesthete" and "obsessed moralist," Sontag declared in "Notes on 'Camp'" that "the two pioneering forces of modern sensibility are Jewish moral seriousness and homosexual aestheticism and irony." If we agree that such categories as "Jewish moral seriousness" and "homosexual aestheticism and irony" actually exist, you could reasonably assert that the two traditions were the antipodes that framed an argument Sontag had with herself all her life. The oscillation between the two marks almost all of her work. She saw herself as a loyal inheritor and servant of a tradition of high seriousness that ennobles and confers dignity upon works that are redolent of truth, beauty, and moral gravitas. Sontag gave us her list: *The Iliad*, Aristophanes's plays, *The Art of the Fugue*, *Middlemarch*, the paintings of Rembrandt, the cathedral at Chartres, the poetry of Donne, Dante, Beethoven's quartets—in short, the whole pantheon of high culture. Sontag offered up a taxonomy of creative sensibilities. She proposed a trinity: the first was high culture; the second was a sensibility whose sign was "anguish, cruelty, derangement," exemplified by such artists as Bosch, Sade, Rimbaud, Kafka, geniuses who understood that, at least in the world we now inhabit, the only honest art was art that was broken, composed of shards, hostage to the insight that at the deep center of human existence lay a Gordian knot of unresolvable issues that no surface coherence could plausibly or honestly treat or reflect or make pretty. The third great creative sensibility was Camp, a sensibility, as she wrote, "of failed seriousness, of the theatricalization of experience."

In Note 37, she wrote, "The first sensibility, that of high culture, is basically moralistic. The second sensibility, that of extreme states of feeling, represented in much contemporary 'avant-garde' art, gains power by a tension between moral and aesthetic passion. The third, Camp, is wholly aesthetic." Seen through this lens, there would always be a conflict between "style" and "content," "aesthetics" and "morality," "irony" and "tragedy."

Perhaps the most striking example of Sontag thinking one way on Mondays, Wednesdays, and Fridays and another on Tuesdays and Thursdays is her view of Leni Riefenstahl. Her critics noted the stunning gulf between her 1965 essay "On Style," which hailed Riefenstahl's films as masterpieces "because they project the complex movements of intelligence and grace and sensuousness" and "transcend the categories of propaganda or even reportage," objects of palpable "beauty, formal composition, and technical achievement," and her eviscerating takedown ten years later in her withering critique titled "Fascinating Fascism," published in the *New York Review of Books*. There she seemed to revise, even to reverse, her earlier opinion, condemning Riefenstahl as a genius propagandist in the service of an evil ideology.

There was, of course, no real contradiction. Both views were true: the films were beautiful and terrible, ravishing and appalling. They were, in every way, exemplary. They reflected and embodied the aesthetic appeal of national socialism. That appeal was part of fascism's intoxicating seduction. Not to see it and not to acknowledge it, not to see how it was possible for people—even for people who ought to have known better—to succumb to it is to miss a very large part of its mesmerizing power. Not to understand this salient factor is to fail to grasp the important observation made so piercingly by Walter Benjamin when he wrote that "the logical result of fascism is the introduction of aesthetics into political life." Further, "All efforts to render politics aesthetic culminate in one thing: war."

Sontag was always torn between the moralist and the aesthete. It was a precocious contest, begun at the very dawn of her consciousness.

She was reading by three. In her teens, her passions were Gerard Manley Hopkins and Djuna Barnes. The first book that thrilled her was *Madame Curie*, which she read when she was six. She was stirred by the travel books of Richard Halliburton and the Classic Comics rendition of Shakespeare's *Hamlet*. The first novel that affected her was Victor Hugo's *Les Misérables*.

"I sobbed and wailed and thought [books] were the greatest things," she once recalled. "I discovered a lot of writers in the Modern Library editions, which were sold in a Hallmark-card store, and I used to save up my allowance and would buy them all." Edgar Allan Poe's stories enthralled her with their "mixture of speculativeness, fantasy, and gloominess." Upon reading Jack London's *Martin Eden*, she determined she would become a writer. "I got through my childhood," she told the *Paris Review*, "in a delirium of literary exaltations."

At fourteen, Sontag read Thomas Mann's masterpiece, *The Magic Mountain*. "I read it through almost at a run. After finishing the last page, I was so reluctant to be separated from the book that I started back at the beginning and, to hold myself to the pace the book merited, reread it along, a chapter each night." She began to frequent the Pickwick bookstore on Hollywood Boulevard, where she went "every few days after school to read on my feet through some more of world literature—buying when I could, stealing when I dared."

She also became a "militant browser" of the international periodical and newspaper stand—now, alas, like so many bookstores and record stores, gone—near the "enchanted crossroads" of Hollywood Boulevard and Highland Avenue, where she discovered the world of literary magazines. She was fond of recounting how, at fifteen, she had bought a copy of *Partisan Review* and found it impenetrable. Nevertheless, as she confessed to me and to others, "I had the sense that within its pages momentous issues were at stake. I wanted desperately to crack the code."

At twenty-six, Sontag moved to New York City, where, for a time, she taught the philosophy of religion at Columbia University. At a cocktail party, she encountered William Phillips, one of *Partisan Review*'s legendary founding editors, and asked him how one might write for the journal. He replied, "All you have to do is ask." "I'm asking," she said.

Soon her provocative essays on Albert Camus, Simone Weil, Jean-Luc Godard, Kenneth Anger, Jasper Johns, and the

Supremes began to spice *Partisan Review*'s pages. Sontag recoiled then—as she would ever after—at what she regarded as the artificial boundaries separating one subject, or one art form, from another.

"I love to read the way people love to watch television," she told *Rolling Stone*. For her, culture was a vast smorgasbord, a movable feast. For her, the choice to be made was never either/or but both/and:

> So, when I go to a Patti Smith concert, I enjoy, participate, appreciate and am tuned in better because I've read Nietzsche. [. . .] [T]he main reason I read is that I enjoy it. There's no incompatibility between observing the world and being tuned into an electronic, multimedia, multi-tracked, McLuhanite world and enjoying what can be enjoyed about rock 'n' roll.

Despite her fascination with the internet—in her later years, her IBM Selectric typewriter was replaced by an Apple computer—she understood that the vast canvas it afforded did little to encourage thoughtful criticism. More: that the increasing velocity of everyday life subverts genuine reflection and banishes the solitude necessary for actual thought.

Sontag's greatest project was her devotion to demolishing, as she put it, "the distinction between thought and feeling, which is really the basis of all anti-intellectual views: the heart and the head, thinking and feeling, fantasy and judgment. [. . .] Thinking is a form of feeling; [. . .] feeling is a form of thinking." This quest can be seen in all her essays and, especially, in her fiction. Her writing, observed Elizabeth Hardwick, her admiring friend and perspicacious literary critic, "has a profound authority, a rather anxious and tender authority—the reward of passion. [...] The tone of her writing is speculative, studious and yet undogmatic; even in the end it is still inquiring."

Others were less impressed, accusing Sontag of "a tendency to sprinkle complication into her writing" and of tossing off "high-sounding paradoxes without thinking through what, if anything, they mean." Greil Marcus found her "a cold writer" whose style was "an uneasy combination of academic and hip, [...] pedantic, effete, unfriendly." Her fiction, despite her last novel, *In America*, winning the 2000 National Book Award, was mostly dismissed by reviewers, largely because the only character whose sensibility Sontag seemed genuinely interested in exploring was her own. Her critics weren't entirely wrong, but neither were they entirely right.

Sontag's style *is* her subject. For it is the way she thinks, how she goes about it, how she offers her readers the chance, as it were, to eavesdrop on a mind thinking as hard and as nimbly as it can that is most compelling about her work. Or, to put it another way, it is not so much her opinions that matter—though of course they do—but rather how she goes about arriving at them, how she renders them, the very warp and woof of her sentences. Wayne Koestenbaum, in his appreciation written soon after her death, understood this well, observing that she "is usually cited for her content rather than her form or style, and yet her paragraphs and sentences bear close and admiring scrutiny as exemplars of [. . .] prose forms that would permit maximum drift and detour." He marveled at what he called "her prose's Mercurochrome aesthetic, her stern, self-conscious, tense sentences." He saw that "her essays behave like fictions (disguised, arch, upholstered with attitudes), while her fictions behave like essays (pontificating, pedagogic, discursive)." Koestenbaum writes that "the ends of her novels are the best parts." Often the same is true of her essays. He offers a number of examples:

The last three sentences of *The Volcano Lover*: "They thought they were civilized. They were despicable. Damn them all." The last two sentences of *Death Kit*: "Diddy has made his final chart; drawn up his last map. Diddy has perceived the inventory of the world." The last sentence of *The Benefactor*: "You may imagine me in a bare room, my feet near the stove, bundled up in many sweaters, my black hair turned grey, enjoying the waning tribulations of subjectivity and the repose of a privacy that is genuine."

And, of course, the famous end of her essay on Riefenstahl and Nazi aesthetics: "The color is black, the material is leather, the seduction is beauty, the justification is honesty, the aim is ecstasy, the fantasy is death."

And here are the concluding lines of her 2001 essay "Where the Stress Falls": "Nothing new except language, the ever found. Cauterizing the torment of personal relations with hot lexical choices, jumpy punctuation, mercurial sentence rhythms. Devising more subtle, more engorged ways of knowing, of sympathizing, of keeping at bay. It's a matter of adjectives. It's where the stress falls."

Sontag kept rules and torments at bay, as Koestenbaum points out, "by generating stressed prose—magnifying, through emphasis and engorgement, the opportunities for attentiveness."

Sontag was an eloquent and stalwart advocate for freedom. She considered herself neither a journalist nor an activist, but rather "a citizen of the American empire." As such, she felt an obligation to accept an invitation to visit Hanoi at the height of the American bombing campaign in May 1968. She had, like so many of us during those turbulent, jumped-up years, participated in many protests against the war. A two-week visit resulted in a fervent essay seeking to understand Vietnamese resistance to American power.

Critics excoriated her for what they regarded as a naive sentimentalization of Vietnamese Communism. Paul Hollander, for one, branded Sontag a "political pilgrim," bent on denigrating Western liberal pluralism in favor of venerating foreign revolutions. That same year, she also visited Cuba, after which she wrote an essay for *Ramparts* magazine calling for a sympathetic understanding of the Cuban Revolution. Two years later, however, she joined Peruvian novelist Mario Vargas Llosa and other writers in publicly protesting the regime's harsh treatment of Heberto Padilla, one of the country's leading poets. She also denounced Castro's punitive policies toward homosexuals.

Ever the iconoclast, Sontag had a knack for annoying both the right and the left. In 1982, in a meeting in Town Hall in New York to protest the suppression of Solidarity in Poland, she declared that Communism was fascism with a human face. She was unsparing in her criticism of much of the left's refusal to take seriously the exiles and dissidents and murdered victims of Stalin's terror and the tyranny Communism imposed wherever it had triumphed.

Ten years later, almost alone among American writers and intellectuals, she would call for vigorous Western—and American—intervention in the Balkans to halt the siege of Sarajevo and to stop Serbian aggression in Bosnia and Kosovo. Her solidarity with the citizens of Sarajevo prompted her to make more than a dozen trips to the besieged city.

Then, in the aftermath of the September 11, 2001, terrorist attacks, Sontag, while she was in Berlin on that infamous date, offered a characteristically bold and singular perspective in the *New Yorker* magazine. "Where is the acknowledgment that this was not a 'cowardly' attack on 'civilization' or 'liberty' or 'humanity' or 'the free world' but an attack on the world's self-proclaimed superpower, undertaken as a consequence of specific American alliances and actions?" She added, "In the matter of courage (a morally neutral virtue): Whatever may be said of the perpetrators of Tuesday's slaughter, they were not cowards." She was immediately pilloried by bloggers and pundits, who accused her of anti-Americanism.

Sontag, in all her political essays and public statements and interviews and deeds, tried valiantly to marshal her remarkable combination of erudition, intelligence, and empathy in the service of an abiding commitment to democratic values. For too long, as Sontag knew, Americans have let our conceit of exceptionalism define our political culture, that (somehow) we had slipped the noose of history. Nowhere was this belief more pronounced than in California. For Sontag, as she often said, California was America's America, where you went to reinvent yourself. Her voluntary migration to New York was an effort to make her home in the one city she thought least American, if by "American" we mean deliberately provincial, uninterested in the rest of the world, anticosmopolitan. Similarly, for Sontag, New York was America's Europe. And indeed, for many years, she divided her time between America and Europe, traveling incessantly. She both championed the American dream of self-invention and was herself a successful example of such a project and, as her critics rightly suspected, its fervent opponent—if by "American dream" one means a country devoted to a dogged suspicion of outsiders and a notorious reluctance on the part of its citizenry to evince even a modicum of interest in the world outside our borders.

There is, however, as 9/11 made clear and as the grotesque assault on *Charlie Hebdo* in Paris made plain, no escape from history. Sontag tried hard to live as Bertrand Russell enjoined us: to "remember your humanity and forget the rest." She sought assiduously to affirm—and to reaffirm—the ideas of secularism, reason, libertarianism, internationalism, and solidarity.

In an interview for the *Paris Review*, published in 1995, Sontag was asked what she thought was the purpose of literature: "A novel worth reading," she replied, "is an education of the heart. It enlarges your sense of human possibility, of what human nature is, of what happens in the world. It's a creator of inwardness." She was the cartographer of her own literary explorations. Henry James once remarked that "nothing is my last word on anything." For Sontag, as for James, there was always more to be said, more to be felt. Alas, these many years since her death, there is only silence from her grave at Montparnasse Cemetery in Paris, alongside Baudelaire and Beckett and Sartre.

And yet and yet: the sound of Susan's voice is still in my head. Her lust for life, her avidity, her pursuit of aesthetic bliss, her detestation of philistinism, her love of learning, her opposition to ethical and aesthetic shallowness, her insistence on being a grown-up, her passion for justice and capacity for outrage, and, always, her hatred of suffering and death are everywhere to be found in her sentences, in her essays, and in her stories. Her exemplary effort to swallow the world, as she concludes her revelatory short story "Unguided Tour," tells the tale:

If I go this fast, I won't see anything. If I slow down—

Everything.—then I won't have seen everything before it disappears.

Everywhere. I've been everywhere. I haven't been everywhere, but it's on my list.

Land's end. But there's water, O my heart. And salt on my tongue.

The end of the world. This is not the end of the world.

I hear most of all her cri de coeur, given to the narrator of her story "Debriefing"—it could be her epitaph, her final aria, as she ends her story with this defiant, throbbing declaration:

> Sisyphus, I. I cling to my rock, you don't have to chain me. Stand back! I roll it up—up, up. And . . . down we go. I knew that would happen. See, I'm on my feet again. See, I'm starting to roll it up again. Don't try to talk me out of it. Nothing, nothing could tear me away from this rock.

[2015]

Orson Welles Meets a Deadline

I N *MY LUNCHES WITH ORSON WELLES,* my old friend Peter Biskind, Hollywood historian extraordinaire, has rescued from Henry Jaglom's jumbled closet the hours upon hours of table-talk Jaglom recorded during his years of acting as amanuensis to the great man. As I hoovered up these edited transcripts of the higher gossip, I thought fondly of my own encounter with Welles—an encounter that would lead to irregular meals (and something of a friendship) at his favored table at Ma Maison.

The story begins with the death of Jean Renoir in Beverly Hills in early 1979. I was then deputy editor of the *Los Angeles Times* Sunday opinion section. The *Times,* in its infinite wisdom, had consigned news of Renoir's demise to an AP wire story buried on page nineteen of the Sunday paper. I was beside myself with unhappiness. Here was one of the great directors of the twentieth century, dying in our backyard, as it were, banished to an ignominious squib on the paper's inside pages instead of being ballyhooed prominently on the front page.

The honor of the paper was at stake, I felt. We needed to act immediately to commission a proper piece, honoring Renoir's life and legacy, to publish in the next Sunday's paper. Only Orson Welles, I felt, could do right by Renoir. But how to contact him? I knew only that Welles made a habit of eating lunch every Wednesday at Ma Maison, but I would need his piece, should he agree to write it, by Wednesday, or Thursday at latest, in order to make the Sunday paper. I remembered that some years before, Welles had been the voice of the Paul Masson Winery, intoning, "no wine before its time." I called the winery and was referred to an ad agency in New York and was, in turn, given the name of Welles's Manhattan agent. I rang and explained my purpose.

"So, you want to reach Orson Welles, do you? Well, a lot of people want to reach him. Listen, kid, here's what I'll do. I'm gonna give you his office number. It's a local number. Area code two-one-three. You're unlikely to reach him, but if you do, will you do me a favor? Will you tell him to call his agent, for cryin' out loud?"

I dialed the number. It rang and rang and rang. Finally, the receiver was slowly lifted off its cradle, and what can only be described as an extraordinarily fey voice drawled hello. It was Welles's assistant. I asked to speak to Welles. "I'm sorry, but Mr. Welles isn't in." "Do you expect him back soon?" "I do not know when he'll be back. You see, Mr. Welles almost never comes in." "Might I leave a message?" "Yes, if you must," the voice said in tones of great exasperation. "But do understand that when Mr. Welles deigns to come into this office, he very often sees the stack of messages piled high on the desk and he sweeps them to the floor."

The next morning, I got to work early. Already at my desk was my boss, Anthony Day, editor of the paper's editorial pages. He was clutching my phone. "Yes, yes. I see him now, just coming in." Cupping the receiver, he looked at me and stammered, "Steve, it's . . . it's Orson Welles. For you!"

I got on the horn and heard, in his inimitable voice, "Mr. Wasserman, this is Orson Welles. I did not know until I received your kind message that my great and good friend, Jean Renoir, had passed away. What, pray tell, would you have me do?"

I told him of the embarrassing and all but invisible notice that Renoir's death had occasioned in the paper, and that we had an obligation to do what we could to remove the stain of shame. Would he write a piece?

"How long? How about two-hundred-fifty words?" he offered.

Given the length of Renoir's life and his considerable achievement, I said a thousand might be better.

"Let's split the difference and agree to five hundred."

As for deadline—he boomed, "I know, I know: you needed it yesterday."

"For you, Mr. Welles, the day after tomorrow would be fine."

As for compensation—he cut me off. "Let us not sully art with talk of money. I count on you to do the right thing. You will do that, won't you?"

I said I'd do my level best.

Wednesday came and went. No piece. We were keeping space open on the front page of the opinion section. By noon on Thursday, we began to sweat. My phone rang. It was Gus, the paper's receptionist-cum-security guard, who manned the front desk in the paper's art deco lobby, worthy of the *Daily Planet*, at the center of which slowly revolved a globe boasting national boundaries not redrawn since the collapse of the Austro-Hungarian Empire. A man saying he was from Mr. Welles's office was waiting for me.

I hurried down. And there, greeting me, was an apparition straight out of *Sunset Boulevard*: a man, kitted out in livery, replete with leather driving gloves, handed me a manila envelope bearing Welles's piece.

As I walked slowly up the stairs to my second-floor office, I read what Welles had written. It wasn't five hundred words; it was nine pages, two thousand words, typed double-spaced on an Underwood Five typewriter, and edited in Welles's hand with a blue felt-tip pen, the last page of which bore his signature. Every sentence had oxygen in it. The lede was unforgettable: "For the high and mighty of the movies a Renoir on the wall is the equivalent of a Rolls Royce in the garage. Nothing like the same status was accorded the other Renoir who lived in Hollywood and who died here last week."

The essay was perfect, all about the uneasy intersection of art and commerce, and, as I read it, I realized it was, of course, as much about Welles himself as it was about Renoir. It was about the trials and tribulations of neglected genius. It was, in a way, a kind of manifesto, a credo of artistic aspiration and principle.

The ending, too, was a doozy (the ellipses are Welles's):

I have not spoken here of the man who I was proud to count as a friend. His friends were without number and we all loved him as Shakespeare was loved, "this side idolatry." Let's give him the last word: "To the question 'Is the cinema an art?' my answer is 'What does it matter?' . . . You can make films or you can cultivate a garden. Both have as much claim to being called an art

as a poem by Verlaine or a painting by Delacroix. . . .
Art is 'making.' The art of love is the art of making love.
. . . My father never talked to me about art. He could not
bear the word."

There was nothing to edit, only to publish it as written. It
appeared in the *Los Angeles Times* on February 18, 1979. It was
the last piece Welles ever wrote.

[2013]

The Russian Avant-Garde:
Promise and Betrayal

*Nothing stands still for us. This is the state which is ours by
nature, yet to which we least incline: we burn to find solid
ground, a final steady base on which to build a tower that rises
to infinity; but the whole foundation cracks beneath us and the
earth splits open down to the abyss.*

—PASCAL

WHEN I WALKED INTO THE exhibition of Russian
avant-garde art held in Los Angeles in the summer
of 1981 and looked at Malevich's canvases of black squares and
blue triangles, Tatlin's constructions of wood and iron, Lissitsky's blueprints for bold new buildings, I was overcome with
sadness. For these early modernist works are emblems of an
innocence I was denied, fragments from my century's adolescence. The palpable exhilaration these objects still exude filled
me with melancholy because I know that I can never believe in
their promise.

Few centuries have dawned with as much promise as the
twentieth century; fewer still have had their hopes shattered so
brutally. In 1900, the future seemed very bright. Science would
conquer religion; reason would banish superstition. An end to
the ancient quarrel between man and nature, man and man,
liberty and necessity, seemed to be within reach. The Machine
Age had arrived.

It is hard now to apprehend the expectations of the men and women who would experience the expansion of capitalism, the founding of the first socialist state, the trauma of economic collapse, and the terrible bloodletting of two world wars. Certainly, their optimism owed much to their youth. By the time of the First World War, the average age of the artists represented in the Los Angeles exhibit was twenty-seven. Born on the cusp of the century, they were fated to act as midwives to the birth of modernism. Realizing that industrialized society demolishes the past, they desired a defiant, aggressive art committed to the notion of progress. They rushed to embrace the future that was speeding toward them.

Nowhere was change more evident than in Russia. The feudal regime of the czars was crumbling; talk of revolution was everywhere. Contentious, intense, and passionate, the Russians were addicted to polemics. The aesthetic squabbles of Russia's artists, like the political quarrels of the country's revolutionaries, were often acrimonious. They were forever issuing proclamations and pronouncements—writing each other out of the movement, branding one another as heretics.

If traditionally three's a crowd and today four's a gang, then in Russia two was an ism. Rayonism, for example, was the offspring of Natalia Goncharova and Mikhail Larionov. They founded a self-proclaimed movement whose influence barely extended itself further than the four walls of their tiny Petrograd apartment. Prewar Russia was a hothouse in which a nearly impenetrable thicket of such isms flourished: Purism, Primitivism, Rayonism, Cubo-Futurism, Suprematism, and later, Productivism and Constructivism.

Despite an initial preoccupation with the traditions of folk art, Russia's artists quickly embraced the new industrial ethos. In 1915, Kazimir Malevich, perhaps the most important figure of the Russian avant-garde, wrote, "The new life of machinery and iron, the roar of motor-cars, the flash of projectors, the snarl of propellers, have awakened the soul." If the revolt against history can be said to date in the twentieth century from the storming of the Winter Palace, then the aesthetic impasse of modernism is anticipated by the art of the Russian avant-garde. What seems remarkable is the bravery of the break with realism and the rapidity with which the limits of abstraction were reached.

Today the aesthetic triumph of the Russian avant-garde is so complete it is no longer evident, its ideological defeat so great it hardly matters. The universal aesthetic language these artists sought to create was condemned by socialism and adopted by the capitalist West. Modern architecture, advertising, packaging, typography, and fashion all owe a debt to their experiments. In their work we can see social, moral, and aesthetic problems that today have become acute. Their art reflects the clash between their search for freedom from necessity and their need for certainties. Too often, their theories were little more than doctrines of submission employing the language of transcendence. In the service of revolution, they helped create an aesthetics of reaction.

Russia's avant-garde, like Italy's Futurists, sought a politics and an art that would quite literally transform the world. They wanted nothing less than a *Gesamtkunstwerk*—a synthesis of all the arts in a single work. The desire to break down the barriers between the work of art and its audience, to offer an inclusive environment, can be seen in Lissitsky's "Proun Room." First built for the 1923 Grosse Berliner Kunstausstellung, it was reconstructed for the Los Angeles exhibition. Imagine a Malevich painting as a three-dimensional box in which all forms have depth and solidity and you have Lissitsky's "Proun Room." "'Proun' [an acronym for the Russian words meaning 'project for the affirmation of the new'}," wrote Lissitsky, "begins on the flat plane, goes on to the construction of three-dimensional models, and beyond that to the construction of every object of our common life." As John Berger has written, "Their works were like hinged doors connecting activity with activity. Art with engineering; music with painting; poetry with design; fine art with propaganda; photographs with typography; diagrams with action, the studios with the street." Their celebration of technology gave rise to a fascination with social engineering.

They saw the world as if it were a movie set on a sound stage, in which everything could be controlled and designed down to the last detail. The film whose crew they joined was the Bolshevik Revolution; Lenin was its director and Eisenstein his cinematographer. Malevich would paint the set that Varvara Stepanova built, Natan Altman would rig the lights, Liubov Popova would design the actors' costumes, Ilya Chashnik would paint the props from cups and saucers to plates and soup tureens, and the Russian people would serve as both participants and spectators. All this according to the new aesthetic principles developed for the new age.

The desire to abolish the distinctions between art and life was not unique to the Russians. To varying degrees, it was shared by artists in Holland, Italy, Germany, and France. Walter Gropius, in his announcement of the founding of the Bauhaus (1919), wrote, "The ultimate if distant aim of the Bauhaus is the *collective* work of art . . . where there is no distinction between structural and decorative art . . . where the many arts are unified in an indivisible whole in which man himself is bound and wins a living consciousness and meaning." Theo van Doesburg, the most prominent theorist of the De Stijl movement, was heavily influenced by the works of the Russian avant-garde. When he returned to Holland from Moscow in 1924, he was convinced that artists could no longer afford to work in the manner of "the majority of painters, in the manner of pastrycooks or milliners." What was required was a method that would rely on "scientific and mathematical (Euclidian or non-Euclidian) data." Malevich had long insisted on the necessity of geometry as the foundation for all art. In 1915, he wrote of his black square that it was "the embryo of all potentials . . . the father of the cube and the sphere. . . . People ought to examine what is painterly, and not the samovar, cathedral, pumpkin, or Mona Lisa."

After 1917, Russia's artists had a chance to put such ideas into practice. Malevich was put in charge of the new nation's art school. Others joined filmmakers to tour the countryside by rail, bringing the revolution's message of hope and faith in the future to the peasants. All Russia became their canvas. Eisenstein recalled the city of Vitebsk in 1920: "All the main streets are covered with white paint splashed over the red brick walls, and against this white background are green circles, reddish-orange squares, blue rectangles . . . Kazimir Malevich's brush has passed over its walls."

All works of art either proclaim or betray a philosophy. Sometimes this is acknowledged by the artist; sometimes it is hidden from the artist himself. In the case of the Russian artists, it was a little of both. They wanted to create an aesthetics for the earthly paradise that was the project of the Bolsheviks. Their quest for a unified world in which national boundaries would disappear, in which humanity would come to share a common political and aesthetic language, represents a very old dream: the myth of the ideal city. Industrial invention gave new life to the Platonic hope of creating a metropolis in which harmony would reign and contradiction would end.

Utopian visions are one of the enduring themes of Western civilization. They are to be found in the urban architectural utopias of the Italian Renaissance, in More's island, in Bacon's Bensalem, in Campanella's seven-walled City of the Sun, in the Futurists' *City of Tomorrow* (1909), and in much of the work of the Russian avant-garde, especially that of Malevich and Vladimir Tatlin, its two most influential figures.

If, as Roland Barthes has observed, "Architecture is always dream and function, expression of a utopia and instrument of a convenience," then almost all architects since the beginning of time have wanted to build the Tower of Babel. Images of a "column of Heaven," of an *axis mundi*, of an *Irminsul* column that supports the sky and links earth and heaven, have been common since the Megalithic Age. They reappeared in the middle of the Renaissance. Michelangelo, for example, composed a sonnet about a giant who "ardently desires the sun" and wants to "reach the sky." Painters too have often been intrigued by this myth. Pictorial representations of the Tower of Babel are to be found in the paintings of Breughel the Elder, his son Peter, Holbein, Delaune, Galle, Merian, Rottenhammer, Valkenborgh, H. van Cleve, and Gustave Doré, to name only a few.

Tatlin, regarded as the father of functionalist aesthetics, or Constructivism, within the Russian avant-garde, was obsessed by this ancient dream. He understood technology's advance meant that work could resume on mankind's greatest unfinished construction project: the Tower of Babel. Barely two years after the October Revolution, he proposed building a "Monument to the Third Internationale." He talked of his tower as a "union of purely artistic form (painting, sculpture, and architecture) for a utilitarian purpose." Tatlin was doubtless inspired by the Eiffel Tower, which he had seen in 1913 when he arrived in Paris to visit Picasso. There he fell under the spell of the world's tallest structure, constructed for the 1889 International Exhibition.

Tatlin's proposed tower, like Eiffel's, had nothing whatever to do with utilitarianism. Indeed, it was its antithesis. But like the engineer Eiffel, Tatlin, the son of a railroad engineer, felt compelled to justify his scheme by touting its supposed social and scientific utility. The rubric of utility was, as Barthes has written of Eiffel, necessary to overcome the doubts of a period dedicated to rationality and empiricism. The notion of a useless object was an anathema. This was as true for the Bolsheviks as it was for the French bourgeoisie.

Tatlin dreamed of a tower to be built in the center of Moscow that would exceed Eiffel's in height by three hundred feet. Made of iron and glass, it was to be in the form of a spiral. On a slanting axis—to be aligned with the earth's own—it was to contain four thermal glass chambers: hemisphere, cylinder, pyramid, and cube. Each geometric form would rotate on its axis at a different rate: once a year, once a month, once a day, once an hour. These structures would house conference centers, the legislature of the International Congress, the administration for the International Proletariat, and a propaganda ministry that would combine telegraph, telephone, radio, and film. On overcast days, Tatlin wanted to project newsreels and revolutionary slogans onto the clouds above. (For several years, Tatlin labored on his great project only to abandon it to pursue the dream of Icarus. For the next thirty years, Tatlin studied winged insects, convinced they provided man with the perfect model of flight. He constructed several models of a tremendous glider, which he called "Letatlin"—a portmanteau formed by the word "to fly" and Tatlin's own name. He devoted his life to a tower that would never be built and to a flying machine that would never fly.)

Architects all over Europe were taken with such ideas. In the same year (1919) that Tatlin began building the first of three models of his tower, Gropius issued a four-page leaflet to announce the founding of the Bauhaus. His opening sentence proclaimed, "The ultimate aim of all visual arts is the complete building! . . . Together let us desire, conceive, and create the new structure of the future, which will embrace architecture and sculpture and painting in one unity and which will one day rise toward heaven from the hands of a million workers like the crystal symbol of a new faith." Bruno Taut and Hans Behne believed with Gropius that one day they would deserve the name "architect"—a word that meant, they wrote, "*lord of art*, who will build gardens out of deserts and pile up wonders to the sky." Architect Eric Mendelsohn also hoped to "bring all the arts back into a unity."

Tatlin's monument was to have enshrined the quintessential modernist symbol of the Russian avant-garde: Malevich's black square. Malevich had hailed his "Black Quadrilateral" as "the face of the new art . . . a living royal infant" and "the icon of my time." When Malevich hit upon the idea of the black square, it struck him with all the force of Rousseau's revelation when he was on his way to Vincennes in 1749. Malevich is supposed to have thought it so important that he was unable to drink or eat or sleep for an entire week. Most of his works displayed in the Los Angeles exhibit seem to have been executed with great haste—as if they were so many proofs piled up to confirm a favored theory. Malevich's black squares are like black holes whose density is so great that its gravity prevents all light from escaping. He regarded them as building blocks of a new age that would renounce appearances for essences. He called his theory "Suprematism" and regarded it as "a new realism." "Through all his productions," Malevich wrote, "man in the hope of arriving at God or perfection seeks to attain the throne of thought as the absolute way in which he will act not as a man but as a god, because on it he is incarnated, becoming ideal."

Both Malevich and Tatlin believed in the notion of aesthetic beauty as revealed in geometric forms and manufactured objects. In 1920, Malevich wrote, "If each form appears as an expression of purely utilitarian perfection, then the Suprematist form too is nothing else but the signs of the . . . utilitarian perfection of the concrete world which is coming." This is an idea at least as old as Plato. It was in *Philebus* that Plato made clear his preference: "understand me to mean straight lines and circles, and the plane or solid figures which are formed out of them by lathes, rulers, and protractors; for these I affirm to be . . . eternal and absolutely beautiful." What is Malevich's black square other than this?

Too much has been made of the alleged differences between Malevich (spiritual) and Tatlin (utilitarian). They, like almost all of their compatriots, were united in their yearning for absolutes, in their desire to discover a single, unifying principle that would explain the secret of the cosmos. Like Marx, who believed that his dictum—"the history of all hitherto existing society is the history of class struggles"—had unlocked the mystery of history, Malevich believed that his black square was the philosopher's stone from which all art was created. Both notions conceal a search for certainty that underlies nearly all of twentieth century art and politics.

For the Russian avant-garde, that search was sustained by the Romanticism they sought to subvert. Malevich's spiritualism, Tatlin's tower of power, Lissitsky's thirst for totality—all have their roots in a sensibility born of Romanticism; only their methods were modern. What they failed to understand was the extent to which their rebellion against Romanticism was itself romantic, a necessary conceit that made possible one of the great revolutions in art.

Their fevered polemics and moral zeal, their lack of irony, their innocent idealism, their epic sincerity, their self-absorption, and, above all, their belief in art as redemption reflect a love of the Romantic enterprise. They paid fealty to reason and science as if they were religious idols—Malevich wanted to replace the Christian cross with his black square icon. Because they believed in science as salvation, they helped create an authoritarian aesthetic.

The art of the Russian avant-garde embodies the two great myths of modern society: the myth of infinite progress and the myth of utopia. Their urban utopias mirrored the romantic nostalgia for an agrarian paradise: the realm of lost innocence. What they did not understand and could not know was that their attempt to forge a universal aesthetic language would puzzle the Russian public and be banned by party bureaucrats. Handed a death sentence by Stalin in 1934—the year in which "socialist realism" became official dogma—the new art was made an orphan and driven into exile to seek a home in the house that capital built. The terrible irony of Russia's avant-garde artists is that they would be murdered (or exiled or spiritually crushed) at home, while the West would welcome their art, even as it spurned their ideas.

This is why when we look at their works—so sincere and so naive—we are moved: precisely because we now live in the future of which they dreamed. Few of them survived to see the century's midpoint. The sadness I felt looking at this gallery of ghosts and the detritus of their work was only matched by the twitchy awareness that their aesthetics were to triumph even as they themselves went down to defeat.

For the ease with which capitalism cultivated the revolutionary forms they had designed for socialism is startling. Of course, the Russians knew that only by winning converts in the West could their work survive. Like Trotsky, they wanted permanent revolution. To that end, Lissitsky travelled throughout Europe, visiting Germany, Czechoslovakia, and France, spreading the gospel of Suprematism. In 1922, he organized an exhibition of six hundred Russian works in Berlin. When Moholy-Nagy saw the show, he said, "Look, they have already done everything."

Russian avant-garde art influenced the architectural designs of Le Corbusier and the experiments of the Bauhaus. Designers like Edward McKnight Kauffer and Raymond Loewy would take the nonrepresentational and geometrical patterns so dear to the Russians and use them in the service of commercial advertising and packaging. Loewy, for example, when asked to create a more enticing logo for an already familiar brand of cigarettes, paid unconscious tribute to Malevich when he altered the background color of a pack of Lucky Strikes from green to white, and placed the Lucky Strike red circle on both sides of the package in order to double its chances of being seen. Capitalism claimed what philistine socialism condemned.

Today the world that exists in the skyscrapers of New York and Singapore, in Tokyo and São Paulo is, in part, a legacy inherited from the Russian avant-garde. The aesthetic that informs contemporary culture is indebted to Russia's early abstractionists. It is an aesthetic in which the universal denies the particular; the cult of essences obliterates the appreciation of appearances; the fetish for uniformity replaces the love of the unique. It refuses to recognize the nobility of contradiction.

[1981]

Sebald's Last Talk

When I was invited by Louise Steinman, the director of the ALOUD literary series, a presentation of the Library Foundation of Los Angeles, to have a public conversation with W. G. Sebald, little did we suspect that it would be his last public appearance. Sebald was at the apogee of his growing renown and would die barely two months later in a traffic accident in England, at the intolerably young age of fifty-seven. Our talk was held before a sold-out audience of more than 130 people in the Mark Taper Auditorium at the downtown Los Angeles Central Library on October 17, 2001.

STEVE WASSERMAN: It's a huge honor to introduce W. G. Sebald. A few years ago, the *Los Angeles Times* gave Sebald its fiction award for the best fiction of the year. Improbably, we had asked Judith Krantz, the glitzy author of *Princess Daisy*, to present the award. I took a perverse and delicious pleasure in compelling Judith to read *The Rings of Saturn*, which she afterward claimed was a very important event in her life. I have no reason to doubt her. The work of W. G. Sebald is, of course, about as un-Californian an exercise in literary achievement as one could imagine since California is a place given to jettisoning the very idea of history weighing upon the brain of the living like a nightmare. It's famously the place that privileges forgetfulness over remembrance and the place where historical amnesia reigns supreme. Resistance to these ideas is at the heart of much of Sebald's work—which overall could be said to be an exercise in grieving, in, to use a German word, *Trauerarbeit*, a work of mourning. One is reminded of the great essay that Freud wrote during the First World War called *Mourning and Melancholia*, which connects melancholy with the inability to work through grief. To understand the past and thereby to exorcise it is Sebald's largest moral and literary ambition. His books are ardent, ravishing, and, singly and taken together, the creation—or perhaps more precisely, the re-creation—of a world from which one feels that its creator has the greatest difficulty in actually extricating himself, a predicament shared by the admiring reader. This exercise in the art of empathy, this joint attempt on the part of the author as well as the complicit reader to recover memory, produces a voluptuous and exquisite anxiety. Walter Benjamin once wrote that melancholy is the origin of true historical understanding. The temperament that produces that degree of obsession is one that prompts such a writer to become an artist of endless speaking, and Sebald's voice, from book to book, is one that simply seems to go on and on. One feels one has embarked, in reading Sebald's work, upon a series of explorations. The result is a literary triumph, altogether exceptional in its emotional expressiveness, its beauty, its sincerity, its moral passion, its concern with contemplative virtues. It's a great honor to present to you—W. G. Sebald.

W. G. SEBALD: Thank you very much. Good evening, ladies and gentlemen. It's a pleasure to be here in this distant place, totally unfamiliar to me. My first impressions are that it would take me probably fifty years to find my bearings, but as I'm being shepherded about, I managed to come to this place on time. I shall read you a short passage from this recent published book, *Austerlitz*. It's set in Wales, this particular passage. As some of you may know, Austerlitz is the name of the main character in this text, one Jacques Austerlitz, who was born in Prague in the 1930s, and this four-year-old boy was taken from there in one of the *Kindertransports* which left various German cities but also the Czechoslovak capital at the time just before the outbreak of the Second World War. He was put on the train by his mother, an actress, and ends up in England, where he arrives at Liverpool Street in London with his rucksack and little suitcase. He is subsequently brought up in Wales by a Welsh Calvinist couple who seek to erase his identity, and he himself later on never looks into the question of his identity until he gets to be near enough sixty years old, at which time he is overtaken by the semimute troubles that clouded his mind for most of his life and begins to investigate his own—to him, so far, covert—past, i.e., he breaks through the barriers which he himself has erected against memory. He is sent to a public school when he is about fourteen years old, when his foster mother becomes gravely ill and later on dies and his foster father disappears in a mental asylum in Denbigh, in Wales. At that public school he befriends a younger pupil called Gerald, and from then on spends his summer vacations and many other times at the home of this friend. The passage that I will read to you is about a revisitation of this place at the point where he, having completed his studies at Oxford, is about to go to Paris to begin his research work. The occasion for returning is a funeral, the funeral of the two eccentric uncles, or great-uncles, who lived in that family, one Alphonso and one Evelyn Fitzpatrick. The boy is called Gerald and the boy's mother is Adela. The father, who was in the Royal Air Force, was shot down over the Ardennes Forest, and so this is a short list of the personages that you will encounter in this brief passage.

[Sebald reads from *Austerlitz*, translated from the German by Anthea Bell. "I think it was in early October 1957, he (Austerlitz) continued abruptly after some time (. . .) which became increasingly morbid and intractable with the passage of time."]

WASSERMAN: One of the most striking aspects of your work is the use of photography. Photographs, of course, have a way of seeming to be truthful, but we all know that very often photographs lie. And yet you litter your work—perhaps "litter" is an unnecessarily pejorative word; I don't mean it that way—but you sprinkle these shards of frozen moments as if to suggest that there is a moment of truth and absence that exists at one and the same time, as a device to snare the reader and as a means of transporting the reader. How have you thought about the arrangement of such photographs, and how did you stumble upon this approach?

SEBALD: Well, I didn't do so deliberately. Photographs are something I've always collected in a random sort of way that began much earlier than my attempts at writing prose fiction. And when I began to write, somehow it became clear to me that they, these images, were part of the material that I had stored up. And so, I, right from the beginning, somehow saw no reason for excluding them from the actual process of writing. It seemed to me unquestionable right from the beginning that they had a right to be there, as very frequently they provided the starting points, or they came from the photo albums of the people I had talked to—sometimes over long periods of time— and summed up experiences and parts of these people's lives which would have been very difficult to convey in words only. So, they seemed to me to have a legitimate place [not only] in the process of production but in the finished product also. And then, subsequently, of course, people have started asking me questions like you have just done, and I had to think a little harder about the reasons for [the] presence of these images in a text. And what you are pointing to is certainly one of the main concerns—namely that the reader of fiction wants to, in a sense, be assured in the illusion, which he knows to be an illusion, that what he is reading is not just an invented tale but somehow grounded in fact. And what better way of demonstrating this than including a photograph—which we tend to all believe, certainly at first sight. That said, the photograph, as you yourself have just indicated, also, of course, opens wide the door to forgery. And, indeed, some images of these books are instances of forgery, deliberate forgery. But they are in the minority—they are perhaps five or four percent of the entire number of images—and the rest are usually from the sources which they suggest they come from, so that it is, in fact, true to say that the relationship between the historic reality behind these fictional stories and the images which are inserted in them is a very close one. The other reason that seems to me increasingly important is the mysterious quality of older photographs. I mean the pictures which we take nowadays on colored films and which get developed in an hour in a Kodak shop hold no secrets at all, so it seems to me. But these old black-and-white pictures which one finds in family albums—not all of them, but you always find one or two amongst the bunch—have a mysterious quality where the subject seems to come out of the image and seems to demand an answer about one thing or another. And this kind of appellative presence that these departed persons still have in these pictures was something that struck me as almost uncanny and that I felt that I had to attend to—and this hasn't gone away. I happened yesterday in Philadelphia to look at three photo albums which an elderly couple who [were] exiled from Germany in the 1930s brought along, and indeed, you know, in those albums, as in so many others, there were some images which one found it very hard to look away from and which have this captivating quality that says to the observer, "Well—what about this? You know I'm no longer here, but I still want an answer."

WASSERMAN: Yes, one has the feeling, flipping through these photographs, of a kind of detective story, almost as if you're looking at photographs taken at the scene of rather mysterious and unacknowledged crimes, similar to the way in which Antonioni in *Blow-Up* used the photograph that you thought was taken of one thing, but upon enlargement revealed quite another thing going on. And one turns the pages of your book with both mounting fascination and a kind of growing horror at what might be discovered in these photographs.

SEBALD: Well yes, they do, if you learn how to read them and if you place them in the right context. The picture which at first sight might be or might seem to be innocent reveals things that perhaps sometimes one would be better off not to know. And this was certainly the case with, say, the photo albums in my own family, because my parents, like all people of that generation, had furnished themselves with small portable cameras. These cameras were then in 1939 taken to war, and albums were made, for instance, of the Polish Campaign, as it was called. And as a small boy I looked through these albums, and I thought there was nothing particularly either exciting or remarkable in them and turned the pages without being disturbed. But when I revisited these albums many years later, the images revealed a different quality because I had comprehended by then the historical context. I asked myself why there were pages on which some of the pictures were missing and only the glue was left behind and [where] perhaps a kind of jocular caption had been written underneath, but which made no sense without the image. And nowadays, of course, you know what the context was and that pictures can tell different stories depending on when one observes or looks at them and who looks at them.

WASSERMAN: And when you asked your father about the missing pictures or the pictures that remained, did you ever trust his answer?

SEBALD: My father generally didn't talk about these kinds of things, and I knew it would be pointless because whenever you raised the topic of that particular past, it would end in family drama and shouting matches, and so after a while, you learned to leave it. There was a zone of silence around that part of our prehistory which was meticulously maintained by practically everyone in Germany in the postwar years, and this is true until this day. The generation of my parents who were involved in that part of our history is now dying out, and so it falls to the next generation to rescue all the historical evidence that can still be retrieved. But mostly you cannot retrieve it by talking to these people. The odd one will give you an answer, but this is very rare.

WASSERMAN: It's a curious thing in *Austerlitz*—which, arguably, might be thought of as an exercise in recovered memory syndrome—that the main character seeks to fill in the absences and hollowed-out portions of his personality, attempts to re-create an identity that is actually tethered to history. The curious thing is that the more he learns, the more overwhelmed he seems to become, until finally, right toward the end of the book, at the very moment when he arguably ought to feel the most liberated for having most accumulated what shards of memory could be gathered, he suffers a breakdown and has to be hospitalized. I wonder if you've ever thought about considering the necessity of forgetting without which no one can move on.

SEBALD: Yes. As a writer interested in these kinds of things and in the habit of talking to people who have been through series of experiences which are highly disturbing, one has to be extremely careful, because the psychoanalytic wisdom that it does people good if they talk about their traumas, or try to retrieve the source of their anxieties, is not always true. And so I think one has to step extremely carefully, and certainly it's an almost biological fact that forgetting is what keeps us going, and that is also exemplified very clearly in the fact that nobody in Germany in the 1950s and 1960s, not even the writers whose job it would have been to do so, has ever written a line or anything worth mentioning about the collective experience of destruction suffered by the Germans, i.e., the bombing of German cities, which was wholesale and which practically everybody experienced. And the only way in which they could rebuild and carry on was to forget, almost by force of will. So naturally, there is a curious dialectic between forgetting and remembering, and they're not just two opposed moral categories, one positive and the other negative, but they're interlaced in an extremely complicated way and in a different fashion in everyone. What is noticeable, though, is that if you do talk to people who have survived political persecution—of whom there are, of course, many in this country and many in England but hardly any in Germany—if you talk to them, you very frequently can find that they manage quite well as long as they hold down a job, as long as they're surgeons in a hospital or . . . I don't know . . . teachers at a university, or whatever it may be. And then, with the arrival of the retirement age, where many people have difficulties in readjusting in any case, they experience a return of repressed memories and find [it] very hard to fight against them. It's also a general phenomenon of growing older that those memories which refer to events that happened last week or last month are often less clear and less sharply

delineated than the memories that refer to one's childhood—
which become increasingly obtrusive and acquire a clarity
which is often highly disturbing. And in the case of those who
have escaped political persecution, who have survived these
difficulties, specific psychological difficulties accentuate generally and very frequently lead to periods of severe disturbance,
of anxiety attacks, and of a general inability to cope.

WASSERMAN: One of the things that I most admire in
your works is the way you have of opening up from the very
specific and then leaping to a very large question. Memorably
in *Austerlitz*, for me, is the passage that has Austerlitz reencoun-
tering his old Prague nanny, Vera. She tells him about the time
when he was a boy, about four years old, when she used to read
to him a picture book, which had the seasons and revealed
the animals throughout the seasons. And one of the pictures
showed the squirrels gathering the nuts to bury for the winter months, and she says to him that whenever they turned the
page and the same scene showed the snow which had covered
everything, that Jacques Austerlitz would always ask, "But how
do the squirrels *know* where to find the nuts?" And then you
ask almost right away, or rather the narrator asks—I perhaps
should not confuse the narrator of the story with you yourself;
that would be a category error, although you seem to invite
such perverse confusion on the part of your readers—"How
indeed do the squirrels know?" "What do we know ourselves?"
"How do we remember?" and "What is it we find in the end?"

SEBALD: We hide things also, but we don't always know how
to recover them, and in that respect we are different from squir-

rels, and either they're superior to us in many ways . . . And that squirrel, incidentally, is, of course, also a reverential gesture toward Nabokov, where squirrels in *Pnin* play a very significant role. As Nabokov is quite important to me, such references turn up occasionally.

WASSERMAN: What other writers have been important to you?

SEBALD: Of contemporary writers relatively few. Nabokov is an exception and he, of course, is as much a nineteenth-century Russian writer as a twentieth-century American writer.

WASSERMAN: Maybe he was the last nineteenth-century Russian writer?

SEBALD: Yes. And in Nabokov's work, particularly, of course, the autobiography, concerned as it is with questions of memory and remembrance. And what I learned from him is precisely that attention to detail—that it's not enough to say that his mother was exiled in Prague, but it's important to remember that her dachshund was also still there and that he wore a muzzle of wire and that it was a sad *émigré* dog. Because Nabokov's father was assassinated in Berlin, his mother kept his wedding ring, but she had grown rather frail in exile in Prague when [he] visited her, and Nabokov remembers that she had the wedding ring of her husband tied to hers with a bit of string because otherwise it would have fallen off her finger. I think memory resides in details of this almost weightless kind. If it wants to come across to the reader as a token of something that is legitimate, then it must be attached to this kind of weightless . . . weightless . . . I'm lacking the word now . . . but that's how I think it must be. The other writers that were important for me were nineteenth-century German prose writers. The prose fiction written in Germany in the nineteenth century didn't quite fit the model of the novel which had evolved in other countries like France and England in the eighteenth and nineteenth centuries. It was not interested to the same extent in social or even political concerns. It was somewhat backward. That nineteenth-century German prose writing was very much attached to the observation of nature, very frequently could be described almost as natural historical writing rather than fiction writing. It was underdeveloped in terms of character construction, and its main concern was the production of flawless prose, so that page by page the prose, as it were, stood in its own right like we expect language to stand in its own right in poetry. And it was quite a useful school to go through. I was attached to these writers, the most prominent of whom are Adalbert Stifter and Gottfried Keller, also because they came from regional backwaters as I do, and I always felt a particular closeness to them.

WASSERMAN: You came from a very small rural community, a hamlet.

SEBALD: Yes, a tiny village in the Alps, three thousand feet above sea level, cut off from pretty much everything in the postwar years. Nowadays, of course, a ski resort—and tennis courts, swimming pools, and everything else. But in those days, it was almost as if you lived in the seventeenth century. I mean, even anthropologically it would have been a hunting ground, because, say, our burial rites in the postwar years were still those of the seventeenth century. I mean, they were archaic. There is a story by Hemingway where he describes a scene in the Alps, possibly in the Vorarlberg, where the narrative figure tells how the bodies couldn't be buried, because the ground was frozen throughout the winter, and they had to keep them in the woodshed, and then you bury them in the spring. And that was indeed the case where I grew up, you know: there were always bodies in the woodshed, and so it means that my early years were shaped by societal mores which certainly from the present point of view in L.A. seem very far removed, to say the least.

WASSERMAN: There is a thread throughout your work of a certain kind of requiem for a lost agrarian world that's been pulverized by an industrial behemoth that has won out almost everywhere.

SEBALD: Yes. One can regret it although one knows it's un-avoidable, because it is just a fact of societal and natural evolution that things should have come to this pass. Well, if you know landscapes intimately—say, the landscape of the Upper Rhine where it comes out of Lake Constance and then turns the corner at Basle and moves northward, or the Danube before it gets to Vienna and after, between Vienna and Budapest—and if you have a recollection, at least a mental one, of what these landscapes looked like fifty, a hundred, or two hundred years ago and see how they have been sanitized now, straightened out, controlled, hemmed in, then you do realize that much has been lost, and what's been lost is some kind of freedom and some form of beauty which we no longer have access to. For instance, I remember very clearly, and I think I make reference to it in one of these books, the Danube, just before it gets to Vienna, in the 1960s, was unregulated—that is to say, in the spring, when the waters were high, the Danube would leave its bed and flood vast areas to either side—the so-called *Donau-Auen*—and it was a singular spectacle, and you could survey it from various vantage points along the river. And these spectacular views don't exist anymore, because in the late 1970s the river was put into a concrete bed—that is to say, weirs and dams were built across it, and the whole thing is now something that nobody really wants to look at. And so, of course, things do get changed all the time and built and concreted over—and much is lost, perhaps inevitably. But that doesn't mean that one should not regret that this kind of development goes on all the time.

WASSERMAN: Let's take some questions from the audience.

AUDIENCE MEMBER: I was just wondering if it was getting close to the time—as it happened to Nabokov—that you might start writing in English.

SEBALD: Oh, I don't think so. But Nabokov had no choice, having moved here and the Russian exile community shrinking further and further. He knew that the time had come to make that move, but he also left testimony of what a traumatic experience it was and how he despaired about ever being able to write a decent page of English prose. It was a very hard time for him, and he was not always the best judge of it because, as you probably know, he nearly burnt the manuscript of *Lolita*. I think it was Vera who rescued it for him.

WASSERMAN: That's because Roger Straus turned it down at Farrar, Straus and Giroux.

SEBALD: One can very easily be mistaken in that way. I have thrown one or two things on the compost heap, and there is reference to that in *Austerlitz*. In the book Austerlitz throws all his papers on the compost heap. I have done the same. It's very difficult to judge; on a good day, if you have two languages, you can manage well in both, and on a bad day you can't manage in either of them. And so, you know, it doesn't make things easier. Writing is a difficult and painstaking business, and one has enough trouble with it in one language, and it also means, of course, moving—as Nabokov did—from one language to another. You usually desert the one that you are leaving because you can't do both at the same time. You can't move to and fro; you must be quite single-minded about it, and I think Nabokov, after moving across, never wrote in Russian again. He still translated, but he never wrote in Russian again.

WASSERMAN: The English translation seemed to me to be superb. You've been very well served by your translators. What, if anything, has been lost in the translation, or, to put it another way: In German is there some resonance or some echo of some quality for your German readers that in English there isn't?

SEBALD: Well, something gets lost inevitably, and the texts are often a pastiche of various levels of time. That is to say, you may have the first narrator who is in the present and who writes the text referring to a narrator who tells [*sic*] him instead, who speaks from a point of view which is in 1939, and then the language used in 1939 clearly is somewhat different from the language used in the present day. And I *can* manage to do that in German by the judicious use of certain bits of vocabulary, which make it clear to certainly a sensitive reader that this is in the 1930s and couldn't possibly [be] in the 1950s. That's very difficult for a translator to get across. So, there are elements of fine grain that get lost. And you do occasionally gain something, but that is the exception rather than the rule. There may be the odd passage where English manages to render things more felicitously than German, but, on the whole, you lose a little bit. Well, it's very easy to lose everything, it doesn't take much: If the prosodic rhythm is not maintained, if the text has two or three blunders or half blunders on every page, readers very soon get irritated, and they don't quite know where the problem comes from. But they find that they're not inclined to read on if it's "bumpy" in any sense. I remember, for instance, how someone once told me I ought to read [Zbigniew] Herbert's book *Still Life with Bridle*, I think it's called in the English translation. The person who recommended it to me was Polish and had read it in the original, and so I read the book in English translation, and I thought it was an abject failure. But I did realize that it had to do almost exclusively with the clumsiness of the translation, which disfigured the whole text, and I then read the French translation of the same book, which was superb. And so, you can see from that one instance that translation really is a very crucial part of getting a book across.

It's not even into another culture, but into some kind of sister culture. So it needs a great deal of care and patience, and in principle it's always possible; if you find the right person to do it, it's possible. But even the right person must be watched very closely.

AUDIENCE MEMBER: In preparation for your latest book—given the experiences of your protagonist—did you read any memoirs or other accounts by adults whose childhood had been spent away from their homes in France or in England? And if you did, what did you learn from these accounts, and which accounts did you learn from?

SEBALD: The fictional figure of Jacques Austerlitz is based on two real-life stories, one which was written up and the other which I know only from listening to that person. That one was a colleague of mine, a London colleague of mine, whom I have known for many years and who over the years has released, as it were, bit by bit, the tale of his life. His life was by no means as tragic as that of Austerlitz, but there are many elements in Austerlitz's biography which correspond to his experiences. And the other one was the life of a woman whom I didn't know personally but with whom I'm corresponding now. She had a television documentary made of her life sometime around 1992 or '93, which I saw by pure chance as I was switching on the television one evening. And I was immediately struck by it, simply, perhaps, because she had come, together with her twin sister at the age of two and a half, from a Jewish orphanage in Munich—which was, of course, for me the nearest bigger town—to England. And the Welsh background—not in detail, but in general outline—is the background of her story. She was indeed taken with her twin sister by a Calvinist fundamentalist Welsh couple and brought up and had her identity erased. She never asked any questions about it, but, having passed the age of fifty, all of a sudden found herself so troubled, so depressed, and so anxious about everything without knowing really why, that she began to ask the kinds of questions which eventually lead to answers. Her story was written up, but I only read the written-up version afterward by some other person whose name I forget. It's a straightforward biographical account full of quite horrific details. But I also read others. Once you have a project like this in mind, you read everything that might have anything to do with it. I read the autobiographical account by Saul Friedländer, who grew up as a small boy in Prague. I think it's called—I read it in German—*When Memory Comes*. And he indeed recounts how he met his nanny again in Prague and how she had, seemingly, not changed at all. There are, of course, also collections of personal accounts and memories from many of the children who came to Britain on these *Kindertransports*. Because in the 1980s, I think, not before, one of their number took it upon herself to bring the children together again, and from that grew various collections of these memories. The organizer of these reunions encouraged them to write accounts of where they came from and what their lives had been like. What is startling about these accounts is how brief they are. Scarcely one is longer than a page, and many of them are no more than two sentences, and from that alone you can judge how hard it is to live with this kind of memory, because telling the tale, of course, does help you to get over the worst implications. So, you can also see, of course, how far flung they became. There are these short, very short, almost potted biographies from New Zealand, from Australia, from practically all states of the United States, from all counties in England. There were many of them.

AUDIENCE MEMBER: From reading your books, I get the feeling that you are looking for a home in the world in some way. It makes me curious about what took you from Germany to England. Do you feel at home anywhere, or do you feel you are a displaced person in the world?

SEBALD: Well, you know, if I said I felt like a displaced person—on a bad day I do, but on the whole, it's not the same, you know. Being vilified in your own country, being driven out, having no possibility to return to it for many years, and when you do have the possibility, you don't want to return to it because what you experienced there is a different kind of problem from the one that I have encountered. I left Germany of my own accord, perhaps for quite complicated reasons which only became clear to me later. But at any rate, I was always able to return there whenever I wanted—it's not very far away from where I live. And so, it would be dramatizing things if I said that I felt displaced. Nevertheless, it is true that if I now return to my native country—which l frequently do almost every month for a day or two, for one reason or another—I do feel out of sorts because, after all, I left this place when I was twenty-one and since then have always lived in what for me are foreign-language environments, either French or German, or rather English. And so, coming back there seems to me a mismatch, because my compatriots still take me for a German aborigine, and, whereas I know that I am not, I have a great distance from them; there are many things in that country that irritate me a great deal. That is not to say that there aren't things in England that irritate me a great deal. So it just makes life more difficult, and inevitably, of course, it is much simpler, you know, or it would have been much simpler for me if I had stayed at home and had opened a bicycle shop somewhere. Then I might have an emotionally more stable life than I have now.

AUDIENCE MEMBER: One of my favorite books is your last book, *The Rings of Saturn*, and that book seems so miraculous in every single paragraph that I suppose you can somehow anticipate what its argument is going to be. If you don't mind, would you tell us how you created the book in that miraculous way?

SEBALD: In the end, it comes down to serendipity. *The Rings of Saturn* had a very peculiar genesis. I had finished one book before, and I wanted to have some time off. So I thought, as it is told in this text, I wanted to go for a walk—which was my primary concern and which indeed I did, and I had to stay overnight here and there, in hotels. I was quite hard up at that time, and I thought, well, I somehow must earn my keep also, so I'm going to write maybe ten very short pieces for the *Frankfurter Allgemeine Zeitung*. They pay quite well, and that would pay for the fortnight being on the loose. And when I returned home, I sat down—I had somehow roughly worked out what I would write about—I sat down, and the short pieces didn't work. I rewrote them again and again, and they wouldn't go into the format, and I gradually realized that they wanted to grow sideways and upwards and in all directions, and that's how that came about. They were supposed to be ten discrete short pieces, and that's why the material there is very heterogeneous: it was never conceived as a work of fiction, although, of course, if you look very closely, it certainly is that.

AUDIENCE MEMBER: I was wondering about the narrative device, in that there's a narrator but most of the story is told by Austerlitz. And yet there's a narrator, so that the result is that we're constantly reminded that Austerlitz is speaking—"he said"; the narrative, the story is constantly punctuated by "Austerlitz said." I was wondering why you chose that structure?

SEBALD: Because we only know what we get told by others. I find it very hard to read the standard novel where you have an omniscient narrator, but you never know who he or she is. They never present their credentials, and they don't show their cards. I want to know who I'm dealing with, and I want to have the moral measure of the person who is telling me something. And you do get that when you talk to real persons, because you can always derive from a person's demeanor an idea of what they are like inside. Whereas if you have a narrator who you see running around in a novel arranging everything but whose face you never see, whose inner thoughts you never hear anything about, then I for one find that problematic. And for that reason, I tend to have a narrator who has some sort of presence in the text. We don't know exactly who he is, but we get a reasonably good idea of what this person's emotional life might be like, and from there you can also then calculate the distance to the story that he tells, and it generally allows you to orientate yourself *vis-à-vis* the figures in the book. So that is the reason for that. And I think if you wanted to sum it up, say, it's my dislike of the standard novel format, which I find very constricting and artificial.

WASSERMAN: I want to thank W. G. Sebald for coming tonight and for giving us his magical and miraculous works.

[2001]

Syberberg's *Hitler*

HANS-JÜRGEN SYBERBERG is the pariah of new German cinema. He has incurred the wrath of most German critics by his refusal to accept the popular view of Hitler as lunatic aberration, and by his indifference to the by now canonized views of art proclaimed and practiced by such leading members of the German avant-garde as Rainer Werner Fassbinder, Werner Herzog, and Volker Schlöndorff.

Syberberg refuses to step beyond the shadow of German history. Unlike his contemporaries, he is haunted, even obsessed, by the romantic ecstasy and intellectual vision that once was so much a part of German culture. For Syberberg, looking into the center of German culture today is like staring into an extinct volcano. His film, *Hitler: A Film from Germany*, is an elegy, not only for Germany, but for all of Western civilization.

"When all is said and done," wrote Martin Bormann at the end, "the Führer is the Führer: Where should we be without him?" To his query, Syberberg responds with a more disturbing question: "Where would Hitler be without us?" His examination of the complicity of millions of Germans who, recognizing in Hitler both the prophet and executor of their hidden ambitions and dark desires, followed him readily, even gladly, in his monstrous attempt to create utopia, is perhaps the most compelling aspect of Syberberg's seven-hour movie.

Shot in 1977 in twenty days on a large sound studio in Munich for $500,000, after four years of preparation, *Hitler* has aroused controversy in France, England, Israel, and, of course, in Germany. It is, as Syberberg says, a film about taboos.

Hans-Jürgen Syberberg is the son of a Prussian landowner who later owned a photography shop in Rostock, a small town near the Baltic Sea. Born in 1935, in Pomerania, which, after the Second World War, became part of East Germany, Syberberg moved to West Germany in 1953, after having worked with Brecht in Berlin for two years. Unlike such West German directors as Fassbinder, Wim Wenders, or Werner Schroeter, Syberberg did not grow up listening to Chuck Berry on the American Armed Forces Radio; instead, his education was more traditional, more classically German, with its emphasis on Schiller, Heine, and Goethe and their fascination with the German demonic.

Syberberg grew up with a deep affection for the Romantic tradition in German culture. But his work with Brecht also inspired a modernist aesthetic. While the Romantic ideal of art as redemption or salvation is usually regarded as antithetical to modernism, which is suspicious of such lofty goals, it is Syberberg's ambitious (and largely successful) synthesis of these two ideals which gives his film its immense artistic power.

"Only the exhaustive is truly interesting," wrote Thomas Mann. The Wagnerian dream of *Gesamtkuntswerk*, the fusion of all the arts in one work, an alliance of work, image, and music, is also Syberberg's objective. But with a difference. Like Brecht,

Syberberg rejects seduction; thus *Hitler* is always conscious of itself as film, as text and quotation. For Syberberg, whose subject is nothing less than humanity's quarrel with God and its place in the cosmos, the only artistic form appropriate to such discourse is the Epic. His aesthetic achievement has been to redeem the Romantic ideal by wedding it to a modernist sensibility.

Syberberg is a man bursting with ideas. He is surprisingly soft-spoken, almost languid in demeanor. What follows is an edited transcript of a taped six-hour interview, begun in California at Francis Ford Coppola's Victorian dacha in Rutherford, and completed in Germany at Syberberg's Munich home.

STEVE WASSERMAN: Why make a seven-hour film on Hitler?

HANS-JÜRGEN SYBERBERG: Because Hitler was utopia. He offered the future like Jesus, like socialism, as a cruel god with sacrifices and obedience. And in a perverse way, he delivered it. And the people followed him. That's the real cruel thing to realize. There were eleven million followers in the Nazi party alone; many more followed.

And—because Hitler was the greatest filmmaker of all times. He made the Second World War, like Nuremberg for Leni Riefenstahl, in order to view the rushes privately every evening for himself, like King Ludwig attending a Wagner opera alone. It is very interesting that the only objects that remain of the Third Reich are fragments of celluloid; nothing else exists—not the architecture of Albert Speer, nor the border of the big German Reich of which Hitler dreamed—only the celluloid record of his existence, of the war and all that. I play with this notion in my film. Perhaps it is a grotesque joke; but underneath this joke there is some horrible truth.

WASSERMAN: Hitler is unquestionably the greatest enigma of the twentieth century. How do you explain him?

SYBERBERG: The question we have to ask is: When did his ideals, the utopia he had in mind, turn into a nightmare? Where was this turning point? When did it become aggressive and wrong? When did everyone see it and didn't, couldn't change? In every man's life there is a point where the desire to achieve the good suddenly becomes horrible. To recognize this moment is the most difficult thing in the world. And, of course, what was it that pushed Hitler?

WASSERMAN: What was it?

SYBERBERG: How can I answer simply? Even a film of seven hours is not long enough.

WASSERMAN: Jean Genet once observed that "Fascism is theater." Do you agree?

SYBERBERG: No, it is much more: Fascism is cinema. For example, Nuremberg is not theater, it is cinema. It was made for Leni Riefenstahl. If you understand the Nuremberg of Riefenstahl, you understand Hitler. If you understand the *Olympiad* of Riefenstahl, you understand Nazism. He built an entire political system as a film. Of course, I speak not about the moral point of view, only about what happened.

WASSERMAN: In your film you say that "Whoever controls film, controls the future." What do you mean by that?

SYBERBERG: It is a play on the slogan of evangelists like Billy Graham who say "Whoever has Christ as a future." Hitler realized, as did the popes and the dukes and the kings of our times, that when they vanish at the end, only the things that they built will remain—castles, cathedrals, and monuments. And so Hitler wanted to build big houses with really big walls that would last one thousand years. But nearly nothing remained. In one generation, everything vanished except celluloid.

WASSERMAN: Walter Benjamin once wrote that "The logical result of fascism is the introduction of aesthetics into political life." Was Hitler an artist?

SYBERBERG: I think that Hitler always thought of himself as an artist, like a painter or a composer. He thought of himself as somebody like Richard Wagner, whose task it was to put all of the arts together, including film, the art of our century. So, in my film, I take Hitler at his word. If he wants to be an artist, okay, let him be that: A man who wants to make a political art of the masses. Hitler wanted to build the Reich as a *Gesamtkunswerk*, like a Wagner opera. But he made it as a film. Again, I am not speaking about the morality of this attempt.

WASSERMAN: Isn't it dangerous to take such an approach?

SYBERBERG: I believe that in order to put someone on trial, you must always be fair. To be fair, I had to give Hitler the opportunity to express what he really wanted. Taking him by his word was the prerequisite of fairness. And if we are right that he was wrong, there's no danger.

WASSERMAN: Obviously a seven-hour film has little commercial potential. How would you describe your film to those that are unlikely to ever see it?

SYBERBERG: That's a problem because it doesn't have a normal narrative story. One can, of course, describe the appearance of some figures, and some things you see and hear. But such a description is perhaps boring. To understand my film, you must imagine what I had to do. There is this war, the history before the war, Germany as the intellectual center of Europe, fifty million people dead, in every family victims, the whole world—East and West—in flames. How to describe that if you want to do everything? And not just to describe, but to *get* it. And not only that. I wanted to speak about us today, even more than about that time. How to do that using the usual instruments of cinema? It took me four years to find a way that could be different.

WASSERMAN: Despite your concern with history, the aesthetic of your film strikes me as antihistorical, even metaphysical.

SYBERBERG: Yes, that is correct. Without such an approach, one can't get to the center of things. Even Einstein, at the end of his life, began to think more about music and spiritual things. There is a point at which science and philosophy meet.

WASSERMAN: But by regarding Hitler as a kind of mythological figure, don't you distort history and thus diminish our understanding?

SYBERBERG: Perhaps the legends of history are more truthful than the reality. Perhaps through an understanding of such myths one can better pierce the center of ideas than through an understanding of the actual history. My film is not actually a film about Hitler as an historical person. Very often I don't follow the actual historical incidents and events; instead I tried always to concentrate on the banality of everyday life. Today Hitler is, for the first time, part of the historical past and can be regarded as a model, like Caesar or Napoleon. And so, my film is not just about Germany, Western Europe, or East and West; it's a film about human conditions in the twentieth century and the turning point of our times, fixed to Hitler as an historical model.

WASSERMAN: But isn't Hitler really the last great romantic visionary of the nineteenth century? Wasn't Hitler's achievement the final destruction of the promise of that century?

SYBERBERG: Yes, I think, in a certain way, you are right. But Hitler was modern too, especially in his use of propaganda and in his way of speaking about the masses. There is no doubt that Hitler destroyed what was and perverted the future. In a strange way, Hitler straddles both centuries, making a mess of both.

WASSERMAN: Over the last few years, there has been a revival of interest in the events of the Third Reich, in Hitler and the Second World War. Television docudramas such as *Holocaust* raise the question of how history is passed on, how the historical memory of people is shaped. What do you think of such attempts?

SYBERBERG: I think it's not the problem to show the killing of people like *Holocaust* did. Why? To show how people are killed? To entertain? To have the possibility to make advertising on television between the killings? Even if you want to educate people in a political way, there's no reason to show them who's guilty, and how they are killed. What for? I believe that people are always so nervous that they resort to the easiest way of looking back at their own history. I think we should be much more patient. And I think that art can be a big help. In my film I try to point out where East and West share a common inheritance. You see, I don't want to be elected and nobody asked me and I don't want to teach somebody how to do and what to do; I only want people to realize that we are the inheritors of a certain legacy from Hitler. For instance, to make money with Hitler is not Nazism, but it is something similar. Hitler always said, "They make money of everything." People now make gold out of the ashes of Auschwitz. For example, the TV movie *Holocaust*. The same people: Jews who perhaps lost members of their family now make money out of the ashes of

Auschwitz. How Goebbels would laugh! Our course, why not make money out of Auschwitz? Even a lot of Jews in Israel say, "Why not? We are living in a free-enterprise system. We make money with everything. Why not with Auschwitz?" But what an idea! I can't. Maybe I'm too German. But, of course, they are right; under the system we live in, it's quite normal. But if that is right, then we could make money with other things too, because then everything is up for grabs.

WASSERMAN: Don't movies like *Holocaust* help ensure that future generations won't forget the barbarity of fascism?

SYBERBERG: No, that's not the problem. If you know that a lot of slaves were killed by the Romans, or you know that many people were killed by Napoleon, it doesn't help to know who's guilty. It's a good story at the end. Maybe it's even a good piece of art. And only if it's good as a piece of art does it have certain possibilities to help humanity. Certain ones, I don't say everything. We know that Hitler and some of his people adored art, but it didn't help. The aesthetic of my film is opposed to the easy moralizing of Hollywood with its cheap stories for the masses on celluloid.

WASSERMAN: Does your film condemn Hitler?

SYBERBERG: No. And I think that's not the problem. It doesn't help anything. If a child is killed in a car accident, what can you do with the guilty driver? Kill him? Will that bring the child back to life? What does it help? I sometimes think that Hitler was a poor guy, much too small for what he wanted. He was not a devil who seduced the German people. No, *they* elected him and he was the poor guy to do their dirty work. A lot of people wanted him subconsciously. Of course they couldn't imagine all of the war's worst, most horrible details. They were too simple; he was their genius.

WASSERMAN: So the German people were to blame for Hitler.

SYBERBERG: What would Hitler have been without us? Without every vote, and later the support of all those who went to Stalingrad, Hitler would not have been possible. We have to realize that this man was really wanted by the people. Though there was a big Communist party, a big Socialist party, they could do nothing against him. Hitler arrived like Fate, like a storm, like an earthquake. Of course, we can't say that nobody knew what Hitler really was, or that nobody did anything to oppose him. Some knew and did a lot against him. Many of the intellectuals, for example. But none of them could prevent Hitler. Even today we are often confronted by dangerous situations that we are powerless to prevent. People become very angry when I speak about these things, because they are used to thinking that human beings are the masters of their fate. It is a good idea to think that we are the master of nature, of politics, and of the arts, but we must always realize that there are certain moments when we are confronted by evil and remain helpless. I cannot today point my finger and say that this one was wrong, and that one was wrong.

WASSERMAN: Did you support the abolition of the statute of limitations in Germany for Nazi war criminals?

SYBERBERG: No. To take revenge is useless; what's done is done. The crimes of the Nazis, thirty-five years later, is very cruel, especially for the victims. I prefer to try to change a man, rather than to take revenge. We must be ready to invent grace again, and to use it.

WASSERMAN: That's all very easy for you to say; but don't the millions who perished in the Holocaust deserve justice? Don't we—the living—have a moral obligation to honor their sacrifice by punishing those of their oppressors who are still alive?

SYBERBERG: I can understand revenge, but it never changes history. It never prevents tragedy from occurring again. Tragedies never happen twice in the same way. Hitler will never happen again. There are other problems today. Putting them in prison doesn't help anything. You cannot change Rudolf Hess even if he stays in prison until he dies. You cannot change him. He is a poor, pathetic man. I believe we are much more guilty to keep him locked up in a cage for more than thirty years. It doesn't help anything. It is wrong to regard the Nazis as barbarians; even those of the SS in the concentration camps. Most of them were ordinary Germans; kind, bourgeois, often of the middle class. Most of them never had a chance to kill a Jew, or even to see one. It is very painful for them to realize now that everything they did then was wrong.

WASSERMAN: How can you possibly make a film about Hitler and hardly mention his victims?

SYBERBERG: It is unfortunately true that the most interesting aspect of a crime is the criminal, not the victim. Without a doubt, what is most interesting is the motive and psychology of the criminal. My film is an examination—a psychoanalysis, if you will—of the victimizer. If one wants to understand the empire of Julius Caesar, one must examine his way of life and way of thinking—not that of Spartacus. It is easy to understand the revolt of slaves, but difficult to comprehend the evil of tyrants.

WASSERMAN: How do you account for Hitler's hold over the vast majority of the German people?

SYBERBERG: The totalitarian temptation is powerful precisely because it promises a future better than the present and superior to the past. Under Hitler, husbands, housewives, even children offered their lives for this future. In my film, I put it very clearly when I say: "If I offered in one hand: the gold of speculation, the full beer belly of a government official, happiness and all the playthings of the world, but, in the other hand: legends and dreams of imagination, the longing for paradise and the music of ideas, then everybody would blindly choose paradise, even if it were a false paradise, greedy for sacrificial blood and ready to offer the best of themselves, involving our hopes with the greatest cruelties for the benefit of lunatic triumphs of the human soul."

History is largely the record of tragedies committed in the attempt to attain utopia. These efforts sacrifice the present on the altar of the future. This idea is the basis of Christianity and of most religions: that now you must bear all manner of sufferings and misfortunes because later you will be in heaven. Even Marxism is based on this notion. This idea gives us the power to destroy everything around us: political systems, people, art, and even nature itself. We must change this way of thinking.

WASSERMAN: How?

SYBERBERG: It is important to begin living for ourselves, not for others. It is here, today, that we have to be concerned with—with the ethics of daily existence. Why not take the chance, just once, to sacrifice the future for the present?

WASSERMAN: One of the more provocative notions in your film is the suggestion that by eliminating European Jewry, Hitler ensured the success of Zionism, and that by establishing the state of Israel, the Jewish people lost what was most precious about their Jewishness—their ability to act as a moral conscience—and became philistines like everyone else.

SYBERBERG: When I was in Israel, I visited the Holocaust museum at Yad Vashem. When I saw all those horrible pictures and, at the same moment, young Israeli soldiers sporting machine-guns standing in front of those pictures of the Holocaust, I felt happy.

WASSERMAN: You felt happy?

SYBERBERG: Happy, yes. My feeling has nothing to do with revenge. I felt really happy to realize that the Jews are like people everywhere: young ones and old ones and not-quite-normal ones, all standing in front of those pictures. But, on the other hand, to see these laughing, beautiful men and sometimes girls in uniform carrying machine-guns as they patrol the streets of Jerusalem—the poor Arabs all around them—it looks like a picture from the Roman Age when the Romans were the chiefs and the Jews were a colony of Rome. Very strange. I am sure there are many powerful Zionist politicians that would agree that Hitler helped them to achieve power as a nation. Perhaps Auschwitz was a needed sacrifice. It's like a cruel joke of history; of course, there is no doubt that nobody wanted Hitler to do all that to help them to establish Israel. It is only now, in retrospect, that one can consider this possibility.

WASSERMAN: What has been the reaction of Jews who have seen the film?

SYBERBERG: A lot of Jewish people come to see the film because Hitler is their problem too. Hitler is their man, their hero, their problem. He is their black messiah. Therefore, they always want to know why and how it could be. I remember that after a screening in Hamburg, a Jewish man, about my age, came up to me and said: "Now I know why I was in a concentration camp." He told me that there is always something secret between the criminal and his victim, and that for the first time he understood what it was. You see, Hitler means nothing if it is only the story of a single stupid man running around with a knife. No, Hitler's story is the story of Germany and its culture, and the entire history of European occidental life. The film touches something very deep inside both Germans and Jews.

WASSERMAN: What has surprised you about the reaction to the film?

SYBERBERG: I think the most astonishing thing is that I was able to make the film in the first place. I am very astonished that it even works, that people go to see it, that people stay through all seven hours of it, and that at the end, they don't kill me.

Perhaps the most interesting reaction was when I came to New York to show the film at Goethe House and then at the FILMEX in Los Angeles. While going through customs at Kennedy, an official noticed the title of the film. Apparently concerned that it might be propaganda, he asked me whether it was for or against Hitler. How could I tell him in only a few words? I assured him that it had nothing to do with propaganda. Nevertheless, he confiscated it. For the next forty-eight hours I tried everything to get it back: telephoning the German consulate, the State Department, everybody. Each person I talked to denied knowing anything about the film, only saying that it might take weeks and a great deal of money to get it out of customs. It was horrible. Really Kafkaesque. Finally, I received a call telling me that the film had been approved for release. I was curious to know on what basis they had determined that the film was not dangerous. I was told that some poor official had screened thirty minutes and pronounced the film "surrealistic." Now I know why surrealism was invented—if only to give such people the idea that art is harmless.

WASSERMAN: Do you secretly admire Hitler?

SYBERBERG: No. Hitler was wrong, but to ask people to give their best is not wrong. If we really want to be human beings, then we have to try again and again, even if before it went badly. We must trust people, to ask them for their best, to give them that freedom. We have to learn the essence of things and learn to discuss the problems of fascism not in a cheap way. Albert Einstein said it very well. He said that we have to think about our nature, think about our individual task, about what we really want, and then change, everyone in his place as individuals. And if we are aware that we can change, then perhaps we can start at a new point. The problem is not to fight power with power and then after the war, we have winners. Perhaps they will be little better than the best of the losers.

WASSERMAN: Are you saying that to dream of paradise in the perverse way that Hitler dreamed of it is wrong, but that to give up the dream itself is an even greater wrong? That one should not stop dreaming just because one has had a nightmare?

SYBERBERG: Yes, absolutely. One must always try it. Otherwise, why live?

WASSERMAN: How has Hitler affected the course of German culture?

SYBERBERG: Germans today are a people without passions, without inventions of their own. That makes me very nervous because until now we lived from such passions. German culture was strong because of that. Before Hitler, there was invention, even genius, in every aspect of life: in technology and science, in philosophy, in the arts, maybe even in politics. Today, Germans don't want to speak about honor of living, much less grandeur; only about the ugly things of life, like drugs taken to kill thinking. Today we lead a debased life divorced from any vision. To imagine Germany without a vision is horrible! Today there is nothing. Without a vision, Germany is nothing; and such a Germany is very dangerous because it is a vacuum.

I believe that a new German culture will arise when we have created a new identity. Today, Germans are not proud of themselves; they feel guilty, but in a bad way. You see, I can feel guilty and be proud, in spite of it. I am full of energy because I am guilty and my work and thoughts are devoted to exorcising that guilt.

WASSERMAN: Do you think art can help provide such a redeeming vision?

SYBERBERG: Yes. But the problem is that Hitler used politics as an art. And now the confusion is very, very great because no one wants to do that again. Today, politics is regarded like a business, not as an art. And, today, art is a business.

WASSERMAN: What role can cinema play?

SYBERBERG: Film has a chance to be something more than entertainment or education. I'm not a teacher; I'm not here to entertain people so that they forget their life. For me, cinema is something more. To ask this question is to ask: Why art? Why? Art is the only thing that remains when we are dead; fragments that remain as documents of our time. And I hope of the best things of our time. Art enables people to understand that there is something more than the daily life of working and money and eating and drinking and sleeping. I am not the founder of a new religion, or party, or message. I have only made a film, a piece of art based on our life. If I did it well, then I think it's already something that helps. The most I can do is to try to construct a work of art, a piece of hope out of the shit of history.

[1980]

Letter from Graz

I T IS USEFUL TO COME HERE, to Austria's second-largest city. Its stolid burghers provide a necessary lesson in human survival. It is a reminder of the fragility of human memory. It offers evidence of the way in which war compels those lucky enough to survive to live a life of resignation and willful amnesia. Nestled amid the mountains of Styria, twenty miles from the Yugoslav border, Graz seems scarcely touched by the economic squalls now buffeting most of Europe. Protected by a generous and constant infusion of Arab petrodollars, the Austria of Chancellor Bruno Kreisky is weathering winter with remarkable nonchalance. Unemployment is among the lowest of any of the industrialized nations of Europe; inflation is almost unknown.

Life here strikes the visitor as banal in its adamant refusal to countenance politics. It proceeds unblemished by the increasingly frigid war of words being waged in the East and the West. The 250,000 citizens of Graz seem oblivious to the preoccupations of politicians who now debate their fate in foreign capitals. People in coffeehouses are more likely to talk about the incompetence of the Yugoslav conductor of the opera, whose orchestra is said to be unhappy almost to the point of open rebellion, than they are about the Soviet SS-20s aimed at them or the proposal to place American Pershing 2s in their neighbor to the north.

This city—with its extensive Renaissance and post-Renaissance core, the largest extant in German-speaking Europe—is picturesque, but the beauty of its buildings conceals the horror of much of its history. Plague, locusts, Turks, and Hitler dominate its fevered past. But this last is not much talked about. The fact that eighty percent of the population enthusiastically backed Hitler, that seventy percent of the city's civil servants were secret Nazis before the *Anschluss* of forty-five years ago, is not mentioned in any of the many guidebooks piled so proudly in the windows of the city's numerous bookstores. Nor, of course, is the fact of the mass murder of all 1,720 of the city's Jews noted. Little is left to record the presence of a community that had thrived since the Middle Ages: a single tombstone inscribed in Hebrew is stuck ignominiously in the wall of a government building, only partly visible from the inner courtyard now used as a parking lot.

Austrian essayist Alfred Polgar once said, "The Germans are first-class Nazis, but lousy anti-Semites; the Austrians are lousy Nazis, but by God what first-class anti-Semites!" (The term *Judenrein* is derived from the membership rules of a turn-of-the-century Austrian bicycle club.) Official policy repudiates this heritage: A museum was opened in the fall on the site of the Mauthausen concentration camp, ninety-five miles north of Graz, to commemorate those who were killed there. But this guilt is not very deep.

Gerhard Roth, born in 1942 in Graz, where he continues to live, is one of Austria's most outspoken writers. Only the Nazi defeat, he believes, has given people reason to regret the past. "Today," he has written, "you can hardly find anyone who has dealt with this era seriously. . . . Personal survival is the victory to be celebrated. The veterans think of the war with almost affectionate memories, the horror has paled, the suffering is quickly forgotten."

Roth's writings, like those of his contemporaries Peter Handke and Thomas Bernhard, have been characterized by John Updike as "short, intense, repellent." They mine "the vein of hysteria . . . where coldness becomes frenzy and alienation becomes terrorism." Death and despair are recurrent themes. "My home city," Bernhard writes of Salzburg in *Der Keller*, the second volume of his autobiography, "is in reality a deadly disease." The statistics of suicide bear him out: two thousand people a year try to kill themselves in Salzburg; ten percent succeed.

It has been said that the silence about the Holocaust was a "necessary quiet" within which former Nazis could be transformed into stalwart citizens of the Western alliance. Perhaps. What is more certain is the hope offered to memory itself by the brave efforts of many of Austria's younger writers to confront the country's bloodied and often blinkered past. They seem determined to come to terms with the sins of their fathers.

Everyone else prefers to remember their grandfathers. Nostalgia for the reign of Franz Josef I (Emperor of Austria, Apostolic King of Hungary, King of Bohemia, King of Dalmatia and Lodomeria, Duke of the Bukovina, Duke of Upper and Lower Silesia, Margrave of Moravia) is palpable. But the nervous splendor, in Frederic Morton's apt phrase, of Hapsburg hierarchy and *fin de siècle* Vienna is long gone. The Austro-Hungarian Empire was dismembered at the end of the First World War. The monarchy collapsed, the feeble attempts at democracy soon faltered, and fascism followed. When the Second World War came to its bloody climax, what was left of Austria found itself occupied by the armies of four nations, including the Soviet Union, which didn't remove its troops until 1985.

Austria has since been called a "torso"—or, even less kindly, a "rump" nation. Ingeborg Day, in her moving memoir of growing up anti-Semitic in Graz, *Ghost Waltz*, muses that "if one can get used to the idea of an empire as a house instead of a body, then it becomes appropriate to call the new Austria a short, dead-end hallway." This is not an easy idea to get used to. Kreisky and his Socialists may manage Austria's affairs with admirable efficiency, but they do so without much conviction. It is the fate of the postwar generation to hunger for conviction even as they remain keenly aware of its dangers.

[1983]

Dear Hitch

A DOZEN YEARS GONE, dear Christopher, and not a day goes by that I don't think of you: boon comrade, peerless writer, stalwart friend. We had so much fun, dreaming up *God Is Not Great*, debating fiercely till wee hours of the morning all the issues of the day, sharpening our rhetorical arrows and stashing them in our respective quivers, looking forward to letting them fly at deserving targets, large and small.

I remember the day in October 1979 when we first met. I was in London for the first time, having permitted myself a holiday a year and a half into my new job as deputy editor of the *Los Angeles Times* op-ed page and opinion section. I made my way to Carlisle Street in Soho to meet Robin Blackburn of the *New Left Review*, who, from time to time, had written for me. I had long admired the *Review* for doing the hard work of salvaging the best of Marxism after the self-inflicted wounds of Stalinism and the implosion of the Bolshevik project and, not least, the unremitting enmity of the capitalist powers. I admired the commitment of its editors and contributors to plumbing with a supple intelligence the nuances of historical circumstance, alive to paradox and irony, in long essays that cast a powerful spotlight on issues and places (often in parts of the world that had long been neglected), throwing them into a sharper and more clarifying relief. Many of the journal's contributors and the galaxy of writers that swirled around them were possessed of an enviable erudition, many of them the beneficiaries of superb English educations. In other words, they knew how to write. Among their number was you. And you struck me as among the most felicitous in your passionate engagement with the issues of the day while wielding your pen in a stylish and witty manner. Reading you never felt like homework. I always emerged smarter, more emboldened. It never mattered whether I agreed with this opinion or that view as you might offer. What mattered most—and I could feel it in the impress of your sentences and the pitch and roll of your arguments—was that I, like all your lucky readers, was being encouraged to think more rigorously, more seriously, more ardently. There seemed in your work no division between intellection and heart. You effortlessly spiced your reporting and commentary with apt quotation from literature and poetry. You especially drew from the deep well of Auden and Larkin. I sensed from the moment I began reading you—first in the *New Statesman*, where you worked as foreign correspondent and then in your spirited provocations for numerous other publications—that you were a rare talent.

Robin and I talked, and as the hours sped by, he suddenly allowed that he had a friend—one Christopher Hitchens—that he thought I should meet, as he was sure we would very much like each other. He asked you to join us at a nearby Chinese restaurant, an establishment Robin took pains to say was, despite its bad food, hugely congenial. I remember only two things from that first meeting: yes, the potstickers were lousy, but you were dazzling. More: I fell in love. Soon you were a frequent contributor to the *Los Angeles Times*.

When you accepted Victor Navasky's invitation to become a Washington-based columnist for the *Nation,* I worried that immersion in tony dinner parties and gatherings in Georgetown manses might blunt your radical edge. I. F. Stone famously and wisely spurned such invitations, convinced that to accept would risk curbing his criticisms in favor of preserving access. He preferred the solitude and anonymity of his study to the seduction of privileged entry to the precincts of the powerful. You, by contrast, never refused an invitation. Hubris (your own) was seen as prophylactic. Ambition and flattery are ever the currency of social success, nowhere more pronounced than in America's capital. I feared you'd succumb to a commonplace careerism. I was wrong. Biting the hand that feeds was always a sign of fealty to first principles. You did not disappoint.

You once told me that shortly after you'd arrived in Washington in the early eighties, you were invited to a cocktail party at the home of Kay Graham, owner of the *Washington Post.* When, taking your leave, you stood under the portico, awaiting a taxi as a hard rain fell, you found yourself sharing an umbrella with a man in a trench coat. To your astonishment, it was Robert S. McNamara, one of the men responsible for the Vietnam War and later the president of the World Bank. You introduced yourself, saying, "Forgive me this intrusion, I'm Christopher Hitchens, a newly arrived journalist from England. I'd like to ask you, if I may, an impertinent question, which if I didn't ask, I'd never forgive myself. Of course, you're under no obligation to answer."

McNamara said, "What's the question?"

"Ever since I've come to Washington, I keep hearing a persistent rumor. It is said that you not infrequently find yourself awakening in the middle of the night, your face wet with tears. People say you weep over Vietnam. Can this possibly be true?"

McNamara stared hard at you and, just as his car and driver were pulling up, said, "Yes." And promptly strode off.

Nearly fifteen years later, I would publish McNamara's tormented memoir, *In Retrospect*. I was then editorial director of Times Books. Peter Osnos, the imprint's publisher and former foreign editor of the *Washington Post*, had got McNamara to confess that "we were wrong, terribly wrong," an admission that, not surprisingly, didn't go far enough for McNamara's fiercest and most unforgiving critics. I'd never forgotten the story of your brief encounter with McNamara, and so wasn't entirely surprised when McNamara decided, at long last, to confess his growing doubts over the course of the war he'd done so much to prosecute. In his book, McNamara told of a momentous demonstration against the war at Harvard in November 1966. He'd been invited to address Richard Neustadt's class at Harvard and then later to give a talk at Henry Kissinger's class. As his car made its way across the campus, he was surrounded by hundreds of protestors. (Years later, Bob Scheer told me that the students were demanding that McNamara debate Scheer, one of the most outspoken voices against the war, who was also visiting Harvard.) McNamara, having attended UC Berkeley in the tumultuous thirties, was not unfamiliar with such protests, and was struck by the passion and anger of the students. He worried that the war had already been lost in the hearts and minds of the next generation of America's best and brightest.

Things threatened to get out of hand. He got out of the car and was led to safety through the underground tunnels beneath Harvard Yard. That evening, at the dinner organized in his honor by Neustadt, McNamara began to think that a study should be commissioned to investigate the origins of the never-ending quagmire that was Vietnam. Thus were the Pentagon Papers born.

Some days later, as he wrote in his book, he was having dinner at Jackie Kennedy's Manhattan apartment on Fifth Avenue. It was a pleasant evening, and afterward they repaired to her well-stocked library and discussed their mutual admiration for the poems of Chilean Nobel Prize winner Gabriela Mistral. Suddenly, Jackie turned to him with a look of pain and consternation. Balling up her fists, she began beating on his chest, crying out, "Bob, Bob, you've just got to stop the slaughter." Alone among the war criminals that made up LBJ's cabinet, McNamara, however feebly, made public decades later his private disquiet. It was, of course, too little and too late. You never tired of me telling this tale.

When later, after nearly nine years as the editor of the *Los Angeles Times Book Review*, I decided to leave the paper—the Tribune Company of Chicago having bought the place from the Chandler family for $8.3 billion some years before, and all the folks who had hired me gone, and it becoming increasingly clear that I was no longer going to be permitted as free a hand as I had gotten used to—you were among the first both to extend solidarity as well as to cheer me on in my new life as literary agent, I having agreed to become a partner in the boutique Boston-based agency of Kneerim & Williams.

I tendered my resignation on Friday the thirteenth of May 2005. It seemed as good as any other day to vamoose. Over the weekend, the phone rang. You intuited that I might need a client or two. What am I, you said, chopped liver?

I jumped at the chance and said I'd be thrilled to represent you, and what was even better, I knew what your next book ought to be. My dear boy, you said, what would that be? A book against God—you've been writing it all your life. For reasons wholly mysterious, I had kept by my bedside for two years a special issue of *Daedalus* entirely devoted to reflections on religion in modern society, for which you'd written a kind of atheist manifesto. It read as a précis for a proper book.

Two months later, I flew to New York and spent seventy-two hours in back-to-back meetings, morning, noon, and night, with two dozen editors and publishers. And while all of them knew your previous books, all were a bit wary, as none of them, whatever their merits (and there were many), had amounted to much more than pamphleteering or collections of previously published essays and sallies, one of which—*Prepared for the Worst*—I had published in 1988. None had broken through to a wider public. Did you have, they worried, the *Sitzfleisch* to write a real book? While your writerly gifts were abundant and your reputation as a fearless critic well established, there was concern that your palpable impatience and restlessness might undermine the tenacity required to deliver a substantive work. Yet so great was the regard for you as a polemicist, quite probably the finest of our generation, as everyone agreed, that the prospect of a book against God found an immediate echo of enthusiasm. But what, prospective editors and publishers wanted to know, what, exactly, was the argument? I didn't yet have a written proposal from you except for the original piece in *Daedalus*, so I simply did my best to channel you. Well, I said, making it up, the book is in three parts: the first demolishes the Judeo-Christian nonsense, the second the Islamic rubbish, and as for the third, if any of us sees one more picture of Richard Gere with the Dalai Lama, aren't we all just going to throw up? *That* was a book everyone wanted to read.

I flew back to Los Angeles. You were in town to give a speech, being put up at the fashionable new monolith of a hotel, the Mondrian, on the Sunset Strip. We agreed to meet for lunch poolside. The whole place looked as if it were an outtake from a remake of Godard's *Alphaville*. Arrayed decorously around the pool, beneath the unforgiving L.A. sunshine, was a clutch of alarmingly beautiful young women, all of whom seemed to have had their body parts surgically rearranged, chaperoned by phalanxes of men, all of whom seemed to be sporting Armani and packing heat. No sooner had we ordered drinks— Johnny Walker Black Label, yours neat, mine with two rocks—you lighting up the first Rothman of the afternoon, me bumming one, as was my disobliging habit, than my Blackberry began to buzz. I stepped away and took the call. It was Jonathan Karp, who was heading up his own imprint, Twelve, at Hachette Publishing Group. We'd seen each other in Manhattan and talked about the God book. He was calling, he said, to ask if, even in advance of seeing a proposal, we might be open to a preemptive offer. How much did he have in mind? It was a sum three times larger than anything you'd ever gotten before. I said I'd talk to you and get back to him. I walked to the lobby—where bellhops, clad in black as if they were in Pol Pot's praetorian guard, lingered—cooled my heels, waited fifteen minutes, and then, my fingers flying over the keyboard of the Blackberry, playing it like it was an electronic thumb piano, texted Karp that the money was insufficient to take it off the table. Karp called back and doubled the offer.

I returned to our poolside table, shared my news, and cautioned that while the money was good, we had yet to submit a written proposal to others, many of whom, like Sonny Mehta of Knopf, I knew to be admirers of your work. With a written proposal we might double, yet again, what Karp was prepared to pay.

I shall never forget your response. You were not, you insisted, the man to write his own flap jacket copy. You'd far prefer just to get on with writing the bloody book than write a proposal. Besides, you said, if the book sells as well as Karp clearly believes it will and you and I hope it will, won't we see the money on the back end? Just so, I said, but such a view suggested a degree of sobriety that is all but extinct in our age of grab-it-now-and-let-the-devil-take-the-hindmost. You inhaled the Rothman and amidst the exhaled smoke said, Steve, in most parts of the world the sum now on the table would be considered indecent. Why don't we just say yes and get on with it?

The deal was struck for a book of sixty thousand words to be delivered in nine months. You delivered ninety thousand in six months. We would go on to see foreign editions in twenty-three countries and the book banned in Malaysia, which fact made you exceedingly happy. Salman Rushdie cracked that the title, *God Is Not Great*, was one word too long. And then a miracle: the Reverend Jerry Falwell collapsed and died in his office (which fact alone almost disproved the entire thesis of your jeremiad), and you were invited on the Sean Hannity show along with Christian straight arrow Ralph Reed. Hannity asked what you thought of the late Falwell, and you bluntly allowed that you found Falwell loathsome in the extreme and called him a con artist, a grifter, and worse. Hannity became apoplectic and denounced your lack of respect for the dead man's family. And you retorted that there was so little to Falwell that had he been given an enema before his expiration, he could have been buried in a matchbox. The blogosphere blew up, and thousands of copies of your book flew out of bookstores. It shot up bestseller lists everywhere, ultimately selling more than five hundred thousand copies.

You were launched, and so was I. Five months later, you were a finalist at the National Book Awards. A black-tie ceremony was to take place at the Times Square Marriott Hotel. Earlier in the day, we'd traipsed along Broadway below West Fifty-Seventh Street to find a clothing store to buy cufflinks for your tux. Suitably attired, we met up with Carol Blue, my dear friend since she was nineteen and now your wife, thanks to my introducing her to you in 1989—thus inadvertently breaking up your first marriage, but hey, everyone has agency, right?—when I sent you to Los Angeles to promote your first book of essays, which I was publishing at Hill and Wang at Farrar, Straus and Giroux.

We gaily trotted off to the hotel. Soon we were engulfed by hundreds of folks crowding into the ballroom. Drinks stations were scattered throughout the lobby. You were encircled by admirers. Keen for a bracing drink, you asked Carol and me to see if we could get one. Twenty minutes later (the lines were long), we made our way back, drinks in hand. We were called to our respective tables. Dinner was served. The awards were announced. First prize was denied. You hid your disappointment well, and we repaired to the Lowell Hotel, where you were staying, for a nightcap.

No sooner had we entered your room than my Blackberry began to thrum insistently against my thigh. I read the message with disbelief: An astonishing story had just been posted on Gawker. Turns out that while Carol and I were busy getting drinks, you had been approached by a young couple who wanted to know more about a screamingly funny column you'd just published in *Vanity Fair*. It described, in painful detail and laugh-out-loud hilarity, your attempt at "self-improvement" by having a Brazilian wax job administered by the woman who was said to have invented the procedure. You got the works: back, crack, and sack. It was, you wrote, almost as excruciating a torment as being waterboarded, which, in the interests of participatory journalism for the benefit of *Vanity Fair*'s readers, you had also endured. How, the woman wanted to know, did you feel now? Smooth, very smooth, you said, and seeing the look of disbelief on her face, you invited her to judge for herself. She was game, and so right there, in the middle of the crowd around you, you unzipped your fly. She put her hand in, lingered, and then withdrew. You looked at her and deadpanned: And the verdict? Smooth, very smooth, she said. Then, spying the incredulous look on her boyfriend's face, you invited: Don't take her word for it. You're welcome to check for yourself. After the briefest hesitation, the boyfriend said he thought he would. The hand went in. The hand withdrew. You said: And?

Smooth, very smooth.

The evening had barely ended when the couple posted their encounter on Gawker, and suddenly the internet had lit up. You, for your part, had said nothing of this to either Carol or me. I drew Carol aside, showed her the story on my Blackberry. She read it quickly and said with what seemed to me loving exasperation, oh God, you can't take him anywhere. What a bad boy he is.

Not everything was easy between us. We sometimes had principled disagreements, but we never let our differences threaten our friendship. After all, I would be best man at your wedding to Carol, and you'd return the favor when I married my second wife. We lived to argue, figuring doing so would sharpen our wits and challenge unexamined presumptions on the grindstone of our devotion to more exacting and thus more convincing understandings. We drank and talked until long hours into the night, enrolling Alexander Herzen and Rosa Luxemburg and Victor Serge, among other heretics of leftist orthodoxy, in the service of our embroilments, and while I encouraged your growing disenchantment with what you called the anti-imperialist left in favor of the antitotalitarian left, I felt you'd dangerously compromised your best instincts by allying yourself with the neocon rush to war in, as you called it, Mesopotamia. I didn't trust your new friendships with warmongers such as Paul Wolfowitz, no matter his near-Talmudic familiarity with the Higher Trotskyism. And yet, I must hand it to you: No one made a better case for American intervention in these benighted lands than you. Your arguments didn't rest on the existence of weapons of mass destruction, but rather on moral grounds. You were convinced that the United States, which had done so much to prop up the despotic vampirism of Saddam Hussein, turning a blind eye to his gassing of the Kurds, whose ambitions for a nation-state of their own you had always supported, bore a special responsibility. Under the Baathist tyranny, Iraq's suffering peoples had become so enfeebled, you argued, that successful resistance was all but impossible. Thus, the United States had an obligation—indeed, as you so vividly put it, a blood debt—to do its utmost to rid Iraq of its dictator, even if that meant sending its own soldiers to fight and die. The *casus belli* was less important, in your view, than the moral imperative. You were eloquent and insistent.

I disagreed on many grounds, not least because I feared that even if the United States were to succeed, the price of victory would be to further deprive the Iraqi people of agency. People, I argued, needed to make their own history, as much for reasons of pride as for reasons of taking responsibility for making right what had gone so grievously wrong and not outsourcing it to nations with little to no understanding of the cultural and religious and political habits and traditions of the region. I worried that if you persisted in advocating American intervention, you'd have blood on your hands.

You went to your death never apologizing for, and never renouncing, any position you'd publicly proclaimed or privately held. It was part of your combative temperament. September 11 and the fatwa against Salman hardened you. You always had a romance with those who fought fascism. And now religious fundamentalists, particularly of the Islamic persuasion, were the new fascists. If it was war they wanted, it would be war they'd get. You were eager to enroll yourself in what you regarded as a just cause. And, increasingly, you made every effort to hoist yourself atop the petard of your own righteousness, seeing in those who questioned your arguments cowards unable to respond to history's call. Public debates became occasions for the hurling of insults. Profanity began to mar your natural eloquence. A pugilistic bent was palpable, and, I found, disturbing. I remember taking you aside just before introducing you to Sam Harris at a dinner I had arranged in Los Angeles, as you were to participate in the *Los Angeles Times* Festival of Books, to urge you, as your friend and publisher and now your agent and, above all, your comrade, to resist the temptation to castigate with unabashed contempt and derision members of the audience who might, during a question and answer period, have the temerity to take you to task. I said you were in danger of becoming a bully, and that you risked losing the audience, who would remember only your denunciatory fury and not the arguments that you were otherwise at pains to marshal. You conceded you recognized the person I described, and that you'd do your best but couldn't guarantee that you'd behave yourself.

From the first, we had found a degree of affinity that claimed us both as comrades in a common struggle to forge an oppositional left worthy of respect, a decent left, a principled left free of the deformities that had so often sullied the effort to right the wrongs of this broken world, to replace structures of oppression with those of liberation. To use our talents in this quest was, we felt, a high calling. And thus, I regarded your exquisite introduction to the volume of your essays I published, the first of your books to appear in the United States, as a kind of credo, almost an act of ventriloquism. I return regularly, dear Christopher, to your good and inspiring words, written last century, words that remain as acutely relevant today as they were when you first presented them to me:

> Nadine Gordimer once wrote, or said, that she tried to write posthumously. She did not mean that she wanted to speak from beyond the grave (a common enough authorial fantasy), but that she aimed to communicate *as if she were already dead*. Never mind that that ambition is axiomatically impossible of achievement, and never mind that it sounds at once rather modest and rather egotistic, to say nothing of rather gaunt. When I read it, I still thought: Gosh. To write as if editors, publishers, colleagues, peers, friends, relatives, factions, reviewers, and consumers need not be consulted; to write as if supply and demand, time and place, were nugatory. . . . Call no man lucky until he is dead, but there have been moments of rare satisfaction in the often random and fragmented life of the radical freelance scribbler. . . . Religions and states and classes and tribes and nations do not have to work or argue for their adherents and subjects. They more or less inherit them. Against this unearned patrimony there have always been speakers and writers who embody [Bertrand Russell's and] Einstein's injunction to "remember your humanity and forget the rest." It would be immodest to claim membership in this fraternity/sorority, but I hope not to have done anything to outrage it. Despite the idiotic sneer that such principles are

"fashionable," it is always the ideas of secularism, libertarianism, internationalism, and solidarity that stand in need of reaffirmation.

And then later, in your introduction to the *Best American Essays 2010*, when you wrote, "I feel relatively confident that neither demand for nor the supply of the well-wrought *feuilleton* will ever become exhausted. We are not likely to reach a time when the need of such things as curiosity, irony, debunking, disputation, and elegy will become satisfied. For the present, we must resolve to essay, essay, and essay again."

In June 2010, you got sick. Diagnosed with stage four esophageal cancer, you faced your illness with exemplary stoicism. I doubt I shall be so brave when my time comes. At the end of September 2011, things got worse. You were back in Houston at the MD Anderson Cancer Clinic. I had visited at the end of September—clutching Proust, which had lain unread on my shelves for forty years but which I'd undertaken, finally, to read all three thousand pages, obsessively, and you, who knew your Proust well, having reviewed the Lydia Davis translation of *Swann's Way* for the *Atlantic*, said from your hospital bed that you envied my waiting till I was in the last third of my life to read him because, you said, only then did I have the requisite life experience to fully understand the melancholy of time's passage—then in October, with Proust still underarm. In mid-December, your son, Alexander, twenty-eight, called me saying you were crying out for my presence. I immediately got on a plane. I arrived on Tuesday night, the thirteenth, and the next day was Wednesday, the fourteenth. Your condition had worsened, and you were down to one hundred twenty pounds;

you had lost a third of your body weight, and you were being ravaged by a virulent pneumonia. You were doped up with morphine. That day, however, you were still lucid and could speak, though wasting away.

I asked how I might help. You said you were "done," that you didn't want any more aggressive medical interventions, and that you were prepared to die. You asked that I tell this to Carol. Wouldn't this news be more convincing coming from you directly? You, not missing a beat, joked that Carol had never much listened to you, and that I, as one of her oldest friends, might be more persuasive.

When I entered the ICU at six thirty that morning, I found Carol at the end of your hospital bed, remonstrating with your chief oncologist. He was trying, without apparent success, to indicate to her that nothing more could be done while not conceding that things were hopeless. Carol said, "I don't think you understand. He's never missed a deadline in his life. Besides, he has his little book on mortality to write." Your eyes blinked open, and seeing me you said, "Steve, believe me, nobody wants to read that fucking book." "But I do, Christopher, I do." "Believe me," you repeated, "nobody wants to read that fucking book."

Later that morning, I was alone with you and Alexander. I'm forever grateful that he was there, otherwise nobody would believe what happened next.

You open your eyes and gesture for a pen and a pad of paper to be brought to you and indicate you want to write something. A yellow legal pad and pen are presented and placed in your hands. You begin writing. You bring the pad up to your face, your brow furrows, you gesture to Alexander to find your reading glasses. You turn the pad like it's an iPad, rotating it one way and then another. I get up and look at it. And it's just chicken scratches. You look at it and let the pad fall to your lap, then look up and say, "Whaddya gonna do?" You sink back into the pillows.

And then comes your Rosebud moment. You whisper a word. I say, "What did you say?"

And you say, quite distinctly, "Capitalism."

"Capitalism? What about it?"

"Downfall."

Those are the last words I hear you utter.

You were true to yourself and to no one else. You followed your own star. Nicking a line of Edna St. Vincent Millay's, you liked to declare as you declined that you'd burned the candle at both ends, and it gave off a lovely light. It did, Hitch, it did. And in that flickering flame, we, your fortunate friends, found a heat that warmed us and illuminated our lives, and even when it was extinguished, we have continued to blow on the embers of the memory of the intensities and curiosities with which you lived. I loved you then. I love you still.

As always, *abrazos*
Steve

[2023]

Sister Souljah Throws It Down

THIS IS A STORY ABOUT SISTER SOULJAH, the late Harry Evans, and me.

I knew Harry reasonably well, having worked for nearly six years (1990–1996) in close proximity to him when he was publisher of Random House and I was editorial director of Times Books, an imprint of Random. Without Harry, I would never have been able to publish Souljah's remarkable first book, *No Disrespect*, a stunningly candid book about how young Black girls can grow up with their integrity intact in a very rough world. I am forever grateful to him. But first, some backstory. Bear with me.

In 1992 Bill Clinton, while seeking to become president, cynically used Sister Souljah's remarks in the aftermath of the Rodney King uprisings in Los Angeles to deride her as a "racist," and to shamelessly ingratiate himself with the centrist and reactionary elements of the Democratic Party in order to burnish his "law and order" bona fides. Robert Scheer was asked by *Playboy* to interview Souljah. Scheer's interview in 1976 with Jimmy Carter, who confessed to having, from time to time, "lust in my heart," had pole-vaulted Scheer into the higher circles of Hefner's kingdom. Scheer spent, in the usual way of such interviews, hours upon hours with Souljah, and emerged from the encounter convinced she'd been given a raw deal. She was far from the bigoted caricature that the media had portrayed. He rang me up and urged—no, insisted—that I reach out to her. He was convinced she had a book in her. About what exactly he didn't know. But he was certain that we'd like each other.

Souljah and I met at an upscale Lebanese restaurant on Third Avenue near Random House's building located on East Fiftieth Street. We got on like the proverbial house on fire. I knew she could rap having bought her album, but I said I didn't know if she could write, and I wasn't in the habit of signing wannabe writers on the back of a napkin to a contract on the basis of a single lunch. Did she want to write a book, and, if so, what would it be about?

She said she'd never read any book by either an African American, or anybody else for that matter, that told the truth about sexual relations between Black men and Black women. She wanted to give it a try. She imagined writing a book filled with characters based on her own coming of age that would be an honest account of the rage and hopes of girls in the ghetto. It would describe the tensions within the Black family, the entanglements of friends, and the entrapments of lovers. It would be an unsparing look at the ferocious struggle for sexual identity and autonomy that, she said, confronts every African American—especially women.

I'd never read such a book either. But could she write it? What, she asked, did I need to see to know? I said it would be great to have a couple sample chapters and an outline, for starters. That's fair, she said. When do you need them? How about, say, in six weeks or so? Fine.

She was as good as her word. A month and a half later, I received sixty pages, double-spaced, full of remarkable stories, told in a compelling voice, full of well-observed detail. I was smitten. Next step: enlist the enthusiasm of my publisher, Peter Osnos. I gave the pages to him to read over the weekend. Monday morning, he called me into his office. He had read every page. She sure can write, he said, but he didn't think that it was a "Times book." Why not? I asked. He didn't really have an answer other than to share his feeling that it just wasn't. He could see I was disappointed. Perhaps, he allowed, I might show it to Sonny Mehta, the head of Alfred A. Knopf, a sister company under the umbrella of the Random House publishing empire.

I took it to Sonny, whom I'd known ever since being introduced to him by Christopher Hitchens when Sonny was still working for Pan paperbacks in London. Sonny had exquisite taste and was known for his strong support of authors. He too promised to read it over the weekend. On Monday, he called me into his office. He said, she sure can write. He'd read every word. The sentences sparkled, but somehow it just didn't strike him as a "Knopf book."

I reported back to Osnos. He said, why don't you show it to Harry. Perhaps he'll take it on. Harry said he'd read it over the weekend. On Monday, he called me into his office. He said, she sure can write. He'd read every word. Who else has read it? he asked. I said both Sonny and Peter had but that, somehow, it wasn't for them. Harry said, tell you what, if Peter doesn't want to do it at Times Books, I'll do it at Random. You be the editor, and I'll make room for it on our list.

I went back to Osnos. Peter was nothing if not competitive. Okay, he said, we'll do it at Times Books, you'll edit it. And so we did, but that wasn't the end of the story.

While Souljah was finishing writing her book, which we would publish in January 1995, I got a phone call from Harry one fine day in the spring of 1994. He wondered if Sister Souljah might be willing to participate on a panel with Erica (*Fear of Flying*) Jong and the elderly philanthropist and blue blood Brooke Astor to discuss George Eliot's *Middlemarch*, which Random House was reissuing in a Modern Library edition to coincide with a PBS broadcast of a British television series of the novel. Harry would moderate the discussion, to take place at the Museum of Television and Broadcasting.

Why Souljah? I asked. Harry said it bothered him greatly that the only time African Americans were asked their opinion was with respect to issues of race. That had to change. I promised to ring Souljah up to ask if she knew the book. She didn't but agreed to read it if I'd be good enough to send a copy to her. Happily, I said. You'll be tempted to give up in the first hundred pages, but don't. Stick with it, I urged. You'll never forget it.

The day of the panel arrived. The place was packed with several hundred people, including Liz Smith, the gossip columnist. The conversation was lively, and Souljah was incisive and compelling in her remarks. At one point, the nearly anorexic Astor turned to Harry, and extending a bony hand, placing it on his thigh, jerking a thumb to her right at Souljah, said *sotto voce*, loud enough for the entire audience to hear, "Where the hell did you find her? She's terrific."

Sure enough, that was the headline in the next day's tabloids, ballyhooed by Liz Smith.

Harry was brilliant. He knew that we needed to change the public perception of just who Sister Souljah was. In one fell swoop, he had masterminded a complete makeover, catapulting Souljah into another regard and helping to make possible the successful publication some months later of her revelatory book.

I remembered a phone call I'd had with Gore Vidal when, a few years earlier, Harry had been appointed to helm Random House. I'd rung Gore, who I knew had known Harry, to ask him what he made of him. Gore's reply was withering and admiring and unfair but not altogether wrong: "Well," he said, "I suppose in the late twentieth century, it doesn't hurt to have as one's publisher a gifted publicist."

As for me, Harry had my back, always. As for Souljah, her astonishing book remains in print twenty-five years later. I treasure her inscription to me: "What can I say to the person responsible for making the deal that put a roof over my head and food on the table for my family. A resounding thank you! You reached out at a time that damn near nobody did. Believe me, that more than counts." Her career as a rapper tanked. But her reputation as a chart-busting writer of the first rank deepened, and her prowess as a much-beloved storyteller of the African American condition won her legions of readers everywhere.

[2020]

Jason Epstein

v.

Benzion Netanyahu

A GIANT HAS FALLEN. His death in 2022 at age ninety-three immeasurably impoverishes American letters. I loved Jason Epstein. We first met forty years ago when he was coming out to Berkeley in the early 1980s to edit Bob Scheer's explosive book *With Enough Shovels: Reagan, Bush & Nuclear War*. They would meet upstairs at Chez Panisse, in the restaurant's congenial café. Scheer introduced Jason to Alice Waters. Jason appeared to lose interest in Scheer's book as the seductions of Alice and her restaurant grew. A deal was done on a napkin. And soon Jason was editing two books. Both would be published in 1982. Scheer was always generous with his acknowledgments, writing of Jason that his book was "very much the product of the goading, lecturing, support, intimidation and above all education that I received from Random House editor Jason Epstein. I have never worked with anyone quite like Jason, whose brilliance and range of knowledge can be devastating when necessary as well as illuminating." Scheer was stunned by "Jason's seemingly endless requests and suggestions for clarification of ideas, improvement of style and introduction of common sense, all of which made this a far clearer and more readable book."

When, nearly twenty years later, I found myself hired as editorial director of Times Books, then an imprint of Random House, I had no sooner settled myself in my office than Jason appeared at my door, offering unsolicited words of advice and a warm welcome. He told me that many people, upon joining Random House, made a mistake, believing the jostling for position and power among the editors was a cutthroat business of opportunism and runaway egos, akin to what people imagined took place among the henchmen clustered around Stalin in the darkest days of the Kremlin. And thus, they became cat's paws to a punishing game of careerism. He didn't deny any of it but said it was a grave error to keep one's ears to the floorboards listening to the tom-toms of corporate machinations. None of that counted, he said. And then, waving an arm at the wall of books in my office, he said that what counted, provided you found a way to both survive and thrive, was the work—and the work was helping others who had something to say. None of us has any claim on immortality, and few of the writers would either. But the work itself was its own reward. And that, he said, was really all that mattered. He was talking to the already converted. I believed it then. I believe it now.

I also remember a disobliging piece that appeared in *New York* magazine bemoaning what the author alleged was the dearth of real editors. Even aging dinosaurs like Jason came in for attack, the author of the screed alleging that Jason was much more interested in eating than he was in editing, that he'd become lazy and had for many years been resting on his laurels. I knew differently. For much of the early 1990s, Jason had been meticulously editing, line by line, the more than two thousand double-spaced pages of the great tome on the Spanish Inquisition that had been the work of a lifetime by the distinguished scholar Benzion Netanyahu, whose command of Hebrew, Latin, Spanish, and English was unrivaled. Netanyahu was the father of several sons, one of whom became the hero of the raid on Entebbe, another of whom became the prime minister of Israel. Jason one day squired Netanyahu around to my office and introduced us, and we later repaired to a nearby restaurant to spend three hours talking about the nuances of fifteenth-century Iberian persecutions, the how and why of the conversos (or secret Jews) and whether their conversions were sincere or opportunistic, and the enduring legacy of the torments visited upon them and what it meant for us in the era of modern fascism and antisemitism. Over the next several years, Jason often talked with me about the challenge of editing this Everest of a book. Netanyahu was, like many pedants, given to unfolding his story by stating a thesis, then engaging in an exegesis, and then summarizing what he'd just told you. Jason spent months and months scratching away in his tiny script, scrupulously editing every sentence. The pages were often dense with his suggested cuts and revisions, seeking, as always, to improve clarity and concision, eliminate repetition and jargon. In the end, he packed it all off to Netanyahu in Jerusalem. For some weeks there was no response. Then one day, Jason appeared at my door, holding in his hand a small piece of paper, a telegram from Netanyahu. It was brutal: "Whose book is this? If yours, take my name off. If mine, restore what you cut." Jason looked at me, shrugged, and mumbled, "Whaddya gonna do? It's his funeral." The book was published at nearly fourteen hundred pages. The reviews were respectful.

Some asked: Where was the editor? In his corner office, hard at work editing another author.

A final story: Jason's second wife, Judith Miller, differed with her husband, to say the least, on the question of the American intervention in Iraq. Judy had lost her job at the *New York Times*, accused of being a stenographer for the hardliners eager for war. Jason, a cofounder of the *New York Review of Books*, began to write a regular series of essays questioning the sense in the attack on Baghdad. One day I summoned up the nerve to ask him about the pillow talk. What can I say, he said, with a Cheshire's cat grin, but that I regularly get to utter the best four words in the English language: I told you so.

[2022]

High Noon with Gore Vidal

I FIRST MET GORE VIDAL in 1979 in Los Angeles while
working as an editor of the *Los Angeles Times* Sunday opinion section. We took an immediate liking to each other, and he
began writing for me, more I always thought out of a lifelong
compulsion to irritate the *New York Times*, which he'd long been
convinced had it in for him, than for any particular affection for
the *Los Angeles Times*. We became friends—he giving me pep
talks at Ma Maison, where we would sometimes meet for dinner,
encouraging me to lead as wide and as fruitful a literary life
as talent and ambition would permit. We saw each other from
time to time at his Hollywood home on Outpost Drive, in New
York at the Plaza Hotel, and once at New Year's in Venice at the
Hotel Palace Gritti, where he complained that Susan Sontag
and he were the only American writers of any distinction that
Bob Silvers would publish in the pages of the *New York Review
of Books*. Three stories from the years of our friendship stand
out.

A conscientious and stalwart paladin for a quartet of US
presidents, Robert M. Gates, having left his CIA directorship,
came knocking on publishers' doors to sell his memoirs. My
bell was rung, and an appointment made. No proposal, beyond a vague letter, was tendered. No previously published

writings were submitted. Gates claimed everything he'd ever committed to paper was top secret, but, he said, he had a well-warranted reputation within the agency as a compelling scribbler of memos. Trying to get a sense of the book he imagined writing, I asked if there were any books by others he admired and might look to as a model. "Rousseau's *Confessions*," he said evenly. Taken aback, I thought, well, one has to start somewhere. "Anything more recent?" I ventured. "Gore Vidal's *Lincoln*," came the reply. I was dumbfounded. What, I asked, was it about Vidal's *Lincoln* he liked? Gates said he'd served a number of presidents, and even though his time in the higher circles was removed by nearly a century and a half from Lincoln's era, no one had better described the pressure cooker tensions among a president's advisers on matters of life and death than had Vidal in his novel. Boy, was I surprised. No sooner had Gates taken his leave than I rang Gore in his palazzo in Ravello. You won't believe who was just in my office. I told him what Gates had said. There was an expensive pause on the telephone. Then Gore erupted: "Wasserman, it's more dire than even you can imagine. So, this is where the Reaganauts got the idea of lifting the writ of *habeas corpus*. They stole it from my *Lincoln*!"

A few years later, I became editor of the *Los Angeles Times Book Review*. Gore's 1999 novel, *The Smithsonian Institution*, was about to be published. It was a modest entertainment, a satire in the manner of *Duluth* and *Myra Breckinridge*. I thought it an occasion to publish a lengthy consideration of Gore's overall achievement as one of America's foremost men of letters.

We commissioned artwork for the front page, and we chose a suitable reviewer.

Vidal was set for a book tour, and he insisted that his publisher have me be his interlocutor at a nationwide Pacifica Radio station hookup before a live audience at the Beverly Hills–based Museum of Television and Broadcasting. Afterward we'd have lunch, just the two of us, at the Polo Lounge at the always congenial Beverly Hills Hotel. I agreed. The interview was set for Monday morning. I also planned to accompany him the following day to the Bay Area, where a similar conversation with Christopher Hitchens would take place before several thousand people at the Berkeley Community Theatre, followed by an intimate dinner at Chez Panisse.

Meanwhile, over the weekend, the review came in. The reviewer was at pains to admire the life and much of the previous work, but as to the current book, alas, the judgment was negative in the extreme.

What to do? The only principle I'd sworn to uphold when I accepted the post was to never reveal, before publication, the nature of a review or the identity of the reviewer. The paper's readers, I felt, deserved to be the first to know.

But all rules are made to be broken. In this instance, I felt that fidelity to friendship trumped professional conceit. I would publish the review as written, of course, but decided that if there was bad news—as indeed there was—I owed it to Vidal that, at the very least, I should be the one to tell him. To say nothing would risk Gore's fury, and he was not a man to be lightly crossed; he'd go around the world warning his innumerable friends and acquaintances to beware of the shameless Wasserman, who would go to great lengths to flatter you during the week and then slip in the stiletto just when you least expected it.

But when, exactly, to give him the bad news? Before our interview? That would spoil the conversation. Lunch would be best. But then, I thought, when exactly? Before the first course, during the meal, or ought I to delay until dessert?

Drinks arrived. I thought, now's the chance, bite the bullet and be done with it. I happened to glance sideways at another table. There, in all his mummified glory, sat Charleton Heston, Vidal's great nemesis. "Don't look now," I said, "but there's Ben-Hur eating his spinach." Vidal, not missing a beat, said, "Oh, Steve, it's the Polo Lounge, the La Brea Tar Pits of Hollywood. It's where all us dinosaurs go to die."

Our salads arrived. I put down my fork and looked up at Gore. "I can't go on a moment longer," I said, "without first telling you that I've got good news and bad news."

"Let's be old-fashioned: first, the good news," he said.

"Well, the good news is we're running a full-page review with a marvelous illustration."

"And the bad news?"

"Our reviewer loves the life and admires many of the past books. As to this particular book, however, not at all."

"And where does the bad news come? Is it in the lede? Or the last paragraph?"

"The penultimate graph, as a matter of fact."

Gore cracked a slight grimace of a smile. "Steve, Steve," he said, "it's all good news. In reviewery, as in real estate, it's all location, location, location. No one reads these things all the way through, only the top and bottom. Relax, it's all good."

He paused and then said: "And your reviewer? A man or a woman?"

"A woman, as it happens."

He shook his head sadly. "Steve, Steve, never give such a book to a woman. They have no ear for irony."

The tradition of backstage work is long, if too little recognized. After all, what would Eugene O'Neill have been without Carlotta? Or Edna St. Vincent Millay without Eugen Boissevain? Or, for that matter, Virginia Woolf without Leonard? For Lord Nelson, it was Emma Hamilton. For F. Scott Fitzgerald, it was Zelda. For Kenneth Tynan, it was Elaine Dundy. For Somerset Maugham, it was Alan Searle. For W. H. Auden, it was Chester Kallman. For Christopher Isherwood, it was Don Bachardy. These are the men and women who manage the money, make sure the household functions, act as first readers and critics, and in so doing help to free their creative partners from being held hostage to the quotidian. Alas, no Nobels are awarded for such contributions to the republic of letters. For Gore Vidal, it was Howard Austen, his longtime companion, who died on September 22, 2003, in Los Angeles of brain cancer at age seventy-four.

Unsung and largely invisible, such companions are the unacknowledged enablers of our great creators. In Austen's case, it was his commitment to the quotidian, to the mundane, to the heroism of everyday life that made him much more than a valet to one of American literature's great divas. For Austen, as for Vidal, rules were made to be broken. He was an original.

Gruff, plain-spoken, and quick-witted, Austen, a life-long chain-smoker, was just twenty-one, a recent graduate of New York University, when he met Vidal, anonymously, at New York's Everard Baths on Labor Day 1950. Red-haired and freckle-faced, Austen worked by day for an advertising agency, Lever Brothers, and by night yearned to become a pop singer. He would go on to become a stage manager for Broadway shows in the 1950s and 1960s. He also dabbled in pictures, assisting the casting of *To Kill a Mockingbird*. He had a talent for many things but reserved his genius for friendship.

His steadfast companionship of half a century to Gore Vidal was a marvel to all who knew him. Friends often wondered how the couple had managed to keep alive so vital a relationship over so long a time. Vidal was in the habit of quipping, "Simple. Like so many old marriages, no sex." Vidal, whose candor was legendary, wasn't joking. After all, the compact they had struck meant that Austen juggled the couple's complicated financial affairs, travel arrangements, and housing needs in Hollywood and Ravello, Italy, thus permitting Gore a degree of solitude necessary to a writer of astonishing productivity and ambition.

Three years before Austen's death, I had lunch with Vidal at the Polo Lounge at the Beverly Hills Hotel. Midway through lunch, Austen arrived, sweating profusely, clutching a portable Olivetti typewriter in each hand. When he had caught his breath, he complained bitterly of having had to search high and low all over L.A. to find for Vidal the preferred writing instrument, now rendered obsolete by the arrival of warp-speed computers. He had managed, he claimed, to buy the Olivettis in East L.A. from *cholos* who ran a barely profitable racket by trafficking in endangered industrial species. He made it sound like a big-bucks drug deal.

It is said that, from time to time over the decades of their life together, Austen, sitting either in their home on Outpost Drive in Hollywood or in their palazzo in Ravello, would, with a sweep of his arm, gesture toward the art hanging on the walls and the various possessions gathered over a lifetime of travel and collecting, and say (with a mischievous gleam in his eye), "You know, Gore, after you're gone, all this will be mine." On one occasion, Gore is said to have replied, "Yes, Howard, that's true, but no one will call."

Gore didn't count on Austen going first. He would outlive Howard by nearly a decade. And for those many years the Great Gore sat alone, the phone ringing, but Howard no longer there to answer for him.

[2022]

Scallops with Jackie

J ACQUELINE KENNEDY ONASSIS will be remembered by most Americans as the remarkable First Lady she was: elegant, beautiful, stoic. By any measure she was a heroic woman, and the trajectory of her life compels our respect. I shall remember her, however, less for her public persona than for her private accomplishments, first and foremost as an editor for many years at Doubleday. For it was in that rather invisible capacity that the republic of letters had a most passionate tribune.

I first met Jackie, as she insisted I call her, soon after I became executive editor of Doubleday in the fall of 1989. One day, she asked me to meet with her in her office. She wanted to know what books I was reading and what books I might suggest she read. Her voice was a beguiling rush of breath as we spoke of favorite authors, the sorry state of literacy in America, the decline of generosity in the country's political culture.

I was charmed. The most famous woman in the world was utterly without pretension, her commitment to ideas and culture serious and sincere. This was a side unknown to most people, despite the best efforts of the tabloid press to pruriently expose every aspect of this very private woman. But, as ever, Jackie—as she had so indelibly demonstrated in the aftermath of John F. Kennedy's assassination in 1963—conducted herself with consummate grace and dignity. Except for a brief interview given to the editor of *Publisher's Weekly*, she never spoke to the press. But for authors and the book-besotted, she had all the time in the world.

Her interests were eclectic; I envied her range. Among the books she edited were the enormously successful *Moonwalk* by Michael Jackson, *The Empire of the Czar: A Journey through Eternal Russia* by the nineteenth-century French aristocrat the Marquis de Custine, *The Diary of a Napoleonic Foot Soldier* by Jakob Walter ("the only account," she wrote me, "of a common soldier in the Napoleonic wars"), and *I Remember Balanchine*, a biography of one of the greatest artists of the twentieth century. Her taste, dedication, and commercial savvy commanded respect from her colleagues. I saw a throughline in the books she had acquired and edited. She concentrated on works by dancers, on Hollywood, on courtly life, and on myth. Many of her books were about being the exotic bird in a gilded cage: the bird wants to escape but can't and so, over time, resigns itself to being always on view. I thought the books reflected her life—a life that had required remarkable self-discipline and rigor not to let the private woman become tainted by the public persona. They were about the rituals and ablutions necessary to perform in that gilded cage, as well as the almost superhuman compartmentalization needed to keep secrets. The most significant theme in the books she published was the hard work that went into the fashioning of a seemingly effortless, stylized outward appearance. The theme in her list was also a theme of her life.

One day at lunch, over scallop salads (of the four plump scallops on her plate, she ate only three), we talked shop. But as was usually the case with Jackie, we found ourselves plunged deeply into a dissection of the country's propensity toward violence, the fracturing of the social consensus, the erosion of citizenship. Suddenly, she turned to me, and putting a slender hand upon my arm, she said, "Tell me, Steve, where did it all go wrong?" She was silent for a moment and then answered her own question. "It was Vietnam, wasn't it?" I didn't disagree. And then we traced the slippery slope that somehow had led from Vietnam to the swaggering films of Arnold Schwarzenegger—movies she refused to see. "I loathe," she said, "everything he stands for."

In a later conversation, she asked what I was publishing. I mentioned a collection of the best of Murray Kempton ("Jack had loved reading him in the *New Republic*," she said) and a wonderfully inspiring biography of Nellie Bly, the early twentieth-century daredevil, reporter, and feminist. Like many people, Jackie dimly recalled the name as part of a popular ditty, nothing more. She was surprised to learn that, at one time, Nellie Bly was perhaps the most celebrated woman in America. Her feats of personal courage and social conscience were peerless. She was an extraordinary inventor of her own life.

Jackie sighed and said, "How remarkable, don't you think, to have lived such a life. It is how I would have liked to live my own."

[1996]

Reading L.A.

A MERICA IS, FAMOUSLY, the republic of reinvention, where peoples the world over have sought an escape from history, a new identity in a land of seemingly endless possibility. California is, as Susan Sontag has said, "America's America," and Los Angeles has for more than one hundred years been a terminus, the destination of desire. Despite its notorious reputation for making a fetish of the body and eschewing the life of the mind, Los Angeles has been a magnet for writers. Hometown for some, refuge for others, it is both a place and a sensibility whose literature reflects a range of affection and disdain among writers who have found here what Carey McWilliams discovered more than half a century ago: a "curious amalgam of all America, of all states, of all peoples and cultures of America."

Writing Los Angeles, edited by David L. Ulin and published by the Library of America, is a nearly nine-hundred-page anthology that, like the city it seeks to represent, is both multifaceted and immense. It offers a panoramic view of a diverse and sprawling literary landscape, featuring brief chronological selections from the work of nearly eighty writers who have sought over the last century or so to make sense of the improbable megalopolis Mike Davis memorably called the "city of quartz," bright, hard, opaque. Ulin has done a masterful job choosing some of the more compelling efforts to evoke a city whose essence has proved maddeningly elusive for most of the writers who found themselves in Los Angeles. Ulin inclines toward many of the usual suspects, from Nathanael West to Raymond Chandler and Joan Didion, whose L.A. is by now so firmly lodged in the frontal lobe of popular imagination that it is all but impossible to experience the city as anything other than a mashup of clichés. Other familiar authors include John Fante, John Rechy, Chester Himes, Christopher Isherwood, Ray Bradbury, Upton Sinclair, Tom Wolfe, Reyner Banham, Gavin Lambert, Wanda Coleman, Carolyn See, Walter Mosley, James Ellroy, and D. J. Waldie. Ulin's compendium is not comprehensive. How could it be? The literary history of Los Angeles is too unruly and rich to be fully represented and enclosed completely within the grid of its latitude and longitude. To those he has left out—both the living and the dead—he offers his regrets.

There are at least two ways to read this Rosetta stone. One is to test one's own experience of L.A. against the reactions of its various writers, to assess where one agrees or disagrees, where they seem to get it right and where they have got it wrong. A second more suggestive (and challenging) approach is to imagine you are a reader who has never visited or lived in L.A., whose only encounter with the city is through the pages of this book, to treat it as if it were a novel written by multiple authors. Read this way, it gives rise to several questions: What is the tale that is told? What is the nature of its main character—the city itself? What changes does it undergo over time? And what, if any, is the moral of the story?

"Cities, like dreams, are made of desires and fears," Italo Calvino wrote in *Invisible Cities*. Nowhere is that truer than in Los Angeles, a city whose very founding and survival rebuke the notion that geography is destiny. For, unlike other cities, Los Angeles is entirely an act of will. It doesn't thrive at the confluence of rivers, or at the mouth of a natural harbor, or in a verdant plain made bountiful by plentiful rainfall. On the contrary, it is, observes John McPhee, "a metropolis that exists in a semidesert, imports water three hundred miles, has inveterate flash floods, is at the grinding edges of two tectonic plates, and has a microclimate tenacious of noxious oxides." To put it another way, Los Angeles has no right to exist. And yet, against all odds, it does.

From the beginning, its chief seduction was the obliteration of the past, the manufacture of desire, and the promise of redemption. Its siren call was most clearly heard through movies, of course. Movies made Los Angeles a virtual destination for people everywhere, projecting images of both a glittering Arcadia and a dark underbelly of anomie and murderous suffocation. But it wasn't only the movies, as *Writing Los Angeles* reveals. Novelists and journalists played their parts, by turns swept away, astonished, and appalled by the spectacle that was L.A. Land speculators, oil men, railroad tycoons, religious cranks, hucksters, and grifters of every stripe combined to make of Los Angeles a beacon for ordinary Americans who sought to liberate themselves from the stifling confinements and corruptions of the industrial East, to flee the idiocies of the rural life, and to renew themselves in a sun-kissed land where they might yet stumble upon the secret of life in their sunset years.

No longer hostage to the past, these immigrants found themselves in free fall. For many—Christopher Isherwood and David Hockney, for instance—the experience was intoxicating. No longer bound by the claustrophobic class and sex constraints of their native England, they found L.A. to be a city of exhilarating velocity and possibility. "Within a week of arriving there in this strange big city," Hockney recalls, "not knowing a soul, I'd passed the driving test, bought a car, driven to Las Vegas and won some money, got myself a studio, started painting, all in a week. And I thought, it's just how I imagined it would be." By contrast, for many Germans fleeing the Nazi conquest of Europe, living in Los Angeles was, as Bertolt Brecht put it, an "exile in paradise." In his bitter and brilliant Hollywood poem cycle, Brecht is at pains to denounce the manifold hypocrisies of the place, the terror lurking behind its shallow smiling exterior: "Alas, the lovely garden, placed high above the coast / Is built on crumbling rock. Landslides / Drag parts of it into the depths without warning." The whole city sought to evade what Brecht called the "stink of greed and poverty." He knew what many other writers had also discovered: Los Angeles is a world unto itself—a mythic city of both abundant promise and tragic disappointment, a city precariously perched on the edge of a continent, a golden mirage of Edenic prosperity that barely conceals a darker edge, an apocalyptic fault line of class and racial tension that splinters its subterranean vaults, threatening its otherwise relentlessly sunny disposition with the specter of disaster.

Los Angeles, on the evidence provided by the authors in *Writing Los Angeles*, is a city that has yet to make up its mind about what it wants to be when it grows up. The one thing it knows for certain is that it wants to get there fast. What emerges in *Writing Los Angeles* is a magical city of the imagination that is as complex, dynamic, and familiar as the real city of palm trees with "scrawny fronds like broken pinwheels," in the words of Robert Towne, who, like others, remembers growing up with "the Santa Anas progressively drying the city into sand and summer smells" and the "smell of pepper trees mentholated more and more by eucalyptus." That more innocent Los Angeles is largely gone, pulverized by the hammer wielded by the present upon the past in its remorseless quest to make way for the radiant future.

No single anthology, however thoughtfully and artfully assembled (as *Writing Los Angeles* surely is), can fully contain that drama. This reader misses, for example, the spice of a number of authors who have written about L.A. with wit and insight: Kate Braverman (*Lithium for Medea*), David Rieff (*Los Angeles: Capital of the Third World*), T. C. Boyle (*The Tortilla Curtain*), Sandro Meallet (*Edgewater Angels*), Yxta Maya Murray (*Locas*), Norman Klein (*The History of Forgetting: Los Angeles and the Erasure of Memory*), Richard Rayner (*Los Angeles Without a Map*), Kem Nunn (*Pomona Queen*), Bret Easton Ellis (*Less Than Zero*), Héctor Tobar (*The Tattooed Soldier*), Susan Straight (*Highwire Moon*), Bruce Wagner (*I'll Let You Go*), virtually any of the novels of Michael Connelly and Robert Crais, as well as extracts from the autobiographical writings of Agnes De Mille, Arthur Miller, and Michael Korda. All such lists are inherently subjective, and every reader will have his or her own favorites. (Ulin himself put several important contemporary L.A. writers into an earlier volume titled *Another City: Writing from Los Angeles*, published by City Lights Books.) The best map to Los Angeles is the one each reader creates by virtue of his or her own reading. Each of us is the cartographer of our own literary discoveries.

[2002]

Chicago Agonistes

WHY CONTINUE TO READ newspapers? After all, newspapers are losing circulation at precipitous rates, giving rise to fears that they may not survive long enough to write their own obituaries. Cutbacks, buyouts, and layoffs are widespread, affecting many of America's most prestigious newspapers, including the *New York Times*, the *Boston Globe*, the *Philadelphia Inquirer*, the *Chicago Tribune*, the *San Francisco Chronicle*, and the *Los Angeles Times*, where it was recently announced that the paper faced an eight percent reduction in its editorial staff. Morale plummets, anxiety mounts.

The growing maturity of the internet and the explosion of the blogosphere suggest that newspapers' demise is inexorable. A perfect storm of technological advances appears to make newspapers fit for the study less of schools of journalism than departments of anthropology. The virtual world is incontestably nimbler and more democratic. It permits a chorus of diverse voices that newspapers can't hope to replicate, if only for reasons of space. Why remain loyal to a medium that every day seems increasingly anachronistic?

Less heralded amid the boosterism of the current moment is the way the World Wide Web offers a portal through which new readers can access the old media more efficiently than ever before. No longer is geography fate. Millions now read reportage online that previously had to land with a dull thud on one's driveway. The killing paradox is that technology has gained for newspapers millions of new readers without finding a way of significantly boosting advertising revenue. Internet devotees trumpet its virtues while refusing to concede that old-fashioned newspapers supply the reporting without which the blogosphere would simply be a virtual balloon filled entirely with hot air. The internet exploits the hard-won authority of traditional news-gathering institutions without offering such perceived dinosaurs a way of avoiding extinction. This is the unacknowledged debt the future owes to a past it strives to vanquish.

Nor is it generally recognized that our best newspapers have been spawning grounds for reporters and editors who know that shoe leather is a prerequisite for discovering how we live the way we do. It is called reporting. It is time consuming and often expensive. It is hard work. It prizes fact over rumor. The internet, by contrast, is a medium that considers one's first thought as one's best thought. In an age of epistemological relativism, opinion, no matter how far-fetched, is thought by many to have the same weight as fact. The internet trades in rumor, exalts snark, prefers rage to reflection. Yet a handful of America's best newspapers have built over the decades deserved reputations and gained the loyalty of readers by remaining hostage not to partisan purposes but rather to that elusive virtue called truth. It was always, of course, a humanly fraught enterprise, filled with pitfalls of ideological and advertising pressures. But the best newspapers sought to resist such dangers, seeking against the odds to navigate a path that would earn them the respect of readers even while incurring the occasional wrath of advertisers, not to mention the displeasure of their owners.

Today, most newspapers are no longer the province of the private barons who owned the press to further their dynastic and civic ambitions. (It would be a mistake, of course, to romanticize the past—one has only to remember the corruptions and self-serving use of the media by such moguls as William Randolph Hearst and Harrison Gray Otis, whose newspapers were sterling examples of what was rightly disparaged as "yellow journalism.") Still, the warp-speed transformation of America's newspapers over the last twenty-five years or so has arguably resulted in a profession that seems increasingly enfeebled, less able than ever before to fulfill its inherent mandate of reporting the news without fear or favor.

How this happened is well told in a shelf full of books, including Ben Bagdikian's prescient *The Media Monopoly* (1983) and Jim Squires's eye-popping memoir *Read All about It: The Corporate Takeover of America's Newspapers* (1993). Squires, the former editor of the *Chicago Tribune*, knew what he was talking about. He'd fought a tough but ultimately losing battle with his newspaper's corporate bosses. Since his book's publication more than ten years ago, things have only gotten worse. Today, many newspapers are owned by private hedge funds whose vampiric commitment to short-term profits trumps whatever conceit they may privately embrace regarding the practice of journalism. Distant owners treat their newspapers much like nineteenth-century imperialists bent on extracting the last shekel out of faraway colonies whose natural resources were to be plundered and then abandoned. Conglomeration intensifies, greed grows, journalism withers.

The *Los Angeles Times* offers an instructive example. It finds itself beset by three separate if overlapping crises: the first is the general crisis of confidence confronted by the entire profession as it grapples with technological change that dramatically alters the way news is delivered; the second is the crisis occasioned by the consequences of the paper's acquisition by the Chicago-based Tribune Co., and the third is the crisis of identity caused by the changing demographics and political economy of its circulation area in Southern California, a region of some eighteen million people that stretches from San Diego in the south to Santa Barbara in the north. These crises have combined to produce near-desperate measures on the part of the paper's owners and managers. The resulting spectacle is exemplary.

The paper's management recently announced it would eliminate eight percent of its editorial staff (some eighty-five positions), through a combination of buyouts and layoffs. This comes on the heels of years of steady downsizing. To be fair, not all of it is to be laid at the door of Tribune Co., the paper's current owner, which bought Times Mirror Co. for $8.3 billion in 2000. The problems that plague the paper are well known. Ken Auletta in a recent report in the *New Yorker* offered a detailed and revealing look at how the paper's editors are seeking to meet its corporate owners' expectations. Tribune Co. insists that the paper deliver annual operating profit margins nearer twenty-five or twenty-six percent than its more customary return of around fifteen or sixteen percent. (In 2004, according to Auletta, the paper reaped an operating profit margin of about twenty percent, a figure that failed to satisfy the Chicago moneymen.) The paper's top managers and editors are determined to do so or die trying. But before they expire, the paper they seek to resuscitate may well be reduced to a husk of its former self. The prospect is not pretty.

Tribune Co. faces a nearly insurmountable challenge. According to some observers, Tribune overpaid the Chandler family—which holds three seats on Tribune's twelve-member board of directors. (It should be noted that the three representatives of the Chandler family who occupy these seats are precisely those whom one former longtime insider at the paper characterizes as "the Bircherite faction of the family, the folks who thought Otis [Chandler, publisher from 1960 to 1980 and credited with the paper's widely admired and prosperous professionalization] was a pinko.") Tribune recently was ordered to pay the IRS back taxes and interest totaling nearly $1 billion stemming from a transaction inherited from the discredited regime of Mark Willes and Kathryn Downing, the former heads, respectively, of Times Mirror Co. and the *Los Angeles Times*, its flagship newspaper. The hoped-for benefits of cobbling together a de facto national newspaper chain—the *Orlando Sentinel*, *Newsday*, the *Hartford Courant*, the *Chicago Tribune*, and the *Los Angeles Times*—in order to attract advertising in America's most promising (and populated) markets has proved elusive. The presumed advantages to be afforded by cross-ownership of a local television station (KTLA-TV) and a major metropolitan newspaper haven't occurred. Indeed, whether the Federal Communications Commission will permit Tribune to consolidate its ownership of the region's largest newspaper and a significant broadcast medium is in doubt.

Meanwhile, Tribune's stock price continues to tumble. Some Wall Street insiders speculate that the price the various parts of the company might fetch, were they to be sold separately, is a sum considerably greater than the worth of the company if left intact. The company appears to be so beleaguered that Dennis FitzSimons, Tribune's CEO, is clinging by his fingernails to his own job, according to John Carroll, a former top editor of the *Los Angeles Times*. Strategies of synergy—that fool's gold of modern corporate hocus-pocus—have come a cropper.

There is also an unquantifiable but important cultural factor: there is a strong feeling within the newsroom at the *Los Angeles Times* that its Chicago masters regard Los Angeles as an alien planet whose denizens are made of different DNA. Chicago's faint and unenthusiastic recognition of the thirteen Pulitzers the paper was awarded during the five years that John Carroll was its editor is a wound that refuses to heal. It's almost as if Mars had conquered Jupiter, but somehow, much to the Martians' bafflement, Jupiter still exercises a larger gravitational pull and looms still brighter in the heavens above. More than one high official of the paper has remarked on the odd but palpable admixture of resentment and envy the paper's Midwestern owners evince when they are in the presence of their West Coast underlings.

As if this weren't enough, the *Los Angeles Times* has for nearly a quarter century faced a set of constraining factors unique to its circulation area that has bedeviled all previous management teams at the paper. These problems antedate Tribune's acquisition in the spring of 2000, chief among them the shifting demographic and economic makeup of the region. Despite the vast reams of internal marketing surveys the paper has routinely commissioned over the years, the *Times* today seems no longer to know who its readers are, much less how to talk to them. Today the paper is ironically an almost perfect reflection of the city it purports to cover: neither really knows what it wants to be when it grows up. Under Otis Chandler, the paper yearned to compete with the *Washington Post* and the *New York Times*. The expansion of its reportorial staff, the opening of dozens of foreign bureaus, the careful attention to accuracy, and the purging of the paper's traditional biased tone raised its stature and catapulted it to the front ranks of America's newspapers. The paper's ascendance coincided with the postwar boom in Southern California's own aspirations. For years, the dream of endless prosperity was synonymous with the California dream. And in the *Los Angeles Times*, many readers could see a faithful reflection of their sunniest hopes about the golden future.

The collapse of the Cold War and the military-industrial complex that had fueled so much of Southern California's economy, providing jobs and patronage; the bitter ethnic divisions that exploded into view during the riots over the Rodney King affair; the rise of a self-absorbed *nouveau riche* Hollywood elite, many of whose members seemed curiously aloof from the city in which they had made their considerable fortunes; together with the growing political clout of the swelling Latino population and the staggering numbers of Asians that flooded into the region were among the more salient factors that combined to hollow out the core readership of white Midwesterners that had been the backbone of the *Los Angeles Times*. Ever since, the paper has been undergoing a slow-motion nervous breakdown, its cultural hegemony broken, its political clout diminished, and the men in charge left bewildered and bereft. The industry they serve is challenged by technologies that render increasingly obsolete and archaic the very means by which news is delivered and advertisers satisfied. And the class for which the paper had traditionally served as tribune is gone, having been replaced by a clique of investors and lobbyists whose interests the paper seems only fitfully interested in aggressively investigating. To be sure, if the talented and ambitious Dean Baquet, the paper's current editor, is permitted to have his way, that may well change, provided, of course, that he has enough strength of character and staff left to do a proper job. His minders, however, are outsiders with no stake in the city's civic future. There is no consensus within the paper as to whom it represents or what, if anything, it should stand for. It has no voice; it lacks gravitas.

Efforts to staunch the hemorrhage of readers grow steadily desperate. The paper's managers oscillate between embracing a strategy that recognizes that the local went global years ago and a strategy that makes a fetish of the local. Today's editors, under pressure from Tribune to arrive at an allegedly closer emotional bond with the paper's prospective readers, have raised the notion of the local to a near dogma. Whatever one thought, for example, of Michael Kinsley's brief-lived efforts to reinvent the editorial and opinion pages of the *Times*, the reasons advanced for his ouster were provincial in character. He was accused of an unseemly devotion to national and international questions and was said to be insufficiently attentive to local and regional issues. It is an irony, of course, that the paper's current managers are almost all outsiders whose experience of and familiarity with Los Angeles prior to being hired by the paper was, to say the least, nearly nonexistent.

The paper's managers have nonetheless declared, in so many words, their intention of making the paper the best possible local paper they can. By doing so, they hope to reverse the circulation slide and to make good on the mantra that has been routinely recited by nearly all previous management teams and which is embodied in the paper's recent but now-abandoned radio advertising jingle: "Find yourself in the *Times*." The notion here is that the paper ought to be a mirror that reflects readers' interests, without which putative subscribers will turn elsewhere for the "emotional bond" that is said by the paper's internal marketing gurus to be the adhesive that binds readers to the paper.

(A better metaphor might have been to liken the newspaper to a telescope: Seen through one end, the device makes visible the invisible, much as discovering a new planet, heretofore unseen by the naked eye, transforms the sense of our place in the cosmos. Or, alternatively, when looked through the other end, the telescope makes the familiar appear strange by throwing the ubiquitous into sharp and distant relief. Together, the double perspectives afforded by looking through both ends make possible a deeper encounter with a more complex reality. This is arguably a better, more accurate metaphor for what journalism does at its best.)

How the notion of newspaper-as-mirror can be success-fully applied at the *Los Angeles Times* at a moment when long-time editorial writers like Sergio Muñoz (former editor of the Spanish-language *La Opinión* and a man widely admired among a broad swath of a Latino community whose members form about a quarter of the paper's readership) are permitted to depart, is puzzling. Others who are leaving include Bill Stall, who was awarded a Pulitzer Prize for editorial writing in 2004, and Kevin Thomas, whose deep knowledge of and pas-sion for movies and championing of independent films and near-Stakhanovite capacity for writing daily stories is legend-ary. They will be missed. So too will longtime editors and writ-ers Claudia Luther and Myrna Oliver, who virtually invented the writing of serious obituaries at the paper. This accom-plishment was something of a heresy at a newspaper that for years seemed reluctant even to note the dead, so firmly was the idea of Los Angeles as an Arcadia for the forever young so well established. The departure of Larry Stammer, the paper's religion correspondent, is also regrettable. These gifted men and women are among the paper's stalwarts who have stoi-cally contributed over the decades to the paper's considerable reputation.

Moreover, their exodus occurs in the context of Tribune's earlier shutdown of the paper's numerous zoned editions, which were designed precisely to appeal to local constitu-encies, not to mention the wholesale gutting of the Orange County edition that saw the loss of scores of jobs.

It is hard to avoid the conclusion that the paper, in a frenetic effort to reinvent itself under the suffocating pressure of its

Chicago overseers, is jettisoning a patrimony of journalistic excellence painstakingly built up over the years at great cost. It is, of course, easier to dismantle than it is to build. A former editor of the paper recently said that it would be naive to think that current publisher Jeff Johnson is calling the shots on his own. The suggestion, if true, reported on LA Observed that Johnson killed an editorial decrying GM's slashing of thirty thousand jobs is ominous. Particularly as it comes in the wake of former chief editor John Carroll's refusal to buckle under GM's pressure when it pulled its advertising from the *Los Angeles Times* in response to a critical column written by Dan Neil, the paper's Pulitzer Prize–winning automobile critic.

None of this should surprise. After all, the men who control the paper's fiscal destiny have never shown any special commitment to Los Angeles, regarding it with all the unbridled avariciousness and ill-concealed contempt that Cortés displayed toward Montezuma and his benighted Aztecs. As John Carroll recently told me, "You've no idea how fast these folks are strip-mining the place. They've already carted away millions of dollars. Their efforts to attract advertising and grow the business have come to nothing. They're Midwestern white men obsessed with only two things: the Chicago Cubs and accounting. They care nothing for journalism. They are Philistines."

When told of this judgment, Jim Squires said, "Philistines is a perfect characterization for that crowd, only the Philistines as a group were smarter. You cannot imagine how intellectually inferior three of the last four chairmen of Tribune Co. were." He compared them to George Bush, remarking that they were "complete frauds as leaders and executives." "Chicago," he said, "is a street-smart town. Cops, crooks, restaurateurs, developers, writers—they are bold and wily. The business executives, on the other hand, are weak and moronic."

Given the persistent floundering at the *Los Angeles Times*, the question must be asked: Are there any adults left minding the store?

[2005]

Good-bye to All That

THE HEALTH OF A SOCIETY is always best measured by how it treats its weakest and most vulnerable citizens. The same test may be usefully applied to America's beleaguered newspapers. Set against the general loss of confidence afflicting the profession is the crisis confronting those few newspapers that bother to regularly review books. Over the past year, and with alarming speed, newspapers across the country have been cutting back their book coverage and, in some instances, abandoning the beat entirely. At a time when newspaper owners feel themselves and the institutions over which they preside to be under siege from newer technologies and the relentless Wall Street pressure to pump profits at ever-higher margins, book coverage is among the first beats to be scaled back or phased out. Today, such coverage is thought by many newspaper managers to be inessential and, worse, a money loser.

Yet a close look at the history of how America's newspapers have treated books as news suggests that while the drop in such coverage is precipitous, it is not altogether recent. In the fall of 2000, Charles McGrath, then editor of the *New York Times Book Review*, the nation's preeminent newspaper book section by virtue of longevity, geography, ambition, circulation, and staff, was already lamenting the steady shrinkage of book coverage. "A lot of papers have either dropped book coverage or dumbed it way down to commercial stuff. The newsweeklies, which used to cover books regularly, don't any longer," McGrath told a *Times* insert profiling the *Book Review*. Indeed, the following April, the *San Francisco Chronicle* folded its book section into its Sunday Datebook of arts and cultural coverage. The move was greeted with dismay by many readers. After six months of public protest—and after newspaper focus groups indicated the book section enjoyed a substantial readership—it was reinstated as a stand-alone section. (Five years later, it would lose two pages in a cost-cutting move that reduced the section, now a broadsheet, by a third to just four pages.) In 2001, the *Boston Globe* merged its book review and commentary pages. Today, the *New York Times Book Review* averages thirty-two to thirty-six tabloid pages, a steep decline from the forty-four pages it averaged in 1985.

That book coverage is disappearing is not news. What is news is the current pace of the erosion in coverage, as well as the fear that an unbearable cultural threshold has been crossed: whether the book beat should exist at all is now, apparently, a legitimate question. Jobs, book sections, and pages are vanishing at a rate rivaled only by the degree to which entire species are being rendered extinct in the Amazonian rain forest. Last spring, Teresa Weaver, the *Atlanta Journal-Constitution*'s longtime and well-regarded book editor, was shunted aside, her original book reviews largely replaced with wire copy. The paper's editor said without shame or chagrin that the move was part of a more general intent to reconfigure the newspaper's coverage of arts, including music and dance. Meanwhile, readers of the *Dallas Morning News* found themselves without a full-time book critic when Jerome Weeks, who had filled the role since 1996, accepted a buyout offer amid a vast restructuring of the paper.

Other papers, including the Raleigh *News & Observer*, the *Orlando Sentinel*, and the *Cleveland Plain Dealer*, also eliminated the book editor's position or cut coverage. The *Chicago Tribune* decided to move its book pages to Saturday, the least read day of the week. Its book editor, Elizabeth Taylor, ever the optimist, said that the very slimness of the Saturday edition would mean that its few pages would loom larger in the eyes of readers and, with any luck, in the esteem of potential advertisers. In June, the *San Diego Union-Tribune* killed its decade-old, stand-alone book section, opting instead to move book reviews into its arts pages. And earlier this year, the *Los Angeles Times*, in a significant retreat from the ambitions that prompted the creation of its weekly *Book Review* in 1975, decided to cut its twelve-page Sunday tabloid section by two pages and graft the remaining stump to its revamped Sunday opinion section. The press release announcing the change sought to allay readers' concerns by proclaiming the paper's intent to expand online coverage (a task made more difficult by the paper's reluctance, so far, to add staff, but instead to increase the burden on the *Review*'s editor and subeditors). The paper also promised to increase the number and prominence of illustrations and photographs, neglecting to note that doing so would further reduce the space allotted for actual words.

For many writers, this threat to the nation's delicate ecology of literary and cultural life is cause for considerable alarm. Last spring, the novelist Richard Ford decried the disappearance of book reviews. Michael Connelly, an ex-*Los Angeles Times* reporter and now a bestselling mystery writer, denounced the contraction of his former paper's book section. Salman Rushdie, in a rare public appearance, went on the *Colbert Report* to voice his displeasure. Writers and readers alike signed petitions circulated by the National Book Critics Circle, hoping to reverse the trend. America's newspapers, they argued, must not be permitted to regard the coverage of books as a luxury to be tossed aside. A widespread cultural and political illiteracy is abetted by newspapers that no longer review books, they charged.

Others, equally passionate, dismiss these concerns as exaggerations, the overblown reaction of latter-day Luddites vainly resisting the new world order now upon us. They foresee—indeed, welcome—an inevitable if difficult adaptation and seek to free themselves of the nostalgia for a past that never was. Newspapers, in this view, are at long last taking steps, however painful, toward a revivified cultural blossoming. To listen to the avatars of the New Information Age, digital technology will democratize debate, empowering those whose opinions have been marginalized by—or, worse, shut out of—mainstream media, and unleash a new era of book chat and book commerce.

The predicament facing newspaper book reviews is best understood against the backdrop of several overlapping and contending crises: the first is the general challenge confronting America's newspapers of adapting to the new digital and electronic technologies that are increasingly absorbing advertising dollars, wooing readers away from newspapers, and undercutting profit margins; the second is the profound structural transformation roiling the entire book publishing and bookselling industry in an age of conglomeration and digitization; and the third and most troubling crisis is the sea change in the culture of literacy itself, the degree to which our overwhelmingly fast and visually furious culture renders serious reading increasingly irrelevant, hollowing out the habits of attention indispensable for absorbing long-form narrative and the following of sustained argument.

These crises, taken together, have profound implications, not least for the effort to create an informed citizenry necessary for a thriving democracy. It would be hard to overestimate the importance in these matters of how books are reported upon and discussed. The moral and cultural imperative is plain, but there may also be a much-overlooked commercial opportunity for newspapers waiting to be seized.

A harsher truth may lurk behind the headlines as well: book coverage is not only meager but shockingly mediocre. The pabulum that passes for most reviews is an insult to the intelligence of most readers. One is tempted to say, perversely, that its disappearance from the pages of America's newspapers is arguably cause for celebration.

In the nine years that I was privileged to preside over the *Los Angeles Times Book Review* (from 1996 to 2005), I grappled with many of these issues. I had a front-row seat at the increasingly contested intersection of culture and commerce. I regularly dealt with such vexing questions as how to balance the reporting of both so-called high and low culture, how to gain more readers and advertisers, how to improve and expand book coverage throughout the pages of the newspaper. It was more than a spectator sport. I was deeply enmeshed in this unfolding drama and had a large stake in its outcome. After all, I had worked for five years as a journalist in the late seventies and early eighties as deputy editor of the paper's Sunday opinion section and daily op-ed page. I left to join the *New Republic*, where I ran its publishing imprint, a joint venture first with Henry Holt and then with Basic Books, departing three years later to become editorial director and publisher of the Noonday Press and Hill and Wang, both divisions of Farrar, Straus and Giroux. In 1990 I was appointed editorial director of Times Books, and it was there, in my eleventh-floor Manhattan office, one sweltering day in August 1996, that I received a telephone call from my old alma mater—the *Los Angeles Times* —wondering if I'd return as the paper's literary editor.

I felt I had no time to waste; life was short and literature long. Moreover, in a nation of nearly three hundred million people, you were lucky at most papers to get a column, or a half page devoted to book reviews, a virtual ghetto that I had long thought was a betrayal of journalism's obligation to bring before its readers the news from elsewhere. Only a handful of America's papers deemed the beat important enough to dedicate an entire Sunday section to it, preeminently the *New York Times*, the *Washington Post,* and the *Los Angeles Times*. The *New York Times*, even after its reduction to thirty-six pages, dwarfed the others. It was the paper to beat. My aim was to be three times as good in one-third the space: to boost the nutritive value of each review and deliver to readers a section on Sunday that would be remembered on Monday.

I wanted to edit the *Los Angeles Times Book Review* in such a way—and with such zeal—that readers might feel the heat of genuine passion for books and ideas in its few pages, which were guaranteed by the paper's top editors at twelve tabloid-sized pages but occasionally went up to sixteen, depending on ad revenue (of which there was barely a trickle) or sometimes on special occasions. Above all, I wanted to treat readers as adults, to shun the baby talk that passes for book chat in all too many of America's newspapers. I wanted to deliver a section aimed squarely and unabashedly at the word-addicted and the book-besotted. To do so, I knew I would have to edit, as Nadine Gordimer once enjoined authors to write, as if I were already posthumous—otherwise I would perhaps lack the necessary courage.

My greatest conceit was my intent to use my new post to answer a single question: Is serious criticism possible in a mass society? If it were possible in L.A., then it would be possible anywhere. I wanted the *Book Review* to cover books the way the paper's excellent sports section covered the Dodgers and the Lakers: with a consummate respect for ordinary readers' deep knowledge and obvious passion for the games and characters who played them. Analysis and coverage in the paper's sports pages were usually sophisticated, full of nuance, replete with often near-Talmudic disputation, vivid description, and sharp, often intemperate, opinion. Its editors neither condescended nor pandered to those of the paper's readers who didn't happen to love sports. No, this was a section aimed directly at fans, and it presumed a thoroughgoing familiarity with the world of sports. Like the *Book Review*, the sports section was nearly ad free and yet nowhere was the demand made that the section ought to gear its coverage to encourage advertising from the very teams its editors and reporters were charged with covering. The sports section, like most sections of the newspaper, if one were to have separately totaled up its costs, lost money. The same was true of the *Book Review*. Nor was the *Los Angeles Times* alone. This was the case at most of America's newspapers.

As I prepared to leave the precincts of book publishing for what I saw as simply another station in the kitchen, I discussed my move with Charles McGrath, who in 1994 had left the *New Yorker* to become editor of the *New York Times Book Review*. He surprised me by saying he rather envied me my new post, telling me that, unlike himself, I wouldn't have to try to cover the waterfront. The few pages given to book reviews in the *Los Angeles Times*, he said, would liberate me from having to provide a full-service consumer guide, which in any case he knew to be a hopeless, even Sisyphean, endeavor.

An unsentimental corollary to his sobriety was presented to me some days later by Joan Didion and her husband, the late John Gregory Dunne. What advice did they have as I prepared to return to my old paper and their former hometown? Didion extended her arm and gripping my forearm with steel in her fingers, said, "Just review the good books." I laughed, and she added, "No, I mean something quite specific: Just because a writer lives in zip code 90210 doesn't mean you have to pay attention. If the work is good, of course, but if it's second-rate, or worse, don't give it the time of day. To do otherwise is a formula for mediocrity, for the provincialization of the *Book Review*."

She was preaching to the converted. If I had a bias— and I did—it was toward paying attention to the unknown, the neglected, the small but worthy (and all-too-often invisible) authors whose work readers would otherwise not have heard about. Books that had already jumped onto the bestseller lists by writers who had become so-called brand names, and who benefited from the enormous publicity machines marshaled on their behalf by established publishers, seemed beside the point. Why bring to readers news they'd already heard?

Besides, review space at the *Los Angeles Times*, as at all other papers, was tight, making hard choices inescapable. Decisions about which books to review were inherently subjective. Given the avalanche of titles that publishers daily sent my way (nearly one thousand a week), it would be triage every day. Between the Sunday *Book Review* and the reviews that appeared in the daily paper, we had room enough to note or review only about twelve hundred books annually (the *New York Times*, by contrast, reviews about three times that number). I would simply have to rely upon my own literary acumen and taste, cross my fingers, and hope that enough of the newspaper's readers would find in themselves an echo of my own enthusiasms. I would try to honor what Mary Lou Williams, the jazz pianist and composer, said about her obligation to her audience and her art: "I . . . keep a little ahead of them, like a mirror that shows what will happen next."

My mission, I was told by Shelby Coffey III, then the paper's editor and the man who hired me, was to focus on books as news that stayed news—books whose pertinence was likely to remain fresh despite the passage of time. Reasonable people might reasonably differ, of course, on how best to do this. But doing it properly, we agreed, meant exercising both literary and journalistic judgment, spurning commercial pressures, eschewing the ostensibly popular in favor of work that would be of enduring worth—insofar, of course, that one can ever be sure of the future's verdict from the decidedly imperfect vantage point of the present. I knew this ambition would likely incur the unremitting hostility of the samurai of political correctness, whether of the right or the left, as well as the palpable disdain of newspaper editors who had convinced themselves that the way to win readers and improve circulation was to embrace the faux populism of the marketplace.

In this view, only the review (or book) that is immediately understood by the greatest number of readers can be permitted to see the light of day. Anything else smacks of "elitism." This is a coarse and pernicious dogma—a dogma that is at the center of the anti-intellectual tradition that is alive and well within America's newspapers. It is why most newspapers barely bother with reviews. And it is why most newspaper reviews are not worth reading. I sought to subvert this dogma. Of course, ideally I wanted what Otis Chandler in his heyday had wanted: mass and class. But if it came down to a choice between the two, I knew I'd go for class every time. In literary affairs, I was always a closet Leninist: better fewer, but better.

Leon Wieseltier, the *New Republic*'s longtime literary editor, has rightly observed that if "value is a function of scarcity," then "what is most scarce in our culture is long, thoughtful, patient, deliberate analysis of questions that do not have obvious or easy answers." He is among the few who have chosen to resist what he condemns as "the insane acceleration of everything," and prefers instead to embrace the enduring need for thought, for serious analysis, so necessary in an increasingly dizzying culture. Wieseltier knows that the fundamental idea at stake in a novel—in the criticism of culture generally—is the self-image of society: how it reasons with itself, describes itself, imagines itself. Nothing in the Eros of acceleration made possible by the digital revolution banishes the need for the rigor such self-reckoning requires. It is, as he has said, the obligation of cultural criticism—and is that too fancy a word for what ought to be everywhere present in, but is almost everywhere wholly absent from, the pages of our newspapers?—to bear down on what matters. It is a striking irony, as Wieseltier points out, that with the arrival of the internet, "a medium of communication with no limitations of physical space, everything on it has to be in six hundred words."

Wieseltier's high-minded sentiments recall the lofty ambitions of Margaret Fuller, literary editor of the *New York Tribune* in the mid-nineteenth century and the country's first full-time book reviewer. Fuller, too, saw books as "a medium for viewing all humanity, a core around which all knowledge, all experience, all science, all the ideal as well as all the practical in our nature could gather." She sought, she said, to tell "the whole truth, as well as nothing but the truth." Hers was a severe and sound standard—one that American journalism would only rarely seek to emulate.

For the most part, early newspaper book reviewing, where it was done at all, was a dreary affair. And discerning observers knew it. In a 1931 assessment of the state of book coverage, James Truslow Adams complained in the *Saturday Review of Literature* that "mass production journalism is doing much to lower the status of reviewing." Nearly thirty years later, little had occurred to revise that judgment. Elizabeth Hardwick's coruscating essay, "The Decline of Book Reviewing," appeared in *Harper's* magazine in October 1959. She called for "the great metropolitan publications" to welcome "the unusual, the difficult, the lengthy, the intransigent, and above all, the *interesting*." Her plea fell on deaf ears.

But soon she would have a chance to take matters into her own hands. Little more than three years later, during the New York newspaper strike begun in December 1962, Hardwick and her then husband, the poet Robert Lowell, would help found the *New York Review of Books*, whose first issue appeared in February 1963. Hardwick and her coconspirators, including Jason Epstein, founder of Anchor Books at Doubleday and an editor at Random House, and his then wife, Barbara, were fed up with the idea that books could be adequately discussed in reviews hardly longer in length than several haikus stitched together. To properly elucidate significant books one needed elbow room, as it were, to stretch out with an idea. One needed a certain rigor. What serious readers craved and what the editors of the *Review* would provide would be reviewers, often poets and novelists, scholars and historians, who had earned, as Hardwick put it, "the authority to compose a relevant examination of the themes that make up the dramas of current and past culture." Further, the editors of the *NYRB* proclaimed, in a credo published in the first issue, that they would not waste time or space "on books which are trivial in their intentions or venal in their effects, except occasionally to reduce a temporarily inflated reputation or to call attention to a fraud." The *NYRB* was intended as an exercise in literary hygiene.

The *NYRB*, alas, was a singular intervention in American letters, and its appearance did little to elevate the ossified and blinkered coverage of books in newspapers. The truth is that there never was a golden age of book reviewing in American newspapers. Space was always meager and the quality low. Nearly a quarter century ago, according to a 1984 study in the *Newspaper Research Journal*, the average American newspaper used three-quarters of a page to one page a week for book reviews. At the time, about fifty thousand books were published annually. (Today, it is more than three times that number.) The *New York Times*, the *Washington Post*, and the *Los Angeles Times* each reviewed about fifteen hundred to two thousand of them. Other major papers—the *Chicago Tribune*, the *Philadelphia Inquirer*, the *Boston Globe*, the *Miami Herald*— reviewed about six hundred to twelve hundred each. Most papers averaged far fewer reviews—about three hundred each. Only three papers thought such coverage warranted an entire, separate Sunday section.

In 1999, Jay Parini, a distinguished critic, poet, and novelist, issued a grim assessment of the state of contemporary newspaper book reviewing. "Evaluating books has fallen to ordinary, usually obscure, reviewers," he observed in the *Chronicle of Higher Education*. "Too often, the apparent slightness of the review leads inexperienced reviewers into swamps of self-indulgence from which they rarely emerge with glory." Moreover, the very brevity of most newspaper reviews "means one rarely has enough space to develop an idea or back up opinions with substantial argumentation. As a result, reviews are commonly shallow, full of unformed or ill-formulated thoughts, crude opinions, and unacknowledged prejudices." The result, Parini concluded, is all too often a mélange of "ill-considered opinion, ludicrously off-the-mark praise, and blame." How little newspaper book coverage had changed. Thirty-six years earlier, disgust with the same ubiquitous, thin gruel had prompted Edmund Wilson to declare in the second issue of the *New York Review of Books*, "The disappearance of the *Times* Sunday book section at the time of the printers' strike only made us realize it had never existed."

Mark Sarvas, among the more sophisticated of contemporary literary bloggers, whose lively site, the *Elegant Variation*, offers a compelling daily diet of discriminating enthusiasms and thoughtful book chat, recognizes the problem. In a post last spring about the fate of newspaper reviews, he wrote, "There's been an unspoken sense in this discussion that Book Review = Good. It doesn't always—there are plenty of mediocre to lousy reviewers out there, alienating (or at least boring) readers. . . . Too many reviews are dull, workmanlike book reports. And every newspaper covers the same dozen titles. . . . There's much talk about the thoughtful 'literary criticism' on offer in book reviews but you don't get much of that literary criticism in eight hundred fifty words, so can we stop kidding ourselves?" But neither does Sarvas find such criticism on the vast Democracy Wall of the internet, which he is otherwise at pains to promote. He confesses that, for him, the criticism that counts is to be found in the pages of such publications as the *New York Review of Books* or the pages of *Bookforum*.

What Sarvas is reluctant to concede but is too intelligent to deny is what Richard Schickel, the film critic for *Time* magazine, eloquently affirmed in a blunt riposte, published in the *Los Angeles Times* in May, to the "hairy-chested populism" promoted by the boosters of blogging: "Criticism—and its humble cousin, reviewing—is not a democratic activity. It is, or should be, an elite enterprise, ideally undertaken by individuals who bring something to the party beyond their hasty, instinctive opinions of a book (or any other cultural object). It is work that requires disciplined taste, historical and theoretical knowledge and a deep sense of the author's (or filmmaker's or painter's) entire body of work, among other qualities." Sure, two, three, many opinions, but let's all acknowledge a truth as simple as it is obvious: not all opinions are equal.

Moreover, the debate over how reviews are published—or, for that matter, the news more generally—is sterile. What counts is the nature and depth and authority of such coverage, as well as its availability to the widest possible audience. Whether readers find it on the web or on the printed page matters not at all. Content rules.

In the fall of 1996, as news of my appointment as editor of the *Los Angeles Times Book Review* was made public, I attended a reception and party at the New York Public Library to mark the centenary of the *New York Times Book Review*. One hundred years after Adolph Ochs started a separate book review supplement as one of his first acts after buying the *New*

York Times in 1896, his descendants gathered to toast a visionary who had done his utmost to ensure that his newspaper would be peerless far into the future as the indispensable chronicler of a city he believed destined to become the financial and cultural capital of the twentieth century.

As I greeted Arthur Sulzberger Jr., who had only recently been named publisher, succeeding his father, he congratulated me on my own new post. I drew him aside, thinking to take advantage of the opportunity to ask him whether the *New York Times Book Review*, the beneficiary of a disproportionate share of book publishing ads by virtue both of its location in the capital of American book publishing and its national distribution, had ever made any money. It had long been rumored in publishing circles that it did not. But who really knew? He looked at me evenly and said, "I think, Steve, someone in the family would have told me if it had." He then said that in the previous year, if one were to have added up the staff's collective salaries (there were then more than twenty full-time editors), the cost of health care, the combined expense of printing, production, and distribution, payments to contributors and illustrators, among other sundry expenses, the section had lost millions.

Readers of the *New York Times* have inarguably benefited from the enlightened views of the paper's owners and editors who have always understood the importance of providing readers with news of the most important and entertaining books being published in the country. They also regard the *Book Review* as something of a loss leader, appealing to the best educated and most prosperous of the paper's readers, many of whom they rightly presume will go wandering among the

Ralph Lauren ads in the money machine that is the paper's Sunday magazine. In his illuminating 1985 three-part series in the *Los Angeles Times* on how newspapers go about reviewing books, David Shaw, the paper's late Pulitzer Prize–winning media correspondent, quoted Mitchel Levitas, then the editor of the *New York Times Book Review*: "We lose money, and we always have, but I don't know how much."

At the time, Levitas's section at the *Times* had a staff of twenty-one, the *Washington Post* had four, and the *Los Angeles Times* made do with two full-time editors. Shaw reported that in the mid-1980s, the *Washington Post* was losing nearly $1 million a year on its Sunday book section. In 1985, the *San Francisco Chronicle* was expecting to lose just under a quarter million dollars on its weekly twelve tabloid pages devoted to books. Levitas's boss, Abe Rosenthal, then the executive editor of the *New York Times*, declared he neither knew nor cared if the *Book Review* lost money. "You can't expect a payoff on reviewing books any more than you can expect a payoff for covering foreign news," he told Shaw. Such a view seems a relic from the Pleistocene era.

I knew very well when I took the job at the *Los Angeles Times* that getting ad revenue from publishers was all but hopeless. I had had to make tough decisions as a publisher myself about where to place ads, and for most books, buying ads in the *Los Angeles Times* didn't make sense. The cost for a single full-page ad in its *Book Review* exceeded the entire advertising and promotional budgets for the vast majority of all books published. Given a choice between advertising in the *New York Times* and the *Los Angeles Times*, publishers invariably and sensibly went for the *New York Times*. After all, the *New York Times* made sure that more than seventy-five thousand copies of its Sunday *Book Review* were separately available in bookstores across the country. Individual subscribers accounted for another twenty-eight thousand copies. In an industry where fifty thousand copies of a book sold within three weeks of publication is enough to make a book a national bestseller, any instrument of publicity that reasonably assures that the news of new books will get into the hands of readers disposed to buy them will always have pride of place with potential advertisers. That is why the prospect of commanding the attention of the one hundred thousand or so readers and separate subscribers to the *New York Times Book Review* offers the single most compelling reason for publishers to advertise in its pages (and to pay a premium for doing so) while ignoring the exorbitant fees more local papers charge. The *Times* offers a national audience in multiple markets and assures delivery to dedicated readers. Local papers can't compete by offering meager coverage whose few pages are lost within the circulars and inserts of the typical Sunday paper.

During the years I edited the *Los Angeles Times Book Review*, it lost about $1 million annually. The pittance the section received in the early years of my tenure, from the ads supplied chiefly by Barnes & Noble and Crown Books, dried up when B&N made a strategic decision to pull the bulk of its advertising from book sections in favor of placing ads in main news sections, and when Crown Books, owned by the feuding Haft family, declared bankruptcy. Nothing that has occurred in the more than two decades since Shaw's 1985 survey suggests that book reviews are clinging to life on anything other than the sufferance of their respective papers' managers. And now that support, always precarious, is at ever greater risk.

The argument that it is book sections' lack of advertising revenue from publishers that constrains book coverage is bogus. Such coverage has rarely made a dime for newspapers. Nor will it. Book publishers have scant resources; their own profits are too slim, and besides, newspapers charge too much for them to afford significant print advertising. Just to pay for the real estate in the chain stores consumes a huge chunk of a publisher's advertising budget. Moreover, their own marketing surveys consistently show that most people who buy books do so not on the basis of any review they read, nor ad they've seen, but upon word of mouth. What's worse is that most people who buy books, like most people who watch movies, don't read reviews at all. For those who do, however, reviews are an invaluable way of eavesdropping, as it were, on an ongoing cultural conversation of critical importance.

The obligation of America's newspapers to cover this conversation—to cover the news of books—ought not to depend on the dollars that are (or are not) to be derived from publishers' ads in the book supplement. It's beside the point. Of course, if one were to make profit the measure of such coverage, then the model to be emulated is less that of the typical newspaper and more the model of a magazine like the *New York Review of Books*, the most profitable and erudite and influential review publication in the history of modern American letters. It enjoys a readership of 280,000—readers who remain loyal to its unflaggingly high standard—and has been in the black for nearly forty years.

At the *Los Angeles Times*, as at other newspapers, readers of the *Book Review* were a minority of the paper's overall circulation. Internal market surveys at the *Times* consistently showed the *Book Review* to be the single worst-read weekly section produced by the paper. I was neither surprised nor alarmed. Since most people didn't read books, I figured of those who did, only a fanatical few would go to any great length to read about them. The regular consumption of book reviews is an acquired taste. Since 1975, when the *Book Review* was created as a separate section at the *Los Angeles Times*, it had almost always been the least read section of the Sunday paper. This was so at other newspapers as well.

This unhappy fact bears scrutiny. Among the paper's most well-off and best-read demographic cohorts—whose members arguably make up any book review's ideal readers—the Sunday *Book Review* was among the more favored of the weekly sections of the *Los Angeles Times*. Ed Batson, the paper's director of marketing research, told me that in 2004, some 1.2 million people had read the *Book Review* over the past four Sundays out of 6.4 million readers. The core readership of what Batson called the paper's "cosmopolitan enthusiasts" amounted to about 320,000 avid and dedicated readers for whom the weekly *Book Review* was among the most important sections of the paper. It was, in part, because of the devotion of this core readership that when, having survived three editorial regime changes, I chose to leave the *Times* in 2005, I believed that my work there had driven a wooden stake through the canard that no one reads or cares about serious criticism in L.A.

If newspapers properly understood such readers and the lifestyle they pursue, they would, in theory, be able to attract advertising from a diverse array of companies, including movie companies, coffee manufacturers, and distillers of premium whisky, among others. Diversification of ad revenue is a key component of a winning strategy of growth. But apart from the *New York Times*, no newspaper has dedicated sales representatives whose sole job is to sell space for book ads. And even the *New York Times*, with three such representatives, finds it hard to drum up significant business.

It is an unfortunate truth that a mass readership will always elude any newspaper section dedicated to the review of books. Nevertheless, I was convinced that because readers of book reviews are among a paper's best educated and most prosperous readers, it might be possible to turn a cultural imperative into a profitable strategy. Such a strategy would require commitment and vision from the overlords of the newspaper—qualities that, if history is any guide, are always in short supply.

The real problem was never the inability of book review sections to turn a profit, but rather the anti-intellectual ethos in the nation's newsrooms that is—and, alas, always was—an ineluctable fact of American news gathering. There was among many reporters and editors a barely disguised contempt for the bookish. Even for those few newspapers that boasted a separate book section, book reviewing was regarded as something of a sideshow. It simply wasn't at the beating heart of the newsroom. Careers were advanced by shoe leather, not by way of the armchair. The suspicion was strong among reporters and editors alike that anyone with enough time could read the pages of a book and accurately report its contents. Such a sedentary activity, however, was a poor substitute for breaking news and getting scoops.

Carlin Romano, the book critic of the *Philadelphia Inquirer*, ran up against this widespread prejudice time and again. "I remember once putting on the cover of my section a translation of *Tirant Lo Blanc*, a Catalan epic, on the dubious argument that maybe, you know, it's the next Cervantes and it will endure in the culture." (Published in 1490, *Tirant Lo Blanc* had, in fact, strongly influenced Cervantes when he wrote *Don Quixote* a century later.) "I got called into the office on that, and someone said, 'Have you gone crazy?'" Romano goes further: "Perhaps the most remarkable aspect of American newspapers in the 1990s is their hostility to reading in all forms." This is the taboo that dares not speak its name.

I wanted to say good-bye to all that. Where everyone else was going faster, shorter, dumber, I was intent upon going slower, longer, smarter, on the perhaps foolhardy presumption that there were enough adults out there in Newspaper Land who yearned to be spoken to as adults. During my years at the helm of the *Los Angeles Times Book Review*, I always did have an ideal literary editor in my head. I often tried to imagine what I might do if I had been, say, the literary editor of the *Times* of London in 1900 when a then obscure Viennese doctor named Sigmund Freud published his first book, *The Interpretation of Dreams*. Suppose I'd had on my desk only two books—Freud's and, say, the next surefire bestselling novel by Mrs. Humphry Ward, the Danielle Steel of her day. Space is, as ever, limited. Mrs. Ward's publisher has announced an unprecedented first printing of 100,000 (the equivalent of at least a half million today), while Freud's book will start off with well under a thousand copies (of which it will take his independent publisher the next six years to sell a paltry 351 copies). I must choose which to review. I like to think I would have chosen the Freud. I like to think that I would have had the perspicacity to ask George Bernard Shaw to undertake it. And I like to think that I would have asked Shaw to write a long essay—some 2,500 words, more if he thought it warranted—in which he would declare the book a masterpiece, of lasting merit, and predict that it would go on to influence the whole of the twentieth century. As indeed it would. Who, today, remembers Mrs. Humphry Ward? Or, for that matter, the editor who chose her book over Freud's?

From time to time, occasions for such choices presented themselves during my tenure as editor of the *Los Angeles Times Book Review*. It was less a matter of serendipity than my own willfulness. Two instances stand out. In 1997, Penguin announced that it would be releasing a volume of Sor Juana Inés de la Cruz's selected writings. Years ago, Carlos Fuentes had told me of this remarkable seventeenth-century Mexican nun and poet. I had never heard of her. Nor was I alone. Much of her work had yet to be translated into English, even some three hundred years after her death. It was, Fuentes said, as if Shakespeare had still to be translated into Spanish. The whole of Spanish literature owed a debt to her work. Thus, I decided that an anthology of her writings, translated by the excellent Margaret Sayers Peden and published under the imprimatur of Penguin Classics, ought to be treated as news. Big news. After all, about a quarter of the readers of the *Los Angeles Times* had Latino roots.

Octavio Paz, Mexico's greatest living poet and critic, contributed a lengthy essay praising Sor Juana. But when I showed the color proof of the cover to my superiors, I was met with baffled incomprehension. Sor Juana who? A nun who'd been dead for almost half a millennium? Had I taken complete leave of my senses?

Dispirited, proof in hand, I trundled up to the paper's executive dining room to brood upon the wisdom of my decision. When Alberto González, the paper's longtime Mexican American waiter, appeared to take my order, he exhaled audibly and exclaimed, "Sor Juana!" "You've heard of her?" I asked. "Of course. Every schoolchild in Mexico knows her poems. I still remember my parents taking me as a small boy to visit her convent, now a museum. I know many of her poems by heart." At which point, in a mellifluous Spanish, he began to recite several verses. So much for my minders, I thought; I'm going to trust Alberto on this one.

After Paz's paean appeared, many people wrote to praise the *Book Review* for at last recognizing the cultural heritage of a substantial segment of the paper's readers. Their response suggested that the surest route to connecting with readers was to give them the news that stays news.

In 1999, Modern Library announced the imminent publication of a new translation of Stendhal's *The Charterhouse of Parma* by Richard Howard, America's most gifted living French translator. Such a translation of one of the classics of Western literature was, I felt, news. And so I commissioned a lengthy essay by Edmund White, which turned out to be so laudatory that

I published it prominently in the Sunday *Book Review*. The next morning, Michael Parks, then the editor of the entire paper, waved me into his office as I happened to walk by. With one eyebrow cocked, he looked at me and said with a kind of weary bewilderment, "Steve, Stendhal? Another dead, white, European male?" I explained my reasons. He didn't seem convinced.

Readers all over Los Angeles, however, came to my aid. Thanks to them, the Stendhal was flying out of local bookstores and rising steadily on the paper's bestseller list. Our review was followed by considerations in the *New York Review of Books* and the *New York Times Book Review*. Sales took off, prompting the *New Yorker*'s Talk of the Town to print an item tracing the trajectory of the book's unexpected success and crediting the *Los Angeles Times* for having helped to spark the sudden national interest.

The prospect of running the *Los Angeles Times Book Review* was irresistible. I was also convinced that the moment was ripe, that Los Angeles had long ago shed the fetish of its provincialism. It was now a big, grown-up metropolis, no longer afraid to wear its neuroses on its sleeve. The percentage of Americans attending the performing arts was rising dramatically. Movies like *Shakespeare in Love* and *The Hours* (and in later years *Babel* and *Pan's Labyrinth*) that might once have been consigned to arthouse ghettos were now finding both a mass audience and Oscars.

Regional theaters and opera companies blossomed even as Tower Records closed its doors. CD sales might have been slipping, but online music was soaring. Almost ten years later,

Peter Gelb, the Metropolitan Opera's general manager, understood this cultural shift better than most and launched a
series of live, high-definition broadcasts of operas like Puccini's
Il Trittico and Mozart's *Magic Flute* shown at movie theaters
across America. His experiment was a triumph, pulling in
thousands of new viewers. As Alex Ross reported in the *New
Yorker*, Gelb's broadcasts "have consistently counted among the
twenty highest-grossing films in America and have often bested
Hollywood's proudest blockbusters on a per-screen, per-day
average. Such figures are a timely slap in the face to media
companies that have written off classical music as an art with
no mass appeal." The truth is that many people everywhere are
interested in almost everything.

Thanks to Amazon, geography hardly matters. It is now
possible through the magic of internet browsing and buying
to obtain virtually any book ever printed and have it delivered
to your doorstep no matter where you live. This achievement,
combined with the vast archipelago of bricks-and-mortar emporiums operated by, say, Barnes & Noble or Borders or any
of the more robust of the independent stores, has given Americans a cornucopia of riches. To be sure, there has also been
the concomitant and deplorable collapse of many independent bookstores—down by half from the nearly four thousand
such stores that existed in 1990. [Borders went bust in February 2011, further reducing the footprint of independent bookstores.] Nevertheless, even a cursory glance at the landscape of
contemporary American bookselling and publishing makes it
hard not to believe we are living at the apotheosis of our culture.
Never in the whole of human history has more good literature,
attractively presented, sold for still reasonably low prices, been

available to so many people. You would need several life-
times over doing nothing but lying prone in a semidarkened
room with only a lamp for illumination just to make your way
through the good books that are on offer.

This is, strangely, a story that has not received near the
attention it deserves. And yet its implications are large, especially if papers are to have a prayer of retaining readers and
expanding circulation. There is money to be made in culture, if
only newspapers were nimble and imaginative enough to take
advantage of the opportunities that lie all around them.

Yet the opposite appears to be the case. In 1999,
Michael Janeway and András Szántó directed a yearlong study
of how America's newspapers covered the arts. Their conclusion: poorly. Funded by the Pew Charitable Trusts and based
at Columbia University's Graduate School of Journalism, the
study found that straightforward listings of upcoming events
make up "close to fifty percent of arts and entertainment coverage" and that "in-house staffing and resources have not been
increased to match an explosion of arts activity." The report
noted that "the visual arts, architecture, dance and radio get
only cursory coverage" and that "the daily Arts & Living section
lags behind both business and sports as a priority at almost
every newspaper, both in its allotment of pages and staff." Yet,
by almost every measure, Americans are a people who spend
vast amounts of time and income pursuing leisure activities of
all kinds, including reading. Sure, book sales might be down
nationally and serious reading a minority pursuit, but other
indicators suggested a persistent and passionate engagement
with the written word.

By the early years of the twenty-first century, for example, book clubs had grown to an estimated five million members. Brian Lamb's CSPAN-2 airs in-depth, commercial-free interviews with and readings by nonfiction authors round the clock every weekend. And I found myself returning to a Los Angeles in which more bookstores were thriving than ever before in the city's history. Indeed, in some years the average per capita sales of books in the Los Angeles metropolitan region had often exceeded—by some $50 million—such annual sales in the greater New York area.

It's almost enough to give one hope. This apparent utopia of readers, however, masks a bitter truth: the arts of reading are under siege. In June 2004, the National Endowment for the Arts released the findings of an authoritative survey based on an enormous sample of more than seventeen thousand adults. Conducted by the US Bureau of the Census and spanning twenty years of polling, it showed that for the first time a majority of Americans no longer had any interest in what, broadly defined, might be called literature. That is to say, fifty-three percent of Americans claimed, when asked, that in the previous year they had not read a novel, play, or poem. This was true for all classes and categories, whatever their age, sex, education, income, region, race, or ethnicity. Still, despite the growth in the population of the country, the survey found that the overall number of people reading literature remained stable at about ninety-six million between 1982 and 2002. Interestingly, the west and northeast regions of the country had the highest reading rates. It wasn't at all clear why, and the report didn't say. Nor did the survey ask whether these same Americans had read history, biography, or self-help, the chief subjects that have historically engaged Americans' attention.

Serious reading, of course, was always a minority taste. We've known that ever since Dr. Johnson. "People in general do not willingly read," he said, "if they can have anything else to amuse them." Today, the entertainment-industrial complex offers a staggering number of compelling alternatives. A substantial number of Americans—scores of millions—are functionally and seemingly happily illiterate. Many more can read but choose not to. Of those who do, most read for the entirely understandable pleasures of escaping the drudgeries of daily life or for moral, spiritual, financial, or physical self-improvement, as the history of American bestsellers suggests. The fables of Horatio Alger, the platitudes of Dale Carnegie, the nostrums of Marianne Williamson, the inspirations of such secular saints as Lee Iacocca—all are the golden jelly on which the queen bees of American publishing have traditionally battened.

Obsessive devotion to the written word is rare. Acquiring the knowledge and technique to do it well is arduous. Serious readers are a peculiar breed. Elizabeth Hardwick, for one, always knew this. "Perhaps the love of, or the intense need for, reading is psychological, an eccentricity, even something like a neurosis, that is, a pattern of behavior that persists beyond its usefulness, which is controlled by inner forces and which in turn controls." For this kind of reading is a profoundly antisocial act: it cannot be done in concert with friends; it is not a branch of the leisure industry, whose entertainments, whether video or computer or sports or rock 'n' roll, can be enjoyed in the mass. How many times, for instance, did you ever say as a child, "Leave me alone! Can't you see I'm reading?"

Twenty-five years ago, the distinguished editor and publisher Elisabeth Sifton announced the discovery of what she dubbed Sifton's Law: "There is a natural limit on the readership for serious fiction, poetry and nonfiction in America that ranges, I would say, between five hundred and five thousand people—roughly a hundred times the number of the publisher's and the author's immediate friends." Sifton's Law was a gloss on Dwight Macdonald's puckish speculation of the late 1940s in which he supposed that there were only about five thousand people interested in serious writing. The problem, he observed two decades later, was that it was likely the same five thousand, but they were all getting quite a bit longer in the tooth.

That suspicion could not have surprised the folks at the Book-of-the-Month Club. They had long been monitoring the steady decline in Americans' reading habits. Back in the middle of the Great Depression, long before the advent of television, much less the internet, the club had hired the Gallup organization to survey reading habits among Americans. In 1937, Gallup found that only twenty-nine percent of all adults read books; in 1955, the percentage had sunk to seventeen percent. Fifteen years later, in 1970, the club evidently no longer could bear to know, and Gallup stopped asking. True, the total income of American publishers continued to rise, but that happy news concealed a more troubling reality: profits reflected inflationary costs passed along in higher list prices, while the number of readers flocking to bookstores continued to decline. That is still the case.

The terrible irony is that at the dawn of an era of almost magical technology with a potential of deepening the implicit democratic promise of mass literacy, we also totter on the edge of an abyss of profound cultural neglect. One is reminded of Philip Roth's crack about Communism and the West: "In the East, nothing is permitted and everything matters; in the West, everything is permitted and nothing matters." In today's McWorld, the forces seeking to enroll the populace in the junk cults of celebrity, sensationalism, and gossip are increasingly powerful and wield tremendous economic clout. The cultural conversation devolves and is held hostage to these trends. The corporate wars over who will control the technology of news gathering and electronic communication and data and distribution are increasingly fierce. Taken together, these factors threaten to leave us ignorant of tradition, contemptuous of the habits of quality and excellence, unable to distinguish among the good, the bad, and the ugly.

But perhaps this is too bleak a view. After all, ninety-six million readers are a third of the country. As John Maxwell Hamilton, a longtime journalist and commentator on Public Radio International's *Marketplace*, writes in his irreverent and trenchant book *Casanova Was a Book Lover*, "People who care about books care profoundly. What they lack in numbers they make up for in passion. A typical mid-1980s study illustrates the fidelity of readers to reading. Only half of the American public, the study found, had read at least one book in the past six months. Of those 'readers,' however, almost one-third devoured at least one book a week."

And the book itself—compact, portable, sensuous—has yet to be bested as our most important information-retrieval system. Even Bill Gates, that Yoda of the virtual world, has been unable to resist its seductions. When, in 1996, he wanted to tell us about *The Road Ahead*, to commit the vision thing, what did he do? He had the Viking Press publish his book. He did not post his Delphic pronunciamentos on his Microsoft site. For Gates knew then—as he knows now, despite his recent insistence that the digital future will carry the day—that the book still retains the patina of authority that only time and tradition can bestow.

What matters in this *Kulturkampf* is a newspaper's ambition, its business acumen, and its cultural imagination. It's a question of allocation of resources, of what a paper's owners and editors think is important for readers to know. It is a question of what, in the judgment of the paper's minders, is news. It's a question of respect for ordinary readers' intelligence and their avidity for culture. Famously, books contain news that stays news. I believed when I was editor of the *Los Angeles Times Book Review*—as I believe now—that there is no more useful framework for understanding America and the world it inhabits. It is through the work of novelists and poets that we understand how we imagine ourselves and contend with the often elusive forces—of which language itself is a foremost factor—that shape us as individuals and families, citizens and communities, and it is through our historians and scientists, journalists and essayists that we wrestle with how we have lived, how the present came to be, and what the future might bring.

Readers know that. They know in their bones something newspapers forget at their peril: that without books, indeed, without the news of such books—without literacy—the good society vanishes and barbarism triumphs. I shall never forget overhearing some years ago, on the morning of the first day of the annual *Los Angeles Times* Festival of Books, a woman asking a UCLA police officer if he expected trouble. He looked at her with surprise and said, "Ma'am, books are like Kryptonite to gangs." What he knew is what so many societies since time immemorial have known: Civilization is built on a foundation of books.

[2007]

The Fate of Books

IS THE PRINTED BOOK ON its way to extinction? Will the e-book win the day? Will writers be able to make a living? Will publishers? Will booksellers? Will there be any readers? Is there life after the Age of Print? The new order is fast upon us, the ground shifts beneath our feet, and as the old sage put it, all that is solid melts into air. What will the future bring?

The only thing we can know for certain, of course, is the past—and even the past is notoriously elusive and discloses its truths in fragments whose meanings provide fodder for endless speculation and debate. The present is a vexing blur, its many parts moving too swiftly to be described with consensual accuracy. As for its significance, or what it portends, only the future can render a credible verdict. The future is, famously, an undiscovered—and unknowable—country.

That has not stopped the avatars of the New Information Age. For these ubiquitous boosters, the future beckons. E-books, they insist, will save an industry whose traditional methods of publishing have been challenged by the new technological forces now sweeping the globe. Robert Darnton, one of our more sober and learned historians of reading and the book, believes that the implications for the ecology of writing and reading, for publishing and bookselling—indeed, for literacy itself—are profound. For we now have, as he notes in his erudite and thoughtful *The Case for Books: Past, Present, and Future*, the possibility to make "all book learning available to all people, or at least those privileged enough to have access to the World Wide Web. It promises," he predicts, "to be the ultimate stage in the democratization of knowledge set in motion by the invention of writing, the codex, movable type, and the Internet." In this view, we are living at one of history's hinge moments.

James Atlas, a former writer for the *New York Times* and the *New Yorker*, and now an independent publisher, says, "Once technology is discovered you can't stop it. We're going to have e-books. We're going to have print-on-demand business. . . . The key word is adaptation, which will happen whether we like it or not." Jane Friedman, former president and chief executive of HarperCollins and a former longtime publishing executive with Alfred A. Knopf, proclaims that digital publishing "is going to be the center of the universe." All the traditional models of publishing, she declares, are broken. Still, the historical role of books in the spreading of knowledge would be hard to overestimate. That role, to say the least, is now in doubt. In analyzing this historic juncture, it is important to retain a sense of proportion, to steer soberly between the Party of the Future, whose members are true believers in the utopia they insist will bring us a new dynamic and open medium that will liberate the creative possibilities of humanity, and the Party of the Past, whose members fear that the dystopian tsunami now rushing toward us signals the death knell of civilization, the trivialization of the word.

*

Once it was the novel that was said to be dying. (Philip Roth, a doyen of the modern republic of letters, recently predicted that in twenty-five years the number of people reading novels would be akin to the number now reading Latin poetry; it will be an eccentricity, not a business.) Today it is the book itself that is thought to be on its way to extinction. Few thought this gloomy prospect was likely, much less to be welcomed. Authors and publishers alike consoled themselves with the thought that new technologies don't always replace older ones, pointing to the comforting example of the way in which the advent of television didn't supplant radio. The challenge was hardly existential.

The attachment to the book as object was also deep, seemingly unshakable. When the late Susan Sontag was a girl of eight or nine, she would lie in bed looking at her bookcase against the wall. She had begun to read her way through the writers published in Random House's Modern Library editions, which she'd bought in a Hallmark card store, using up her allowance. Gazing at that bookcase, she recalled, was "like looking at my fifty friends. A book was like stepping through a mirror. I could go somewhere else. Each one was a door to a whole kingdom." Will the invisible library nesting within the Kindle beckon in quite the same way? As a teenager, Sontag would visit Thomas Mann in his home in Pacific Palisades in Los Angeles. She would later recall the visit vividly as an encounter between "an embarrassed, fervid, literature-intoxicated child and a god in exile." Over cookies and tea, while smoking one cigarette after another, Mann spoke of Wagner and Hitler, of Goethe and *Doctor Faustus*, his newest book. But what struck Sontag were the "books, books, books in the floor-to-ceiling shelves that covered two of the walls" of his study. Neither of them knew that only a few years before, in 1945, the first faltering steps had been taken to create a Frankenstein called Memex, the first e-book.

Sixty-five years later, there seems little doubt that a critical mass, or tipping point, is being reached. Ever more dedicated e-readers are being invented and marketed, with ever-larger screens. So, too, are computer tablets that can serve as giant e-readers, and hardware will not be very hard: a thin display flexible enough to roll up into a tube is soon to be on offer to consumers. Randall Stross of the *New York Times* asks the right question: "With the new devices in hand, will book buyers avert their eyes from the free copies only a few clicks away that have been uploaded without copyright holder's permission? Mindful of what happened to the music industry at a similar transitional juncture, book publishers are about to discover whether their industry is different enough to be spared a similar fate."

Certainly in the United States there is a growing anxiety among publishers. The *New York Times* reports that hardcover book sales, the foundation of the business, declined thirteen percent in 2008 versus the previous year. Last year, sales were down fifteen percent through July, versus the same period of 2008. Total e-book sales, though up considerably, remain small, at slightly less than $82 million, or less than two percent of total book sales through July 2009. "What happens," asks an executive of the Association of American Publishers, "when twenty to thirty percent of book readers use digital as the primary mode of reading books? Piracy's a big concern."

US sales of e-readers are growing. An estimated three million e-readers were sold in 2009, and it is expected that six million will be bought this year. Sales in 2009 for print books in Europe's major markets of France, Germany, and the UK held flat from 2008. E-readers haven't taken off in Europe due to the lack of wireless connectivity, but all that will change soon with Amazon's move to make the Kindle available outside the United States. In the fall of 2009, the Kindle 2 became the first e-reader available globally. Stephen Marche, the pop culture columnist for *Esquire* magazine, writing in the pages of the *Wall Street Journal*, considers this fact "as important to the history of the book [as were] the birth of print and the shift from the scroll to bound pages." He insists that the "e-reader . . . will likely change our thinking and our being as profoundly as the previous pre-digital manifestation of text. The question is how."

As vessels of knowledge and entertainment, books were unrivaled. It was unthinkable that they could one day disappear. Nor was it contemplated that bookstores too might vanish. Jason Epstein, a cofounder of the *New York Review of Books*, ended his incisive 2001 book on publishing and its discontents by hailing the indispensable function of bookstores: "A civilization without retail booksellers is," he wrote, "unimaginable. Like shrines and other sacred meeting places, bookstores are essential artifacts of human nature. The feel of a book taken from the shelf and held in the hand is a magical experience, linking writer to reader." Boy, was he wrong. Millions succumbed to the ease of e-readers. And tell it to the thousands of independent bookstores whose owners have gone out of business.

In the United States, bricks-and-mortar bookstores continue to disappear at a rate rivaled only by the relentless destruction of the Amazonian rain forest. Twenty years ago, there were about four thousand independent bookstores. Today, only about fifteen hundred remain. [By 2023, the number, against all expectation, had rebounded by nearly a thousand to an estimated twenty-five hundred.] Even the two largest US chain bookstores—themselves partly responsible for putting smaller stores to the sword—are in a precarious state: Borders is said to be teetering on the brink of bankruptcy [and indeed would go out of business in 2011], and Barnes & Noble is trying desperately to figure out ways to pay the mortgage on the vast real estate it occupies across the nation. [Since 2019 when James Daunt, the managing director of the UK's Waterstones chain, became CEO of Barnes & Noble, his strategy of empowering regional managers to more closely curate their respective stores' selection and displays appears, at least for the moment, to have staunched the fiscal hemorrhage and put the chain on a more sustainable path.]

The contrast with Europe is stark. There are important structural differences in bookselling in America and in Europe. A recent report in the *Wall Street Journal* notes that many of Europe's major publishing markets, except for the UK, are bolstered by laws requiring all bookstores, online retailers included, to sell books at prices set by publishers. Nowhere is the fixed-price tradition, now 120 years old, as deeply rooted as in Germany. The system protects independent booksellers and smaller publishers from giant rivals that could discount their way to more market share. Thus, Germany with a population of slightly more than eighty-two million, less than a third the size of the United States with its three hundred million citizens, boasts seven thousand bookshops and nearly fourteen thousand publishers. The *Wall Street Journal* quotes Gerd

Gerlach, owner of a small Berlin bookshop named after the nineteenth-century poet Heinrich Heine, as saying, "The smaller publishers get to publish quality works they never could afford to do without the fixed book price. Everyone benefits, not least the reader." Together, German companies published in 2008 more than ninety-six thousand new titles.

Marshall McLuhan, that manic exaggerator and media seer, noted long ago in his *Gutenberg Galaxy* that something is always gained, and something is always lost, when a new technology vanquishes an old one. In the transition from scrolls to the codex, from quills dipped into inkwells, their marks inscribed upon parchment, to the invention of movable type to the typewriter and then onto the computer, something is gained, and something is lost. What is most vulnerable is an entire world view, a mentality, a way of thinking. Readers in the fifteenth century, for example, had, according to Robert Darnton, a hard time accepting the invention of printing with movable type. He cites the example of Niccolo Perotti, a sophisticated and erudite Italian classicist, to make the point. Perotti confessed his doubts in a private letter written in 1472, less than twenty years after Gutenberg's invention:

> Now that anyone is free to print whatever they wish, they often disregard that which is best and instead write, merely for the sake of entertainment, what would best be forgotten, or better still be erased from all books. And even when they write something worthwhile, they twist it and corrupt it to the point where it would be much bet-

ter to do without such books, rather than having a thousand copies spreading falsehoods over the whole world.

He was not alone in his concern. Anthony Grafton and Meg Williams, in their book *Christianity and the Transformation of the Book*, point to the remarkable fifteenth-century Benedictine scholar Trithemius, who assembled a library half the size of the Vatican's and was the author of *In Praise of Scribes*, a polemic in favor of writing things out and against printing them. For Trithemius, printed books could never rival the beauty and uniqueness of a copied text—copying, he thought, prompted a state of contemplation that was spiritually beneficial; hand-produced books were, he believed, inherently holy. As Darnton sees it, book culture reached its highest peak when Gutenberg modernized the codex, and, he argues, the codex is superior in some ways to the computer. You can, he says, annotate it, take it to bed, and store it conveniently on a shelf. He finds it hard to imagine that a digitized image of an old book will provide anything comparable to the excitement of contact with the original. Moreover, he argues, for historians it will always be important to get the feel of a book—the texture of its paper, the quality of its printing, the nature of its binding. Such physical aspects provide clues about its existence as an element in a social and economic system. Digital reproduction fails to convey the texture of the printed page, its layout, its typography, which suggest subtle shifts in ways of viewing the world— nothing can be pinned down with precision but nonetheless there is something in the physical aspect of the book itself that underpins human experience and that historians strive to understand.

Darnton also rightly fears the obsolescence that is built into the electronic media: "Bits become degraded over time. Documents may get lost in cyberspace." He insists on the point: "All texts 'born digital' belong to an endangered species. The obsession with developing new media has inhibited efforts to preserve the old." History offers a cautionary precedent: "We have lost," he notes, "eighty percent of all silent films and fifty percent of all films made before the Second World War."

What is most threatened, most in danger of being lost by the digital revolution, however, is our nearly six-hundred-year-old literary culture. The role of publishers is up for grabs. As Elisabeth Sifton, one of our most astute and experienced editors, in a recent piece in the *Nation* observes,

Publishers and writers have for centuries conspired and fought over words, sentences, chapters, fonts, illustrations, paper, trim size, binding materials, jacket design. Publishing decisions made distinctive differences to literature in every century. A publishing rationale lay behind Descartes' wish that *Discours de la methode* have an unusually small format. The publisher of *The Charterhouse of Parma* wanted to issue it quickly and needed it shorter; Stendhal concurred—hence the rushed compression of its ending (a flaw the consummate professional Balzac noticed). G. B. Shaw insisted on a specific typeface ('I'll stick with Caslon until I die,' he said, Caslon being the font Benjamin Franklin also used for setting the Declaration of Independence); Edmund Wilson on an unusual trim size; John Updike on all physical aspects of his books. If you speak of the death of books, you are speaking of the extinction of this shared culture of choice, correction, revision and presentation, along with its craft skills. If you talk of the future of books, you must somehow anticipate how it might continue.

But is it true that the internet, as Sifton insists, has devolved from "the pure, open-access Eden that the Internet's founders claimed they wanted" to a "habitat unnatural for the true life of the mind, politics or art"? There is little doubt, of course, that we live in an increasingly noisy culture. Gaining attention among a wide public for deserving work is increasingly difficult. Does the web make this easier or harder? At first blush, it appears to make it possible to publish books much the way the military is said to have developed "smart bombs," heat-seeking devices that when launched fly directly to their intended targets.

The real fear is that, as Sifton has also observed, the nature of reading itself has been fundamentally changed. Reading on the web, she writes, "is of a completely different order than reading in a book." Doing one's schoolwork on a computer, growing up texting and posting, it is said, produces a qualitatively different way of listening and comprehension. "Teachers and writing instructors report big changes in their students' habits of attention and modes of expression," reports Sifton. This is why, she concludes, "we must still ask . . . what kind of imaginative energy, what kind of reading—or readers—will Kindle, the Sony Reader, [or the Nook] or other electronic devices attract in years to come? And what kind of writing?"

The historian David A. Bell, writing of "The Bookless Future" in the *New Republic* in 2005, shares this concern. He writes, "The Internet revolution is changing not only what scholars read, but also how they read—and if my own experience is any guide, it can easily make them into worse readers." Why? Because, argues Bell, the computer encourages sampling and surfing, and this is where the greatest dangers lie, because "information is not knowledge; searching is not reading; and surrendering to the organizing logic of a book is, after all, the way one learns." Thus, it is possible to search for keywords, for many apt quotations, which can be conveniently harvested, cut, and pasted. What is lost is the experience of reading a work in its entirety. The computer, concludes Bell, encourages one to read in exactly the wrong way, leaving the user with little but a series of disembodied passages. But even a cursory look at the history of reading reveals that people have been reading in precisely this way for a very long time. Darnton cites one William Drake, "a voracious reader and bit player in the conflicts that convulsed England from 1640–1660. Drake understood reading as digestion, a process of extracting the essence from books and of incorporating them into himself. He favored bite-sized bits of text, which could be useful in their application to everyday life. Reading, he felt, should be aimed at helping a man get ahead in the world and its most helpful chunks came in the form of proverbs, fables, and even the mottoes written into emblem books" and carefully copied into the commonplace journals Drake so scrupulously kept. He was not alone. "Early modern Englishmen seem clearly to have read in the same way— segmentally, by concentrating on small chunks of text and jumping from book to book, rather than sequentially, as readers did a century later, when the rise of the novel encouraged the habit of perusing books from cover to cover." "Segmental reading," concludes Darnton, "compelled its practitioners to read actively, to exercise critical judgment, and to impose their own patter on their reading matter."

Our ancestors, as historians of reading have noted, lived in different mental worlds and so too must they have read differently. We know, as Darnton has written, that "reading itself has changed over time. It was often done aloud and in groups, or in secret and with an intensity hard to imagine today." It was one thing to unfurl a scroll, it was quite another to leaf through a codex. "Texts shape readers' responses. Typography as well as style and syntax determine the ways in which texts convey meaning. The history of reading is arguably as complex as the history of thinking." Or, to put it another way, just as different languages offer entirely different ways of understanding the world, so too must different ways of reading suggest different ways of apprehending the world. Reading is, writes Darnton, a mystery: "How do readers make sense of the signs on the printed page? What are the social effects of that experience? And how has it varied?" And how will the arrival and ubiquitous spread—indeed the likely coming hegemony of the World Wide Web—affect and shape the very ecology of communications and our habits of attention and comprehension? Does the ethos of acceleration prized by the internet diminish our capacity for deliberation and enfeeble our capacity for genuine reflection? Does the daily avalanche of information banish the space needed for actual wisdom? "Change is good" is the mantra heard everywhere. Perhaps, but arguably only up to a point.

Although the printed book continues to dominate the marketplace, it no longer holds pride of place as the only possible kind of book. Today, if Bill Gates were to offer up a new visionary work, he might well first post his prognostications as an e-book. Few readers would consider his sentences any less worthy or his ideas somehow less serious by having been conveyed through a technology invented the day before yesterday.

The fear that literature itself is under siege may also be misplaced. Perhaps new forms of literary accomplishment will emerge, every bit as rigorous and as pleasurable and as enduring as the vaunted forms of yesteryear. After all, does anyone hold the haiku in contempt? Perhaps the discipline of tapping 140 characters on Twitter will one day give birth to a form as admirable and as elegant as haiku was at its height. Perhaps the interactive features of graphic display and video interpolation, hyperlinks, and the simultaneous display of multiple panels made possible by the World Wide Web will prompt new and compelling ways of telling each other the stories our species seems biologically programmed to tell. And perhaps all this will add to the rich storehouse of an evolving literature whose contours we have only just begun to glimpse, much less to imagine.

We're not yet there, of course. The predicted paperless world has yet to materialize. By one measure, the old world of book publishing is robust: According to Bowker's Global Books in Print, 700,000 new titles appeared worldwide in 1998, 859,000 in 2003, and 976,000 in 2007. Soon a million new books will be published every year. One is tempted to say that almost no new work, however mediocre, goes unpublished. And now that technology has democratized the means of production, the cost of producing a book is within reach of nearly every aspiring author. The arrival and increasing sophistication of the internet is steadily democratizing the means of distribution, rendering traditional bookstores increasingly irrelevant.

The debate over how books are published is, of course, terribly important for publishers worried about profit margins, the habitual ways of conducting their business, and the looming threat of obsolescence. Authors and their agents are understandably anxious. For many readers, however, much of this debate is sterile. For them, what counts is whether and how books will be made available to the greatest number of consumers at the cheapest possible price. Whether readers find books in bookstores or on the web or can access them on an application on the smartphones that are already in their pockets by the billions matters not at all. Content and cost and ease of access rule.

Jason Epstein, in a particularly lucid and sober assessment of book publishing's likely future, writes in a recent issue of the *New York Review of Books* of his conviction that "e-books will be a significant factor in the uncertain future, but actual books printed and bound will continue to be the irreplaceable repository of our collective wisdom." [Epstein was right. Despite predictions of an e-book tsunami, by 2024 e-books constituted just thirteen percent of the overall book market.] He ends on an uncharacteristically sentimental note—and here he speaks for many of us—when he confesses, "I must declare my bias. My rooms are piled from floor to ceiling with books so that I have to think twice about where to put another one. If by some unimaginable accident all these books were to melt into air leaving my shelves bare with only a memorial list of digital files left behind, I would want to melt as well for books are my life. I mention this so that you will know the prejudice with which I celebrate the inevitability of digitization as an unimaginably powerful, but infinitely fragile, enhancement of the worldwide literacy on which we all—readers and nonreaders—depend."

[2010]

Size Matters

FROM THE START, Jeff Bezos wanted to "get big fast." He was never a "small is beautiful" kind of guy. The Brobdingnagian numbers tell much of the story. In 1994, four years after the first internet browser was created, Bezos stumbled upon a startling statistic: the internet had been growing at the rate of 2,300 percent annually. In 1995, the year Bezos, then thirty-one, started Amazon, just sixteen million people used the internet. A year later, the number was thirty-six million, a figure that would multiply at a furious rate. Today, more than 1.7 billion people, or almost one out of every four humans on the planet, are online. Bezos understood two things: One was the way the internet made it possible to enable anyone anywhere with an internet connection and a computer to browse a seemingly limitless universe of goods with a precision never previously known and then buy them directly from the comfort of their homes. The second was how the internet allowed merchants to gather vast amounts of personal information on individual customers.

The internet permitted a kind of bespoke selling. James Marcus, who was hired by Bezos in 1996 and would work at Amazon for five years, later published a revealing memoir of his time as Employee #55. He recalls Bezos insisting that the internet, with "its bottomless capacity for data collection," would "allow you to sort through entire populations with a fine-tooth comb. Affinity would call out to affinity: your likes and dislikes—from Beethoven to barbecue sauce, shampoo to shoe polish to *Laverne & Shirley*—were as distinctive as your DNA and would make it a snap to match you up with your 9,999 cousins." This prospect, Marcus felt, "was either a utopian daydream or a targeted-marketing nightmare."

Whichever one it was, Bezos didn't much care. "You know, things just don't grow that fast," he observed. "It's highly unusual, and that started me thinking, 'What kind of business plan might make sense in the context of that growth?'" Bezos decided selling books would be the best way to get big fast on the internet. This was not immediately obvious: bookselling in the United States had always been less of a business than a calling. Profit margins were notoriously thin, and most independent stores depended on low rents. Walk-in traffic was often sporadic, the public's taste fickle; reliance on a steady stream of bestsellers to keep the landlord at bay was not exactly a surefire strategy for remaining solvent.

Still, overall, selling books was a big business. In 1994 Americans bought $19 billion dollars' worth of books. Barnes & Noble and the Borders Group had by then captured a quarter of the market, with independent stores struggling to make up just over another fifth and a skein of book clubs, supermarkets, and other outlets accounting for the rest. That same year, 513 million individual books were sold, and seventeen bestsellers each sold more than 1 million copies. Bezos knew that two national distributors, Ingram Book Group and Baker & Taylor, had warehouses holding about 400,000 titles and in the late 1980s had begun converting their inventory list from microfiche to a digital format accessible by computer. Bezos also knew that in 1992 the Supreme Court had ruled in *Quill Corp. v. North Dakota* that retailers were exempt from charging sales tax in states where they didn't have a physical presence. (For years, he would use this advantage to avoid collecting hundreds of millions of dollars in state sales taxes, giving Amazon an enormous edge over retailers of every kind, from bookstores to Best Buy and Home Depot. In recent months, however, Amazon, under mounting pressure, has eased its opposition and reached agreements with twelve states, including California and Texas, to collect sales tax.) "Books are incredibly unusual in one respect," Bezos said, "and that is that there are more items in the book category than there are items in any other category by far." A devotee of the culture of metrics, Bezos was undaunted. He was sure that the algorithms of computerized search and access would provide the keys to a consumer kingdom whose riches were yet undiscovered and barely dreamed of, and so he set out to construct a twenty-first-century ordering mechanism that, at least for the short term, would deliver goods the old-fashioned way: by hand, from warehouses via the postal service and commercial shippers.

One of Amazon's consultants was publishing visionary Jason Epstein. In 1952 Epstein founded Anchor Books, the highbrow trade paperback publisher; eleven years later, he was one of the founders of the *New York Review of Books*, and for many decades was an eminence at Random House. His admiration for Bezos was mixed with a certain bemusement; he knew that for

Amazon to really revolutionize bookselling, physical books would have to be transformed into bits and bytes capable of being delivered seamlessly. Otherwise, Bezos would have built only a virtual contraption hostage to the Age of Gutenberg, with all its cumbersome inefficiencies. But Epstein could not fathom that the appeal of holding a physical book in one's hand would ever diminish. Instead, he dreamed of machines that would print on demand, drawing upon a virtual library of digitized books and delivering physical copies in, say, Kinkos across the country. The bookstores that might survive in this scenario would be essentially stocking examination copies of a representative selection of titles, which could be individually printed while customers lingered at coffee bars awaiting the arrival of their order. Ultimately, Epstein would devote himself to this vision.

Bezos looked elsewhere, convinced that one day he could fashion an unbroken chain of ordering and delivering books, despite the deep losses Epstein warned he'd have to sustain to do so. But first he had to insert the name of his new company into the frontal lobe of America's (and not only America's) consumers. Like all great and obsessed entrepreneurs, his ambitions were imperial, his optimism rooted in an overweening confidence in his own rectitude. He aimed to build a brand that was, in Marcus's phrase, "both ubiquitous and irresistible." A decade before, while a student at Princeton in the mid-1980s, he had adopted as his credo a line from Ray Bradbury, the author of *Fahrenheit 451*: "The Universe says No to us. We in answer fire a broadside of flesh at it and cry Yes!" (Many years later, the octogenarian Bradbury would decry the closing of his beloved Acres of Books in Long Beach, California, which had been unable to compete with the ever-expanding empire of online bookselling.) A slightly built, balding gnome of a man, Bezos often struck others as enigmatic, remote, and odd. If not exactly cuddly, he was charismatic in an otherworldly sort of way. A Columbia University economics professor who was an early boss of Bezos's said of him, "He was not warm. . . . It was like he could be a Martian for all I knew. A well-meaning, nice Martian." Bill Gates, another Martian, would welcome Bezos's arrival to Seattle, saying, "I buy books from Amazon.com because time is short and they have a big inventory and they're very reliable." Millions of book buyers would soon agree.

As the editor of the *Los Angeles Times Book Review*, I had watched Bezos's early rise with admiration, believing that whatever complications he was bringing to the world of bookselling were more than compensated for by the many ways he was extending reader access to a greater diversity of books. After all, even the larger sixty-thousand-square-foot emporiums of Barnes & Noble and Borders could carry no more than 175,000 titles. Amazon, by contrast, was virtually limitless in its offerings. Bezos was then, as he has been ever since, at pains to assure independent bookstores that his new business was no threat to them. He claimed that Amazon simply provided a different service and wasn't trying to snuff bricks-and-mortar stores. Independent booksellers weren't so sure.

In the mid- to late 1990s, when online bookselling was in its infancy, Barnes & Noble and Borders were busy expanding their empires, often opening stores adjacent to long-established community bookstores. The independents were alarmed by these and other aggressive strategies. The chain stores could give customers deeply discounted offerings on a depth of stock made possible by favorable publishers' terms not extended to independents. Clerks at the chains might not intimately know the tastes and predilections of the surrounding neighborhood, but the price was right: lower was better, lowest was best.

The death toll tells the tale. Two decades ago, there were about four thousand independent bookstores in the United States: today, less than half that number. And now, even the victors are imperiled. The fate of the two largest US chain bookstores—themselves partly responsible for putting smaller stores to the sword—is instructive: Borders declared bankruptcy in 2011 and closed its several hundred stores across the country, its demise benefiting over the short term its rival Barnes & Noble, which has itself shrunk, uncertain of its future. The very idea of owning a bookstore strikes most savvy investors as forlorn.

For many of us, the notion that bricks-and-mortar bookstores might one day disappear is unthinkable. That sentiment is likely to strike today's younger readers as nostalgia bordering on fetish. Reality is elsewhere. For these readers, what counts is whether and how books will be made available to the greatest number of people at the cheapest possible price. Whether readers find books in bookstores or a digital device matters not at all; what matters is cost and ease of access. Walk into any Apple store (temples of the latest fad) and you'll be engulfed by the near frenzy of folks from all walks of life who seemingly can't wait to surrender their hard-earned dollars for the latest iPhone or iPad, no matter the constraints of a faltering economy. Then try to find a bookstore. Good luck. If you do, you'll notice that fewer books are on offer, the aisles wider, customers scarce. Bookstores have lost their mojo.

*

The bookstore wars are over. Independents are battered, Borders is dead, Barnes & Noble weakened but still standing, and Amazon triumphant. Yet still there is no peace; a new war rages for the future of publishing. The recent Justice Department lawsuit accusing five of the country's biggest publishers of illegally colluding with Apple to fix the price of e-books is, arguably, publishing's Alamo. What angered the government wasn't the price, but the way the publishers seemed to have secretly arranged to raise it. Many publishers and authors were flabbergasted, accusing the Obama administration of having gone after the wrong culprit. Scott Turow, president of the Authors Guild, denounced the suit, as did David Carr, the media critic of the *New York Times*, who said it was "the modern equivalent of taking on Standard Oil but breaking up Ed's Gas 'N' Groceries on Route 19 instead." On its face, the suit seemed an antitrust travesty, a failure to go after the "monopolistic monolith" that is, as the *Times* put it, "publishing's real nemesis." In this view, the biggest threat is Amazon's willingness to sell e-books at a loss in order to seduce millions of unwitting consumers into the leviathan's cornucopia of online goods and services. What is clear is that "legacy publishing," like old-fashioned bookselling, is gone. Just as bookselling is increasingly virtual, so is publishing. Technology democratizes both the means of production and distribution. The implications for traditional publishers are acute.

Amazon, not surprisingly, is keen to sharpen its competitive edge, to use every means at its disposal to confound, stymie, and overpower its rivals. It is well positioned to do so: the introduction of the Amazon Kindle in 2007 led to a startling surge in e-book sales, which until then had been insignificant. Soon it was not unusual to see e-book sales jump by 400 percent over the previous year. An estimated three million e-readers were sold in 2009, the year Amazon began to sell its Kindle 2, the first e-reader available globally. Bezos called the Kindle a response to "the failings of a physical book. . . . I'm grumpy when I'm forced to read a physical book because it's not as convenient. Turning the pages . . . the book is always flopping itself shut at the wrong moment." Millions of people agreed, and millions of Kindles were bought (though Amazon refuses to reveal exact numbers). Competing devices—including the Nook and the iPad, to name but two of the most prominent—began to proliferate and to give Amazon's Kindle a run for its money, thanks to the e-book pricing arrangement between some publishers and Apple that attracted the ire of the Justice Department. Barely a year after Apple launched the iPad, it had sold more than fifteen million worldwide. In 2009, only two percent of Americans had an e-reader or a tablet; by January 2012, the figure was twenty-eight percent. And Amazon, despite watching its market share drop from ninety percent of the American e-book market in 2010 to about fifty-five to sixty percent today, reached a milestone just under three years after the Kindle was introduced. "Amazon.com customers now purchase more Kindle books than hardcover books," Bezos crowed, "astonishing when you consider that we've been selling hardcover books for fifteen years, and Kindle books for thirty-three months."

*

One thing is certain, and about it publishers agree: e-book sales as a percentage of overall revenue are skyrocketing. Initially such sales were a tiny proportion of overall revenue; in 2008, for instance, they were under one percent. No more. The head of one major publisher told me that in 2010, e-book sales accounted for eleven percent of his house's revenue. By the end of 2011, it had more than tripled to thirty-six percent for the year. As John Thompson reports in the revised 2012 edition of his authoritative *Merchants of Culture*, in 2011 e-book sales for most publishers were "between eighteen and twenty-two percent (possibly even higher for some houses)." Hardcover sales, the foundation of the business, continue to decline, plunging thirteen percent in 2008 and suffering similar declines in the years since. According to the Pew Research Center's most recent e-reading survey, twenty-one percent of American adults report reading an e-book in the past year. Soon one out of every three sales of adult trade titles will be in the form of an e-book. Readers of e-books are especially drawn to escapist and overtly commercial genres (romance, mysteries and thrillers, science fiction), and in these categories e-book sales have bulked up to as large as sixty percent. E-book sales are making inroads even with so-called literary fiction. Thompson cites Jonathan Franzen's *Freedom*, published in 2010 by Farrar, Straus and Giroux, one of America's most distinguished houses and one of several American imprints now owned by the German conglomerate Holtzbrinck. Franzen's novel sold three-quarters of a million hardcover copies and a quarter million e-books in the first twelve months of publication. (Franzen, by the way, detests electronic books, and is also the guy who dissed Oprah when she had the gumption to pick his earlier novel, *The Corrections*, for her popular book club.) Did Franzen's e-book sales depress his hardcover sales, or did the e-book iteration introduce new readers to his work? It's hard to know, but it's likely a bit of both.

The inexorable shift in the United States from physical to digital books poses a palpable threat to the ways publishers have gone about their business. Jason Epstein got it right in 2010 when he wrote, "The resistance today by publishers to the onrushing digital future does not arise from fear of disruptive literacy, but from the understandable fear of their own obsolescence and the complexity of the digital transformation that awaits them, one in which much of their traditional infrastructure and perhaps they too will be redundant." Traditional publishers, he argued, have only themselves to blame, many (perhaps even most) of their wounds having been self-inflicted. They have been too often complacent, allergic to new ideas, even incompetent. Their dogged and likely doomed defense of traditional pricing strategies has left them vulnerable to Amazon's predatory pricing practices. Peter Mayer, former CEO of Viking/Penguin and now owner and publisher of the independent Overlook Press, agrees: "Publishers clearly need to newly prove to readers and authors the value that publishers add." That value, he concedes, is no longer a given.

The inability of most traditional publishers to successfully adapt to technological change may be rooted in the retrograde editorial and marketing culture that has long characterized the publishing industry. As one prominent literary agent told me, "This is a business run by English majors, not business majors." A surpassing irony: For years many of us worried that the increasing conglomeration of publishers would reduce diversity. (We were wrong.) We also feared bloated overheads would hold editors hostage to an unsustainable commercial imperative. (We were right.) But little did we imagine that the blunderbuss for change would arrive in the form of an avaricious imperium called Amazon. It is something of a surprise to see so many now defending the practices of corporate publishers who, just yesterday, were excoriated as Philistines out to coarsen the general culture.

Epstein, for one, doesn't fear Amazon, writing that the company's "strategy, if successful, might force publishers to shrink or even abandon their old infrastructure." Thus will publishing collapse into the cottage industry it was "in the glory days before conglomeration." Epstein insists that the dialectic Amazon exemplifies is irreversible, "a vivid expression of how the logic of a radical new and more efficient technology impels institutional change."

Not very long ago it was thought no one would read a book on a computer screen. That assumption is now demonstrably wrong. Today, whether writers will continue to publish the old-fashioned way or go over to direct online publishing is an open question. How it will be answered is at the heart of the struggle taking place between Amazon and traditional publishers.

Jeff Bezos got what he wanted: Amazon got big fast and is getting bigger, dwarfing all rivals. To fully appreciate the fear that is sucking the oxygen out of publishers' suites, it is important to understand what a steamroller Amazon has become. Last year it had $48 billion in revenue, more than all six of the major American publishing conglomerates combined, with a cash reserve of $5 billion. The company is valued at nearly $100 billion and employs more than 65,000 workers (all nonunion); Bezos, according to *Forbes*, is the thirtieth-wealthiest man in America. [In 2023, Amazon's valuation stood at nearly $1.4 trillion and had about 1.5 million full-time and part-time employees; Bezos, for his part, is the third-wealthiest person on the planet.] Amazon may be identified in the public mind with books, but the reality is that book sales account for a diminishing share of its overall business; the company is no longer principally a bookseller. Amazon is now an online Walmart, and while fifty percent of its revenues are derived from music, TV shows, movies, and, yes, books, another fifty percent comes from a diverse array of products and services. In the late 1990s, Bezos bought IMDb.com, the authoritative movie website. In 2009 he went gunning for bigger game, spending nearly $900 million to acquire Zappos.com, a shoe retailer. He also owns Diapers.com, a baby products website. Now he seeks to colonize high-end fashion as well. "Bezos may well be the premier technologist in America," said *Wired*, "a figure who casts as big a shadow as legends like Bill Gates and the late Steve Jobs."

With the introduction last fall of the Kindle Fire, Bezos is pushing an advanced mobile portal to Amazon's cloud universe, which hosts web operations for a wide variety of companies and institutions, including Netflix, the *New York Times*, NASA's Jet Propulsion Laboratory, Tina Brown's *Newsweek/Daily Beast*, PBS, Virgin Atlantic, and the Harvard Medical School, among others. As *Wired* put it, when you buy the Kindle Fire, "you're not buying a gadget—you're filing citizen papers for the digital duchy of Amazonia." For his part, Daniel Ellsberg of Pentagon Papers fame has renounced his "citizenship," pulling the plug on his Amazon Prime membership and calling for a boycott of Amazon after he discovered that the company had buckled under pressure from Washington and scrubbed WikiLeaks from its web servers. Not unlike small independent bookstores, bricks-and-mortar retailers such as Walmart, Home Depot, and Best Buy are feeling the ground give way beneath them. Target is fighting back, declaring that it will no longer sell Kindles, clearly dismayed by Amazon's brazen promotion of a price-checking app as a means of competing with many of the goods that Target sells.

Amazon has sixty-nine data and fulfillment centers, seventeen of which were built in the past year alone, with more to come. For the thousands of often older migratory baby boomers living out of RVs, who work furiously at the centers filling customer orders at almost literally a breakneck pace, it is, by all accounts, a high-stress job. These workers are the Morlocks who make possible Amazon's vaunted customer service. Last fall, the *Morning Call* investigated their plight in one of Amazon's main fulfillment warehouses in Allentown, Pennsylvania. It found that some employees risked stroke and heat exhaustion while running themselves ragged trying to fulfill quotas that resemble the onerous conditions so indelibly satirized by Charlie Chaplin in *Modern Times*. Ambulances were routinely stationed in the facility's giant parking lot to rush stricken workers to nearby hospitals. Amazon, for its part, says such problems are exceptional, and indeed, by OSHA's standards, incidents of this kind are not the norm. Pursuing greater efficiencies, Amazon in March bought Kiva Systems Inc., a robot manufacturer, for $775 million. Kiva, founded in 2003 and backed by, among others, Bain Capital Ventures, claims that three to four times as many orders per hour can be packed up by a worker using its robots. For Bezos the Martian, the human factor is pesky. Now a more automated solution looms.

In spring 2011, Amazon announced that it was hiring publishing veteran Larry Kirshbaum, former CEO of the Time Warner Book Group, to head Amazon Publishing in New York. Kirshbaum was all but condemned by many of his publishing comrades as an apostate. Others were puzzled: Why, they wondered, would Amazon, having so spectacularly led the e-book revolution and done so much, in the words of one of its spokesmen, to "re-invent reading," seek to become a player in the rearview world of publishing books on paper? Doing so would require building an entire infrastructure of editors, publicists, and even sales representatives who would be charged with convincing America's booksellers—by now allergic to the very idea of aiding their most agile adversary—to carry its books. Indeed, Barnes & Noble, among other booksellers, promptly said it would not sell any book published by Amazon. (It should be remembered that B&N had once tried to become a publisher itself through its purchase of Sterling Publishing, raising howls of "conflict of interest" from publishers. The perennial question of whose ox is being gored fairly begs to be asked here.) For its part, Amazon swiftly struck an alliance with Houghton Mifflin Harcourt to handle placing its books in physical stores. In a transparent subterfuge aimed at protecting its tax avoidance strategies, Amazon intends to publish many of its books under a subsidiary imprint of Houghton's called New Harvest, thus keeping alive the increasingly threadbare fiction that it has no physical presence in states where it does business online.

Nine months after Kirshbaum's hire, judging by the number of deals concluded, his nascent operation rivals two of publishing's largest companies, the French-owned Hachette and the Murdoch-owned HarperCollins. Like his boss, Kirshbaum wants to get big fast. It remains to be seen, however, whether spending a reported $800,000 to acquire Penny Marshall's Hollywood memoirs is ultimately profitable; several of the publishers I spoke to thought not and professed little anxiety at Amazon's big foot approach. They are not inclined to join the hysteria that largely greeted Kirshbaum's defection, feeling that a recent *Bloomberg Businessweek* cover story depicting a book enveloped by flames had exaggerated by several orders of magnitude the actual threat posed by Amazon's new venture. If Amazon wants to burn the book business, as the magazine's headline blared, publishing books the old-fashioned way struck them as a peculiar way of going about it. Was there really a "secret plot to destroy literature," as the magazine alleged? It seemed far-fetched, to say the least.

At the same time, Amazon's New York foray might be seen as an effort to lure "legacy writers," assuring them of a hardcover trophy and a state-of-the-art digital edition, and as such part of an overall strategy to overcome resistance among established bestselling authors to publish with the online retail giant. As one senior publishing executive said, forty to sixty percent of the sales for the Stephen Kings, Lee Childs, and John Grishams are still derived from Barnes & Noble, Walmart, and

Costco. Such authors, he said, "were they to walk away from
their traditional publishers, would be leaving a considerable
fortune on the table." But as Amazon's six other publishing
imprints (Montlake Romance, AmazonCrossing, Thomas and
Mercer, 47North, Amazon Encore, the Domino Project) have
discovered, in certain genres (romance, science fiction, and
fantasy) formerly relegated to the moribund mass-market
paperback, readers care not a whit about cover design or even
good writing and have no attachment at all to the book as object. Like addicts, they just want their fix at the lowest possible
price, and Amazon is happy to be their online dealer.

James Marcus sees a particular irony in Amazon's entry
into book publishing. "When I first worked at Amazon in the
mid-1990s," he recalls,

> we were advised to think of publishers as our partners.
> I believe this directive was in earnest. But even then, a
> creeping contempt for the publishing industry was
> sometimes discernible. Weren't they stodgy traditional-
> ists, who relied on rotary phones and a Depression-era
> business model? Well, the company is now a bona-fide
> trade publisher. There's no predicting how these books
> will fare, especially with many retailers refusing to sell
> them (an embargo that won't, of course, affect e-book
> sales, where Amazon still rules the roost). But Bezos may
> now discover that cutting out the middleman isn't all it's
> cracked up to be—that it's surprisingly easy to fail in the
> neo-Victorian enterprise of publishing, especially when
> it comes to finding readers for worthy books. Perhaps it's
> time for him to acquire a rotary phone, available in five

retro colors and eligible for two-day Prime shipping on his very own site.

Amazon's entry into publishing's traditional casino is a sideshow. More worrisome, at least over the long term, is the success of Amazon's Kindle Single program, an effort to encourage writers to make an end run around publishers, not only of books but of magazines as well. That program offers writers a chance to publish original e-book essays of no more than thirty thousand words (authors agree to a bargain-basement price of no more than $2.99 in exchange for a seventy percent royalty and no advance). It has attracted Nelson DeMille, Jon Krakauer, William Vollmann, Walter Mosley, Ann Patchett, Amy Tan, and the late Christopher Hitchens, as well as a slew of lesser-known scribblers, some of whom have enjoyed paydays rivaling or exceeding what they might have gotten were magazines like *Vanity Fair* or the *New Yorker* to have commissioned their work. Royalties are direct deposited monthly, and authors can check their sales anytime—a level of efficiency and transparency almost unknown at traditional publishers and magazines.

The boundaries are blurring all over publishing as various actors have belatedly roused themselves to the necessities and blandishments of the online world. The literary agency William Morris Endeavor, for example, has launched 212 Books, an e-publishing program designed to showcase its clients, such as David Frum, a former speechwriter for President George W. Bush, whose first novel is unsurprisingly called *Patriots* (first serial rights have been placed with the *Huffington Post*).

Endeavor is also bringing out as a direct e-book the hapless James Frey's *Final Testament of the Holy Bible*. J. K. Rowling, an empire unto herself, is releasing the Harry Potter series on her own terms and making it available through her own website, Amazon, Apple, and every other conceivable digital "platform" in the known universe. Sourcebooks Inc., a medium-sized independent publisher based in Naperville, Illinois, is starting an online bookstore to sell its romance novels directly to readers for a monthly fee. Other creative online inducements for writers are being hatched at several publishers, including Little, Brown.

Such efforts have scant chance of preventing Amazon from bulldozing any real or perceived obstacles to its single-minded pursuit of maximum clout. It is big enough to impose increasingly harsh terms on both its competitors and its clients. As reported by the *Seattle Times*, it has even begun to compel tiny indie publishers to abandon their traditional short discounts and embrace punitive larger trade discounts. When Karen Christensen of Berkshire Publishing Group refused, Amazon "stopped placing orders, affecting ten percent of her business."

The Independent Publishers Group, a principal distributor of about five hundred small publishers, recently angered Amazon by refusing to accept the company's peremptory demand for deeper discounts. Amazon promptly yanked nearly five thousand digital titles. Small-press publishers were beside themselves. Bryce Milligan of Wings Press, based in Texas, spoke for most when, in a blistering broadside, he lambasted Amazon, complaining that its actions caused his sales to drop by forty percent. "Amazon," he wrote, seemingly wants to kill off the distributors, then kill off the independent publishers and bookstores, and become the only link between the reader and the author.... E-book sales have been a highly addictive drug to many smaller publishers. For one thing, there are no "returns." ... E-book sales allowed smaller presses to get a taste of the kind of money that online impulse buying can produce. Already e-book sales were underwriting the publication of paper books-and-ink at Wings Press. ... For Amazon to rip e-book sales away is a classic bait-and-switch tactic guaranteed to kill small presses by the hundreds. . . . There was a time not so long ago when "competition" was a healthy thing, not a synonym for corporate "murder." Amazon could have been a bright and shining star, lighting the way to increased literacy and improved access to alternative literatures. Alas, it looks more likely to be a large and deadly asteroid. We, the literary dinosaurs, are watching to see if this is a near miss or the beginning of extinction.

But Amazon isn't the only player willing to play hardball. Random House, for example, quietly began in March 2012 to charge public libraries three times the retail price for e-books, causing Nova Scotia's South Shore Public Libraries to call for a boycott and accuse the German-owned conglomerate of unfair e-book pricing. It gets worse: according to the *New York Times*, "five of the six major publishers either refuse to make new e-books available to libraries or have pulled back significantly over the last year on how easily or how often those books can be circulated."

Jacob Stevens, the managing director of Verso, the distinguished independent press spawned by the London-based *New Left Review*, says of Amazon, "Having our backlist instantly and immediately available has so far outweighed the problems. For me, the problems become worse as Amazon moves from 'just' being a big player in selling books to vertical control of entire sections of the industry. It all gets a bit Big Brother. It's easy to imagine Amazon muscling existing publishers out of the picture altogether and inviting authors and agents to deal directly with them. What would that do for the richness and diversity of our culture?"

And yet Amazon gives $1 million a year, in grants of about $25,000 apiece, to a wide range of independent literary journals and nonprofit organizations, including the *Kenyon Review*, the online *Los Angeles Review of Books* and even *One Story*, the nonprofit literary magazine devoted to the short story, which recently celebrated its tenth anniversary by honoring Ann Patchett, an outspoken critic of Bezos's business practices and a co-owner of an independent bookstore in Nashville. Amazon's contributions outstrip by a large factor any advertising dollars sent my way by traditional publishers during the nearly nine years I ran the *Los Angeles Times Book Review*. Of course, such largesse—less than a pittance of its $5 billion cash reserve—may be meant to ensnare its most articulate critics in a web of dependency. If so, Amazon will likely be surprised, as the editors of such journals have well-deserved reputations for biting the hand that feeds, and they prize their contrarian sensibilities.

Another bookselling veteran made uneasy by Amazon's colossal success is Andy Ross, who—having succeeded the venerable Fred Cody as the owner of Cody's Books in Berkeley until online competition forced its flagship location to close in 2006, after fifty years in business—now works in Oakland as a literary agent. "Monopolies are always problematic in a free society, and they are more so when we are dealing with the dissemination of ideas, which is what book publishing is about," he told me:

> In the realm of electronic publishing, Amazon until recently controlled about ninety percent of the market, a monopoly by almost anyone's definition. Most people bought their e-books in the proprietary Kindle file format that could only be purchased from Amazon and only read on the Kindle reader that was manufactured by Amazon. Other makers of e-book readers designed them to accept the open-source e-pub format that allowed customers to have a wider choice of retailers to supply them with e-books. Since then, Amazon's market share has been declining, but sixty percent of all e-books in America continue to be sold by Amazon in the Kindle file format. Amazon simply has too much power in the marketplace. And when their business interest conflicts with the public interest, the public interest suffers.

It's a fair point—one that also plagues Peter Mayer of Overlook Press: "All sides of this argument need to think deeply—not just about their businesses, but also about their world.

I grew up in a world in which many parts together formed a community adversarial in a microcosmic way but communal in a larger sense: authors, editors, agents, publishers, wholesalers, retailers, and readers. I hope, worried as I am about the current trajectory [of publishing], that we do not look back one day, sitting on a stump as the boy does in Shel Silverstein's *The Giving Tree*, and only see what has become a largely denuded wasteland."

[2012]

Two years later. . .

Hardly a month goes by without news of Amazon's continuing assault on the publishing industry. Nearly two-thirds of all e-books are bought through the online retailer. Its share of all new books sold is forty percent—a whopping increase from twelve percent in just five years. Peter Hildick-Smith, head of Codex, a leading book audience research firm, declares that Amazon is "the most powerful book retailer today by far." Traditional publishers are in an uproar, fearing that the Seattle-based firm will render them obsolete by enabling writers to end-run old-school "gatekeepers" by going directly to readers digitally.

The rise of the internet was initially seen as a revolutionary boon, transforming a backward carriage trade into a modern engine of knowledge distribution, with a promise of democratizing literacy. Thus was the rise of Jeff Bezos's Amazon celebrated in many precincts. Books now could be ordered from anywhere and swiftly delivered. Plus, the prices charged were the lowest to be had. Convenience, cost, and excellent customer service won millions of readers, happy to throng in Bezos's big tent.

Two years ago, I took a close look at the behemoth that Amazon had become. While big is not always bad, there was much about Amazon that was troubling: its labor practices, for one; its cutthroat business dealings, for another. Bezos once joked that Amazon ought to approach small publishers "the way a cheetah would pursue a sickly gazelle"—a remark, we now learn, that led to an effort inside Amazon dubbed the Gazelle Project, designed to extract concessions from the weakest publishers (it's since been euphemistically renamed the Small Publisher Negotiation Program). Brad Stone's revelatory book *The Everything Store: Jeff Bezos and the Age of Amazon*, as well as recent reports in the *New Yorker* by George Packer and in the *New York Review of Books* by Steve Coll, echo my original analysis and deepen my worst fears.

Today, Amazon so dominates the marketplace that it feels free to bulldoze the competition, dictating terms to suppliers and customers alike. With respect to publishing and bookselling, Amazon is increasingly a vertically integrated company, at once a bookseller, a reviewer, even a publisher, and as such it poses a uniquely disturbing threat. It has achieved a worrying hegemony, having successfully laid siege to traditional bricks-and-mortar bookstores not only in the United States but also in Europe. In Germany, Austria, and Switzerland, Amazon has forced the media conglomerate Bertelsmann to shutter its core book clubs and retail stores. Sarah Simon, a media analyst with Berenberg Bank in London, says Bertelsmann's bookselling business "has been largely superseded by online sales, where Amazon is the market leader." Amazon is also going after other important publishers like Piper, Carlsen, and Ullstein, all owned by the Swedish Bonnier Group. According to a recent report in *Der Spiegel*, Amazon is demanding that its share of the profit from every e-book sale rise from thirty percent of the retail price to fifty percent. Christian Schumacher-Gebler, the CEO of Bonnier Media Deutschland, worries that "Amazon is undermining our ability to survive." Amazon is now engaged in a widely reported and increasingly bitter and potentially industry-defining struggle with Hachette, the French company that owns Little, Brown, among other American imprints. As a negotiating tactic to extract higher fees from the firm, it has refused to sell many Hachette titles. Amazon used a similar tactic with Time Warner's Warner Bros. Studio by refusing to take preorders for selected movie titles to get better terms for the sale of movie discs, which it sells for little or no profit in order to compete with stores like Walmart and Best Buy.

The entire ecology of publishing is at risk. Conglomeration proceeds at a dizzying pace: Random House and Penguin (which includes, among other imprints, the Viking Press) merge; Hachette buys the Perseus Group. Little fish are gobbled up by bigger fish, and they, in turn, face even larger predators. There is blood in the water. But the Obama Justice Department, seemingly mesmerized by visions of a digital utopia, is oddly blind to the threat to publishing posed by Amazon's growing monopoly. Attorney General Eric Holder and his staff seem to regard Amazon as a benign giant whose machinations, so far, offer more benefits than disadvantages. Amazon, for its part, insists that it has only readers' interests at heart and is merely providing books at the lowest possible price, absorbing huge losses to do so. Increasingly, this claim is revealed as a self-serving stratagem; as Coll writes, "The more

Amazon uses coercion and retaliation as a means of negotiation, the more it looks to be restraining competition." Antitrust issues are not only about price and market share, but also the antidemocratic implications for both competition and the larger culture. When will the Justice Department wake up? There is precedent, after all. In 1948, the Supreme Court, in *United States v. Paramount Pictures, Inc.*, ordered the breakup of the old Hollywood studio system.

Amazon is hardly an online bookstore anymore. Books are a small fraction of its overall business—just seven percent. From the start, Amazon understood that books were a loss leader whose chief benefit was to induce millions to enroll in the online Walmart the company wanted to become. Today, even the CIA finds itself compelled to outsource some of its data collection by availing itself of Amazon's powerful cloud servers, in a deal estimated at $600 million.

I remain optimistic that our species will continue to tell itself stories, for that's the way we extract meaning from our otherwise unruly lives. But just as utilities are rightly regulated because they provide an essential service everyone needs— water, gas, electricity—so too has the time come for closer scrutiny and regulation of a company that, like Standard Oil a century ago, provides an indispensable service for a modern economy and a healthy culture. As Amazon gains market share, its self-proclaimed conceit that unfettered growth is invariably in the consumers' interest is every day less convincing. A narrow definition of those interests doesn't serve the public interest. Just as a responsible energy policy must strike a balance between the benefit to individuals and the consequences to the environment, so must a similar calculus be applied to

Amazon. (The French are exemplary here, having long recognized that books, like bread, are indispensable for any civilization worthy of the name; they subject both to price controls, thus permitting independent bookstores and bakeries to survive and thrive.) One can support Amazon's right to offer readers the widest array of books at the most reasonable price. But such a right is not to be exercised at the expense of the fragile and essential contributions of authors, editors, and publishers to the general culture. Amazon ought no longer to be permitted to behave like a parasite that hollows out its host. A serious Justice Department investigation is past due.

[2014]

In Defense of Difficulty

I T IS A COMMONPLACE TO BEMOAN the vanishing of serious criticism in our popular culture. The past, it is said, was
a golden age. More than twenty-five years ago, Russell Jacoby
put it sharply in *The Last Intellectuals* when he decried the
disappearance of the "public intellectual" since the heyday
of the fevered debates over politics and literature that broke
out among Depression-era students in the cafeteria at New
York's City College. Much had gone awry: "A public that once
snapped up pamphlets by Thomas Paine or stood for hours
listening to Abraham Lincoln debate Stephen Douglas hardly
exists; its span of attention shrinks as its fondness for television
increases."

The rising price of real estate was also to blame, for it
had led to the gentrification of America's bohemian enclaves,
like Greenwich Village in New York and North Beach in San
Francisco, spawning grounds for generations of disaffected
intellectuals and artists, who now could no longer afford
independence. Jacoby's verdict was harsh and sweeping: "The
eclipse of these urban living areas completes the eclipse of
the cultural space." Universities, too, were at fault. They had
colonized critics by holding careers hostage to academic
specialization, requiring them to master the arcane tongues
of ever-narrower disciplines, forcing them to forsake a larger

public. Compared to the Arcadian past, the present, in this view, was a wasteland.

It didn't have to be this way. In the postwar era, a vast project of cultural uplift sought to bring the best that had been thought and said to the wider public. Robert M. Hutchins of the University of Chicago and Mortimer J. Adler were among its more prominent avatars. This effort, which tried to deepen literacy under the sign of the "middlebrow," and thus to strengthen the idea that an informed citizenry was indispensable for a healthy democracy, was, for a time, hugely successful. The general level of cultural sophistication rose as a growing middle class shed its provincialism in exchange for a certain worldliness that was one legacy of American triumphalism and ambition after the Second World War. College enrollment boomed, and the percentage of Americans attending the performing arts rose dramatically. Regional stage and opera companies blossomed, new concert halls were built, and interest in the arts was widespread. TV hosts Steve Allen, Johnny Carson, and Dick Cavett frequently featured serious writers as guests. Paperback publishers made classic works of history, literature, and criticism available to ordinary readers, whose appetite for such works seemed insatiable.

Mass-circulation newspapers and magazines, too, expanded their coverage of books, movies, music, dance, and theater. Criticism was no longer confined to such small but influential journals of opinion as *Partisan Review*, the *Nation*, and the *New Republic*. *Esquire* embraced the irascible Dwight Macdonald as its movie critic, despite his well-known contempt for "middlebrow" culture. The *New Yorker* threw a lifeline to Pauline Kael, rescuing her from the ghetto of film quarterlies and the art houses of Berkeley. Strong critics like David Riesman, Daniel Bell, and Leslie Fiedler, among others, would write with insight and pugilistic zeal books that often found enough readers to propel their works onto bestseller lists. Intellectuals such as Susan Sontag were featured in the glossy pages of magazines like *Vogue*. Her controversial "Notes on 'Camp,'" first published in 1964 in *Partisan Review,* exploded into public view when *Time* championed her work. Eggheads were suddenly sexy, almost on a par with star athletes and Hollywood celebrities. Gore Vidal was a regular on Johnny Carson's *Tonight Show*. William F. Buckley Jr.'s *Firing Line* hosted vigorous debates that often were models of how to think, how to argue, and, at their best, told us that ideas mattered.

As Scott Timberg, a former arts reporter for the *Los Angeles Times*, puts it in his recent book *Culture Crash: The Killing of the Creative Class*, the idea, embraced by increasing numbers of Americans, was that drama, poetry, music, and art were not just a way to pass the time or advertise one's might, but a path to truth and enlightenment. At its best, this was what the middlebrow consensus promised. Middlebrow said that culture was accessible to a wide stratum of society, that people needed some but not much training to appreciate it, that there was a canon worth knowing, that art was not the same as entertainment, that the study of the liberal arts deepens you, and that those who make, assess, and disseminate the arts were somehow valuable for our society regardless of their impact on GDP.

So what if culture was increasingly just another product to be bought and sold, used and discarded, like so many tubes of toothpaste? Even Los Angeles, long derided as a cultural desert, would by the turn of the century boast a flourishing and internationally respected opera company, a thriving archipelago of museums with world-class collections, and dozens of bookstores selling in some years more books per capita than were sold in the greater New York area. The middlebrow's triumph was all but assured.

The arrival of the internet by century's end promised to make that victory complete. As the *Wall Street Journal* reported in a front-page story in 1998, America was "increasingly wealthy, worldly, and wired." Notions of elitism and snobbery seemed to be collapsing upon the palpable catholicity of a public whose curiosities were ever more diverse and eclectic and whose ability to satisfy them had suddenly and miraculously expanded. We stood, it appeared, on the verge of a munificent new world—a world in which technology was rapidly democratizing the means of cultural production while providing an easy way for millions of ordinary citizens, previously excluded from the precincts of the higher conversation, to join the dialogue. The digital revolution was predicted to overthrow the old monastic, self-selecting order of cultural gatekeepers (meaning professional critics). Thus would critical faculties be sharpened and democratized. Digital platforms would crack open the cloistered and solipsistic world of academe, bypass the old presses and performing arts spaces, and unleash a new era of cultural commerce. With smart machines, there would be smarter people.

Harvard's Robert Darnton, a sober and learned historian of reading and the book, agreed. He argued in *The Case for Books: Past, Present, and Future* that the implications for writing and reading, for publishing and bookselling—indeed, for cultural literacy and criticism itself—were profound. The web would make possible greater access to knowledge for ordinary people and represent a great evolutionary leap in the human mind. Others, echoing this view, were convinced the future couldn't be brighter.

Others, such as Evgeny Morozov and Jaron Lanier, were more skeptical, echoing the prescient warnings of earlier critics like Theodore Roszak and Neil Postman. They worried that whatever advantages might accrue to consumers and the culture at large from the emergence of such behemoths as Amazon, not only would proven methods of cultural production and distribution be made obsolete, but we were in danger of being enrolled, whether we liked it or not, in a warp speed culture that would destroy essential traditions of argument and narrative. They feared that the digital tsunami now engulfing us may even signal an irrevocable trivialization of the word. Or, at the least, a sense that the enterprise of making distinctions between bad, good, and best was a mug's game that had no place in a democracy that worships at the altar of mass appeal and counts its receipts at the almighty box office.

Karl Kraus, the acerbic *fin-de-siècle* Viennese critic, once remarked that no nation's literature could properly be judged by examining its geniuses, since genius always eludes explanation. A better metric is the second rate, which is to say, the popular literature and art that make up the bulk of what people consume. The truly extraordinary defy taxonomy. More fruitful by far would be to map the ecosystem of the less talented, for whom craft and tenacity and ambition are no insult. By that measure, postwar America's middlebrow culture, a culture whose achievements often mistook the second rate for top-tier work—see, for example, the novels of Herbert Gold, Herman Wouk, James Michener, Edna Ferber, Irving Stone, and John Steinbeck, to name a few—appears almost to have been a golden age. Or, as Timberg says, a silver age, at the least. What is missing today is a cultural ecology that permits the second rate to fail upwards.

That failure is a body blow against the broader culture. The world that had once permitted such efforts to flourish is gone. Today, America's traditional organs of popular criticism—newspapers, magazines, journals of opinion—have been all but overwhelmed by the digital onslaught: their circulations plummeting, their confidence eroded, their survival in doubt. Newspaper review sections in particular have suffered: jobs have been slashed, and cultural coverage vastly diminished. Both the *Los Angeles Times* and the *Washington Post* have abandoned their stand-alone book sections, leaving the *New York Times* as the only major American newspaper still publishing a significant separate section devoted to reviewing books.

Such sections, of course, were always few. Only a handful of America's papers ever deemed book coverage important enough to dedicate an entire Sunday section to it. Now even that handful is threatened with extinction, and thus is a widespread cultural illiteracy abetted, for at their best the editors of those sections tried to establish the idea that serious criticism was possible in a mass culture.

The arrival of the internet has proved no panacea. The vast canvas afforded by the internet has done little to encourage thoughtful and serious criticism. Mostly it has provided a vast Democracy Wall on which any crackpot can post his or her manifesto. Bloggers bloviate and insults abound. Discourse coarsens. Information is abundant, wisdom scarce. Leon Wieseltier has decried the inherent insidiousness of the internet, noting that "where the mind is rushed . . . neither thought nor creativity will ensue. What you will most likely get is conformity and banality. Writing is not typed talking."

Today we inhabit a remarkably arid cultural landscape, especially when compared with the ambitions of postwar America, ambitions which, to be sure, were often mocked by some of the country's more prominent intellectuals. Yes, Dwight Macdonald famously excoriated the enfeeblements of "mass cult and midcult," and Irving Howe regretted "this age of conformity," but from today's perspective, when we look back at the offerings of the Book-of-the-Month Club and projects such as the Great Books of the Western World, their scorn looks misplaced. The fact that their complaints circulated widely in the very midcult worlds Macdonald condemned was proof that trenchant criticism had found a place within the organs of mass culture. One is almost tempted to say that the middlebrow culture of yesteryear was a high-water mark.

The reality, of course, was never as rosy as much of it looks in retrospect. Cultural criticism in most American newspapers, even at its best, was almost always confined to a ghetto. Most newspapers consigned arts and books coverage to barely more than a single broadsheet at best. Editors encouraged reporters, reviewers, and critics to win readers and improve circulation by pandering to the faux populism of the marketplace. Only the review that might immediately be understood by the greatest number of readers would be permitted to see the light of day. Anything else smacked of "elitism"—a sin to be avoided at almost any cost.

This was a coarse and pernicious notion, one that lay at the center of the country's longstanding anti-intellectual tradition. From the start of the republic, Americans have had a profoundly ambivalent relationship to class and culture, as Richard Hofstadter famously observed. He was neither the first nor the last to notice this self-inflicted wound. As even the vastly popular science fiction writer Isaac Asimov understood, "Anti-intellectualism has been a constant thread winding its way through our political and cultural life, nurtured by the false notion that democracy means that 'my ignorance is just as good as your knowledge.'" The ambition to smuggle more serious standards into the instruments of mass culture was always challenging, even when a rising middle class made possible the notion of increasing cultural sophistication.

Today such an ambition seems absurdly quixotic. Perhaps it always was. After all, the very idea of cultural and intellectual discrimination is regularly attacked for the sin of "snark," and notions of authority and expertise are everywhere under siege. The necessity of literary hygiene as a way of keeping a culture honest and astute is in danger of being forgotten. Too few remember William Hazlitt's essay on "the pleasure of hating." Hazlitt complained that "the reputation of some books is raw and *unaired*," and rightly saw that "the popularity of the most successful writers operates to wean us from them, by the cant and fuss that is made about them, by hearing their names everlastingly repeated, and by the number of ignorant and indiscriminate admirers they draw after them." Today what is needed, more than ever, is what Wieseltier has called "the higher spleen."

A good recent example is Francine Prose's lacerating take-down of Donna Tartt's bestselling and widely admired novel, *The Goldfinch*, or the late Christopher Hitchens's mighty evis-ceration of Henry Kissinger. Or, in an earlier period, Susan Sontag's defenestration of Leni Riefenstahl's fascist aesthetics at a time when her Nazi past had been largely forgotten. None of these critics banished difficulty or avoided complexity of thought; on the contrary, they tried hard to think seriously and deeply, to express themselves with vigor and clarity, without shirking the moral obligation to treat readers as adults. They understood the necessity of making distinctions between the excellent, the mediocre, and the dreck. Doing so, they knew, was a critic's highest calling.

When did "difficulty" become suspect in American culture, widely derided as antidemocratic and contemptuously dis-missed as evidence of so-called elitism? If a work of art isn't somehow immediately "understood" or "accessible" by and to large numbers of people, it is often ridiculed as "esoteric," "ob-tuse," or even somehow un-American. We should mark such an argument's cognitive consequences. A culture filled with smooth and familiar consumptions produces in people rigid mental habits and stultified conceptions. They know what they know, and they expect to find it reinforced when they turn a page or click on a screen. Difficulty annoys them, and, hav-ing become accustomed to so much pabulum served up by a pandering and invertebrate media, they experience difficulty not just as "difficult," but as insult. Struggling to understand, say, Faulkner's stream of consciousness masterpiece *The Sound and the Fury* or Alain Resnais's Rubik's Cube of a movie *Last Year at Marienbad* needn't be done. The mind may skip trying to solve such cognitive puzzles, even though the truth is they strengthen it as a workout tones muscles.

Sometimes it feels as if the world is divided into two classes: one very large class spurns difficulty, while the other, very much smaller, delights in it. There are readers who, when encountering an unfamiliar word, instead of reaching for a dictionary, choose to regard it as a sign of the author's contempt or pretension, a deliberate refusal to speak in a language ordinary people can understand. Others, encountering the same word, happily seize on it as a chance to learn something new, to broaden their horizons. They eagerly seek a literature that upends assumptions, challenges prejudices, contests conceits.

The second group is an endangered species. One reason is that the ambitions of mainstream media that, however fitfully, once sought to expose them to the life of the mind and to the contest of ideas have themselves shrunk. We have gone from the heyday of television intellection, which boasted shows hosted by, among others, David Susskind and David Frost, men that, whatever their self-absorptions, were nonetheless possessed of an admirable high-mindedness, to the sound-bite rants of Sean Hannity and the inanities of clowns like Jimmy Fallon. Once upon a time, the ideal of seriousness may not have been a common one, but it was acknowledged as one worth striving for. It didn't have to do what it must today, that is, fight for respect, legitimate itself before asserting itself. The class that is allergic to difficulty now feels justified in condemning the other as "elitist" and antidemocratic. The exercise of cultural authority and artistic or literary or aesthetic discrimination is seen as evidence of snobbery, entitlement, and privilege lording it over ordinary folks. A perverse populism increasingly deforms our culture, consigning some works of art to a realm somehow more rarefied and less accessible to a broad public. Thus is choice constrained and the tyranny of mass appeal deepened in the name of democracy.

Consider, by contrast, Theodor Adorno's exemplary response to his good friend Gershom Scholem upon receiving Scholem's translation of the *Zohar*, the masterpiece of Kabbalah, as mysterious as it is magnificent. In 1939, Adorno, living in exile in New York after fleeing Nazi Germany, wrote Scholem, who had long since settled in Jerusalem:

I'm not just being rhetorical when I say that the *Zohar* translation you sent me gave me more joy than any gift I have received in a long time. Don't read into this remark anything pretentious, because I am far from claiming to have fully grasped the text. But it's the kind of thing whose indecipherability is itself an element of the joy I felt in reading it. I think I can say that your introduction has at least given me a topological notion of the *Zohar*. A bit like someone who goes high into the mountains to spot chamois bucks but fails to see them, because he's a nearsighted city dweller. After an experienced guide points out the precise spot where the bucks congregate, he becomes so thoroughly acquainted with their territory that he thinks he must be able to discover these rare creatures immediately. The summer tourist cannot expect to glean anything more than this from the landscape, which is truly revealed only at the price of a lifetime's commitment—nothing less.

The ideal of serious enjoyment of what isn't instantly understood is rare in American life. It is under constant siege. It is the object of scorn from both the left and the right. The pleasures of critical thinking ought not to be seen as belonging to the province of an elite. They are the birthright of every citizen. For such pleasures are at the very heart of literacy, without which democracy itself is dulled. More than ever, we need a defense of the Eros of difficulty.

[2015]

A Writer's Space

WHAT DO WE THINK we mean when we say, "a writer's space"? Is such a space different than, say, any other citizen's space? Is the space of a writer a physical place—the place where the writing is done, the den, the office, the hotel room, the bar or café, the bedroom, upon a desk or table or any available flat and stable surface?

Or is the "writer's space" an inner region of the mind? Or is it a psychological place deep within the recesses of the heart, a storehouse of emotions containing a jumble of neurological circuitry? Is it the place, whether physical or spiritual, where the writer tries to make sense of otherwise inchoate lives? In either case, is it a zone of safety that permits the writer to be vulnerable and daring and honest so as to find meaning and order in the service of story?

Perhaps it will be useful to begin at the very dawn of writing, when prehistory became history. Let's think, for a moment, about the clay tablets that date from around 3200 BC on which were etched small, repetitive, impressed characters that look like wedge-shaped footprints that we call cuneiform, the script language of ancient Sumer in Mesopotamia. Along with the other ancient civilizations of the Chinese and the Maya, the Babylonians put spoken language into material form, and for the first time people could store information, whether of lists of goods or taxes, and transmit it across time and space.

It would take two millennia for writing to become a carrier of narrative, of story, of epic, which arrives in the Sumerian tale of Gilgamesh. Writing was a secret code, the instrument of tax collectors and traders in the service of god-kings. Preeminently, it was the province of priests and guardians of holy texts. With the arrival of monotheism, there was a great need to record the word of God, and the many subsequent commentaries on the ethical and spiritual obligations of faithfully adhering to a set of religious precepts. This task required special places where scribes could carry out their sanctified work. Think of the caves of Qumran, some natural and some artificial, where the Dead Sea Scrolls were found, or later the medieval monasteries where illuminated manuscripts were painstakingly created.

Illiteracy, it should be remembered, was commonplace. From the start, the creation of texts was bound up with a notion of the holy, of a place where experts—anointed by God—were tasked with making scripture palpable. They were the translators and custodians of the ineffable and the unknowable, and they spent their lives making it possible for ordinary people to partake of the wisdom to be had from the all-seeing, all-powerful deity, from whom meaning, sustenance, and life itself was derived.

We needn't rehearse the religious quarrels and sectarian strife that bloodied the struggle between the Age of Superstition and the Age of Enlightenment, except perhaps to note that the world was often divided—as, alas, it still sadly is—between those who insist all answers are to be found in a single book and those who believe in two, three, many books.

The point is that the notion of a repository, where the writer (or religious shaman, adept, or priest) told or retold the parables and stories of God, was widely accepted. It meant that, from the start, a writer's space was a space with a sacred aura. It was a place deemed to have special qualities—qualities that encouraged the communication of stories that in their detail and point conferred significance upon and gave importance to lives that otherwise might have seemed untethered and without meaning. The writer, by this measure, was a kind of oracle, with a special ability, by virtue of temperament and training, to pierce the veil of mystery and ignorance that was the usual lot of most people and to make sense of the past, parse the present, and even to predict the future.

This idea of the writer was powerful. It still is. By the time we enter the Romantic Age, the notion of a writer's space has shed its religious origins without abandoning in the popular imagination the belief that writers have a special and enviable access to inner, truer worlds, often invisible to the rest of us. How to put it? That, by and large, artists generally, of which writers are a subset, are people whose epidermises, as it were, are more porous than most people's. And thus they are more vulnerable, more open to the world around them, more alert, more perspicacious. Shelley put it well when he wrote that, "Poets are the unacknowledged legislators of the world." Think Virginia Woolf.

By the end of the nineteenth century, writers in their person and in their spaces are widely celebrated and revered, imbued with talents and special powers that arouse admiration bordering on worship. It is said that when Mark Twain came to London and strode down the gangplank as he disembarked from the ship that had brought him across the Atlantic, dockworkers that had never read a single word of his stunning stories burst into applause when the nimbus of white hair atop the head of the man in the white suit hove into view. Similarly, when Oscar Wilde was asked at the New York customs house if he had anything to declare when he arrived in America in 1882 to deliver his lectures on aesthetics, he is said to have replied, "Only my genius."

Many writers were quickly enrolled in the service of nationalist movements of all kinds, even as many writers saw themselves as citizens in an international republic of letters, a far-flung fraternity of speakers of many diverse languages, but united in their fealty to story. Nonetheless, the space where they composed their work—their studies and offices and homes—quickly became tourist destinations, sites of pilgrimage where devoted readers could pay homage. The objects on the desk, writing instruments and inkwells, foolscap and notebooks, the arrangement of photographs and paintings on their walls, the pattern of wallpaper, the very furniture itself, and preeminently the desk and chair, favorite divan and reading sofa, lamps and carpets, all became invested with a sacredness and veneration previously reserved only for religious figures. Balzac's home, Tolstoy's dacha, Hemingway's Cuban finca are but three of many possible examples. Writers were now our secular saints.

Somehow it was thought that by entering these spaces, the key to unlocking the secret of literary creation could be had, and that by inhaling the very atmosphere that celebrated authors once breathed, one could, by a strange alchemy or osmosis, absorb the essence that animated the writer's imagination and made possible the realization of native talent.

This almost mystical space is not reserved to the worthy dead. Famous living authors are similarly regarded. How else to explain the palpably zealous efforts by many readers and aspiring writers to attend readings and book festivals, to be closer to the avatars of stories that give our lives meaning? The human desire, however understandable, to find oneself within the inner and invisible circle that surrounds celebrity, is accompanied by the conceit (or hope) that entering that space will provide a passport to a world more alive and more authentic, even wiser perhaps than the one most us know. And that somehow the admired author's mojo will rub off. Entering a writer's space is seen as a near-magical shortcut to the absorption of craft and insight.

Patti Smith, for one, has made such pilgrimages a central pillar of her lifelong quest for ecstatic and artistic inspiration. Traveling with her sister on her first visit to Paris in the spring of 1969, she arrived "with a handful of precious addresses of cafés and hotels" where the existentialists hung out and where Rimbaud and Verlaine presided over their circle of scruffy bohemians, and where Baudelaire "smoked hashish and penned the opening poems in *Les fleurs du mal.*" Nearly fifty years later, she recalled how "the interiors of our imaginations glowed, as we walked back and forth before these places synonymous with poets. Just to be near where they had written, sparred, and slept."

I am myself not immune to such hocus-pocus. For a long time, I found myself under the spell of Susan Sontag. In a way, I still am. I confess: I wanted to be Susan Sontag when I grew up. Living as I did the entire summer of 1974 in her Manhattan apartment, the walls lined with her eight thousand books, I hoped that the space that was hers would be filled with molecules that would almost biologically enter my body, animate my circulatory system, awaken my brain, and spur an avid, even relentless curiosity about the world and about literature with a capital L. That space harbored the writer's elixir that I believed could be mine if only I were to drink it all up at Chez Sontag. I admired the way this girl from the San Fernando Valley and from the outskirts of Phoenix had invented herself, had read her way through the great books, and had become a fearless Joan of Arc of the Higher Seriousness. It was a space that I, too, wanted to inhabit.

Of course there isn't only one writer's space. There are many writers, and we must acknowledge their many variegated spaces. Kafka sold insurance and wrote the stories that he instructed his best friend, Max Brod, to burn upon his demise. Fortunately, Brod betrayed him.

"Why is one compelled to write?" asks Patti Smith in her book *Devotion*. "To set oneself apart, cocooned, wrapped in solitude, despite the wants of others. Virginia Woolf had her room. Proust his shuttered windows. Marguerite Duras her muted house. Dylan Thomas his modest shed. All seeking an emptiness to imbue with words. The words that will penetrate virgin territory, crack unclaimed combinations, articulate the infinite."

Every writer is different. The path to telling stories about our world is hard-won, and the space that's necessary to allow us to find our respective voices differs. The world we carry in our heads is arguably the most important space of all. It is a space whose suffocations and seductions compete for our attention. They shape the way we look at things, the way we shape the stories we tell. In the end, a writer's space is determined by the circumstances bestowed by geography and family, gender, ethnicity, culture and class and the goddesses of serendipity and fortune, and—not least—by the self-inventions, temperament, and aspirations of those of us willing to sacrifice ourselves on the altar of our own arrogance—an arrogance that inevitably constructs a space that both welcomes the world and seals us off from it, leaving us prisoners in disguise, unacknowledged victims of the necessary conceit that we are authors of our own space.

[2017]

Credo

To laugh often and much,
To win the respect of intelligent
People and the affection of children;
To earn the appreciation of honest
Critics and endure the betrayal of false
Friends; To appreciate beauty, to find
the best in others; To leave the world
a bit better, whether by a healthy child,
a garden patch or a redeemed social
condition; To know even one life has
breathed easier because you have lived.
This is to have succeeded.

—RALPH WALDO EMERSON

Index

ABOUT THE AUTHOR

STEVE WASSERMAN was born in 1952 and graduated from UC Berkeley in 1974 with a degree in criminology. After a brief stint as assistant editor of *City Magazine of San Francisco*, he became deputy editor of the op-ed page and opinion section of the *Los Angeles Times* and was later appointed editor of the paper's Sunday *Book Review*. He was a principal architect of the annual *Los Angeles Times* Festival of Books. He was also editorial director of New Republic Books; publisher and editorial director of Hill and Wang at Farrar, Straus and Giroux and of the Noonday Press; executive editor of Doubleday; and editorial director of Times Books at Random House. Later, he was a partner of Kneerim & Williams, a literary agency, where he represented numerous authors, including James Fenton, Christopher Hitchens, Russell Jacoby, Frederic Raphael, Linda Ronstadt, Robert Scheer, and David Thomson. A founder and codirector of the Los Angeles Institute for the Humanities at the University of Southern California, he has taught advanced nonfiction writing at USC's Professional Writing Program and taught cultural criticism at the Graduate School of Journalism at UC Berkeley. He is a fellow of the New York Institute for the Humanities and a former adjunct professor in NYU's department of cultural reporting and journalism. In 2002, he chaired the nominating jury for the Pulitzer Prize in general nonfiction, and in 2004 he was a member of the nominating jury for the Pulitzer Prize in fiction. He also served for nearly a decade on the jury for the annual literary prize awarded by the Commonwealth Club of California. Most recently, he was editor at large for Yale University Press until 2016, when he became publisher of Heyday, an independent, nonprofit press founded in 1974. He lives in Berkeley, California.

A NOTE ON TYPE

This book is set in Athelas. Inspired by classic British book-making, Athelas features tasteful curves and serifs, eschewing hard edges in favor of a spacious, tranquil feel. Athelas was created in 2008 by the founders of TypeTogether, Veronika Burian and José Scaglione, who designed the font specifically for use in fine books printed on high-quality paper.